The Working Class in American History

Editorial Advisors
DAVID BRODY
HERBERT G. GUTMAN
DAVID MONTGOMERY

Worker City, Company Town

Worker City, Company Town

Iron and Cotton-Worker Protest in
Troy and Cohoes, New York, 1855-84

Daniel J. Walkowitz

UNIVERSITY OF ILLINOIS PRESS
Urbana   Chicago   London

ILLINI BOOKS EDITION, 1981

© 1978 by the Board of Trustees of the University of Illinois
Manufactured in the United States of America

LIBRARY OF CONGRESS CATALOGING IN PUBLICATION DATA

Walkowitz, Daniel J
    Worker city, company town.

    (The Working class in American history)
    Bibliography: p.
    Includes index.
    1.   Iron and steel workers—New York (State)—
Troy—History.   2.   Textile workers—New York (State)—
Cohoes—History.   3.   Cotton manufacture—New York
(State)—Cohoes—History.   4.   Troy, N.Y.—Social
conditions.   5.   Cohoes, N.Y.—Social conditions.
I.   Title.   II.   Series.
HD8039.I52U67   301.44′42′0974741   78-18305
ISBN 0-252-00915-0

To my parents

Selda and Sol Walkowitz

In memory

Contents

Acknowledgments

THE MATERIAL in this book had a previous existence as a doctoral dissertation directed by Herbert G. Gutman at the University of Rochester. The present manuscript bears only faint resemblance to the thesis, but Professor Gutman's encouragement—as well as his own substantial historical work—have always been important to me. Indeed, the Rochester history department faculty in the 1960s constituted the most intellectually stimulating faculty I have experienced within the halls of academe.

This work could not have been completed without the dedication and service of the staffs at many libraries in this country and in England. In particular, I would like to thank R. E. Starkey, director of the Troy Public Library, and Audrey Smith, senior reference librarian at the New York State Education Library in Albany, for their always courteous and helpful assistance. Edward Vandecar, M.D., Cohoes's city historian, was kind enough to let me see his unpublished chronology of the city's history. In addition, research was completed with the aid of the thoroughly professional staffs at the following libraries: Rush Rhees Library at the University of Rochester, Rensselaer Polytechnic Institute Library, Troy Public Library, Russell Sage Library, Rensselaer County Historical Society, Siena College Library, New York State Education Library at Albany, Alexander Library at Rutgers University, University of London Library at Senate House, London School of Economics Library, and the British Museum. Two research assistants, Larry Cohen and Waverly Lowell, collated and cross-referenced some of the data, and Chelley Theodore did some of the preliminary map work for the text. The prefatory poem, "Mike McChanic's Relatives," was provided by Herbert Gutman. The Rutgers Research Council gave generous financial support for many of the research and typing expenses. Finally, excerpts and data from two previously published journal articles are scattered throughout the first half of the manuscript and are used with the journals' permission. The two articles are: "Working-Class Women in the Gilded Age: Factory, Family and Community Life among Cohoes, New York, Cotton Workers, 1860–1880," *Journal of Social History* 5, no. 4 (Summer 1977):464–90, and "Statistics and the Writing of Working-Class Culture: A Statistical Portrait of the Iron Workers in Troy, New York, 1860–1880," *Labor History* 15, no. 3 (Summer 1974):416–60.

Various colleagues, friends, and students read part or all of the manuscript in various stages of its evolution, consistently offering thoughtful advice that I accepted or rejected, of course, at my own peril. The best work is often a collective effort, however, and they have left an indelible mark on this manuscript. Not everyone can be mentioned here, but I am grateful to all. I have been especially fortunate to have had the advice and supportive friendship of Barbara Abrash, Howard Green, Ron Grele, and many Rutgers graduate students. In addition, an early draft of this book was read by Joseph Held, John Modell, John Gillis, and Peter Stearns—each of whom offered detailed criticisms and suggestions, while Rudolph Bell reviewed some of the statistical material, especially that on the standard of living. I owe a special debt, however, to my comrades in England. They were a constant source of strength to me during a difficult personal time. On a later draft, Stephan Yeo struggled over the introduction with me, Martha Vicinus read and edited the middle chapters with care and intelligence, and Raphael Samuel massaged my spirit—much as he has with a whole generation of English social historians—and regularly challenged me with new ideas. Gareth Stedman Jones read the final draft with the astuteness which historians have come to expect from him.

Finally, two people made inestimable contributions to this book. Milton Cantor perceptively read a final draft and meticulously edited it. The manuscript reads much the better for his efforts, and several of the more interesting connections in this volume are spin-offs from his suggestions. Those that are not are often Judith R. Walkowitz's contributions. She reworked countless versions of this material with me, consistently providing incisive criticism, support, and encouragement. Always sharing her time and ideas with me, she was a partner in the best sense of the word.

But this book most belongs to my parents, Selda and Sol Walkowitz, to whom it is dedicated. Even though both died during its completion, something of their struggle for peace and social justice lives on in this history.

"MIKE McCHANIC'S RELATIVES"
(to the tune of "Yankee Doodle")

I'm Uncle Samuel's big step son,
  My father's name is Labor;
My constant visitor is Dun,
  And Want my nearest neighbor.

My mother's maiden name was Toil,
  My sister's name is Slavery;
And, though I never share the spoil,
  I'm famed in war for bravery.

Who were the men who fought and tell,
  By cannon ball or sabre;
Or starved in southern prison cell,
  But the stalwart sons of Labor?

My kind stepmother's name is Trade,
  Her son is Opposition;
She bows to him, the fickle jade,
  Which alters my condition.

They say of trade [sic] he is the life,
  Yet he lowers and degrades men;
Mrs. Reduction is his wife,
  And they're the death of tradesmen.

Their eldest child is Ten Per Cent,
  An apt and cunning scholar,
Who hacks and hacks away, content
  To whittle down my dollar.

But there's a remedy they say,
  And in my fist I'll stick it;
Go to the polls election day,
  And vote the People's ticket.

I'll leave my relative's cunning lot
  To his majesty Satanic;
So, politicians! forget me not,
  I'm sturdy Mike McChanic.

John Brophy, Troy, September, 1884;
published in *John Swinton's Paper*,
September 21, 1884

Introduction

On december 28, 1880, the *Troy Daily Times* reported, Francis Murphy's Christian Temperance Revival gained perhaps its most impressive local convert when Dugald Campbell, the head of the Liquor Dealers' Association, took the pledge.[1] Campbell's leadership of the association, however, only begins to explain the importance of this conversion. He was also an elder statesman of the region's labor movement, readily recognized throughout the working-class communities of both Troy and Cohoes as the onetime iron molder who was a fiery labor organizer and land reformer, as well as a tavern owner, poet, and lecturer.

Little is known of Campbell's early life beyond the fact that he was born in Scotland in 1820.[2] What led him to become a labor organizer is unclear, but in 1857, when a Philadelphia iron molder, William Sylvis, sought to organize the molders into a national union, Campbell's support was solicited. Campbell, who was apparently in Jersey City at that time, responded favorably and helped organize a local there; at some point he even became its president.[3]

After the Civil War, Campbell surfaced again in the pages of the *Iron Molders' International Journal*, writing letters from Jersey City and Peekskill, New York, strongly supporting the Cooperative Movement and the Eight-Hour Movement. In September, 1866, he attended the National Labor Union Congress, but complained that molders were poorly represented and that the Eight-Hour issue was lost among other resolutions pressed by the delegates. To Campbell, delegates did not seem willing to place common problems above their own special concerns or self-interest.[4] Discouraged, he turned back to the Iron Molders' International Union. He

1

urged that apprenticeship regulations be enforced, that sons of molders be given priority employment "as fathers will inculcate good union principles," and that benevolent benefits be extended beyond death.[5] Moving to Troy shortly thereafter, he was now committed to building a strong local movement; while national efforts may have lagged, labor organizations thrived there.

Several features of the Troy labor movement attracted Campbell. First, the city itself was the home of the largest and strongest molders' union local, and had built one of the first and most active cooperative foundries in the country. By 1869 Campbell seems to have married a young Irish woman and begun a family.[6] Still a molder, he also served as local correspondent to *Finchers' Trade Review* and as superintendent of the Troy collarmakers' union cooperative, one of the nation's first female unions.

By the mid-1870s, Campbell and his growing family had settled into the city's social life. He joined the Third Street Baptist Church. Now in his mid-fifties, he left the foundry—since the work had become too strenuous—and ran a saloon. As the *Journal* of the Iron Molders' International Union explained it: "Dugald Campbell, so well known for his grip the poetic muse had on him at one time, as well as for his Horace Greeley style of writing, has never deserted the cause, but hard work got rather the better of him, and he now tries to keep the boys' spirits up in Troy, by furnishing them spirits to put down."[7] But the poetic muse had not deserted him, and Campbell had not deserted the labor movement. He continued to help organize the Troy Industrial Council and simultaneously completed a volume of romantic poetry, *Blue Ribbon Lays*. In succeeding years he assumed the proprietorship of the Holly Tree Inn and became head of the Liquor Dealers' Association. After taking the pledge, however, Campbell became a leading temperance advocate, editing and publishing a temperance newspaper in 1880 and 1881.

Campbell's last years were devoted to the struggle for the rights of working men and women. He seemed to appear on a different platform almost every evening. During the bitter, protracted 1882 strike in Cohoes's Harmony Mills, for example, he spoke on five different occasions: he gave a temperance lecture, addressed the 'Irish Land League and urged contributions to aid Irish tenant farmers, promised a rally of striking cotton workers the support of the Central Labor Union of New York, lectured at Egberts Hall on "A Night Wi' Burns" (giving the same lecture delivered earlier at New York's Clarendon Hall as part of his statewide lecture tour on Robert Burns's life and poetry), and spoke at a political rally celebrating the election of a Cohoes strike leader to the New York State Assembly.[8] At his death in 1884, he left his thirty-three-year-old wife, Anna, six children, and a volume of poetry. Campbell's modification of a familiar pauper's epitaph rightly stands as his own:

> Rattle his bones,
> Over the stones,
> He's only a molder,
> Nobody owns.[9]

While Dugald Campbell's leadership positions distinguish him within the Troy working class, his biographical sketch tells us something of the less articulate, for it discloses that network of working-class associations and activities which developed during the post–Civil War years and which informed the attitudes and behavior of those engaging in labor protest at this time. Though he was a Scot, Campbell's life is paradigmatic of the associational experience of the predominantly Irish and French-Canadian immigrants to this region. This organizational experience provides some insight into the continuing process of adaptation by which the worker community became an effectual social and political unit in industrial society.

The relationship between adaptation to new circumstances and protest against those circumstances is complex. Adaptation and protest seem to be in opposition, but they are not mutually exclusive responses to socioeconomic conditions; instead, they are dialectically and inextricably linked aspects of human behavior. Adaptation in fact represents a neutral historical process in which protest occurs. By adapting, a group modifies to meet the requirements of the changing social and political environment, perhaps to accommodate to that environment, but perhaps to change it. The specific social context in which the group finds itself is crucial. An immigrant family and kinship network may reorganize itself—that is, adapt—in the New World, but whether or not it supports a strike will depend on many factors, including alternative sources of family income or a sudden family crisis (e.g., illness) that might necessitate an immediate return to work.

Historians have concluded that adaptation usually precedes and facilitates protest.[10] The study of Troy and Cohoes confirms the central thesis of Edward Shorter and Charles Tilly that "there is little doubt that the efflorescence of strikes came in direct consequence of . . . [an] improved associational foundation."[11] Two other observations by Shorter and Tilly are also pertinent here. Regional collective action changes over time as the dominant industrial sector changes; in addition, the nature of the city is a major source of territorial variation in conflict.[12] These changing patterns, they note, require knowledge of local conditions and particular mentalities that lie hidden in the histories of local communities. The study of Troy and Cohoes can provide a window into the complex world of local particularities that influence protest patterns. In addition, Cohoes is what Shorter and Tilly call a mono-industrial company town, while Troy is a poly-industrial city.[13] Their French strike statistics suggest that larger cities provided associational possibilities which more readily supported collective action. Such data cannot, of course, speak to the experience of workers whose history falls outside the statistical "average"—such as striking Cohoes cotton workers in the early 1880s. The study of Troy and Cohoes illuminates the thesis that adaptation generally precedes protest, but it also illustrates how local traditions and circumstances can affect particular patterns of protest.

As immigrants like Dugald Campbell settled into growing cities such as Troy, they had to establish a network of voluntary associations, build churches, develop community social and political bases, and perhaps even reshape their ethnic mores. Campbell's life and associations suggest the configuration of the working-class community that emerged in these cities. His strong ties to the labor movement extended to the Baptist Church and, through the saloon, to the local area in which he lived. His poetry helped maintain an ethnic consciousness on "Scotch Hill" in the ninth "iron" ward. And his temperance activities may have aided work discipline, but they also made for a sober, more financially self-reliant union member.

Worker priorities, suggested by Campbell's, often contrasted with those set by the business community. Class positions were not always as clearly defined as this suggests, since ethnic bonds (for instance, between the working-class and middle-class Irish who were not manufacturers) often proved equally important. Nevertheless, basic divisions and conflict did emerge; and the disorder that they produced in the 1870s and 1880s provides the major focus for the social history of Troy and Cohoes. Such conflict cannot be understood simply as a labor conflict, for workers had ethnic, religious, and political identities as well. Ethnic associations such as the Fenians and political organizations such as the Working Men's party helped cement ties between ironworkers and the rest of the worker community. Manufacturers opposed this network of worker associations with their own ethnic, religious, and political groupings, such as Troy's Law and Order League, which would advance their own interests. The study of labor protest in these cities must include these larger political and social dimensions whenever possible.

Finally, the history of the Troy and Cohoes working class suggests how protest patterns were shaped by both internal and external dynamic processes. Internally, the changing relationship of class and ethnicity affected workers' ability to organize socially and politically. Political and nationalist associations had previously served a variety of interests, including those of their primarily immigrant working-class constituency. Increasingly, however, with the emergence of an immigrant or migrant middle-class leadership, these associations more narrowly served ethnic rather than class interests. Externally, the dynamics of industrial capitalism meant more than the introduction of new technology; capitalism also involved repeated efforts by manufacturers to impose a work discipline, increase productivity, and lower costs. Locked into the competitive pressures produced by continual price fluctuations, workers and manufacturers had to struggle within the marketplace and with each other to maintain or improve their competitive edge.

Troy and Cohoes are good historical laboratories in which to test these theories concerning adaptation and protest. Troy was among the first industrial cities in America, while Cohoes early became a "company town," possessing for a time in the 1870s the largest cotton mill in the world, the Harmony Mills' "Mastodon" (No. 3) Mill. Although other cities could make equal claims to the distinction, one prominent historical archeologist has recently characterized this region as "the birthplace of America's Industrial Revolution."[14] Cohoes's Harmony Mills, with 5,000 operatives, constituted one of the nation's largest textile firms, dominating the political economy of the city. Most important, a five-month strike in 1882 received widespread local and national newspaper coverage, and it provided the opportunity to examine large-scale worker protest in a company town.

Troy had the advantage of being just across the Hudson River from Cohoes, thereby providing an example of contrasting behavior within one political and economic region. It was also the home of a local of one of the country's strongest unions, the Iron Molders' International Union No. 2, which labor historians have considered to be in the forefront of the immediate post–Civil War union movement.[15] Troy's was the nation's largest and most powerful molders' local; its members were instrumental in organizing the workforce of both cities and were deeply involved in Troy's political processes. Not only did they provide the organizing impetus for much of the region's working class, but they also were central to the famous molders' lockout of 1866. Finally, what Troy's Republican newspaper frequently characterized as the city's "reign of terror" in the 1870s and 1880s occurred with dramatic clarity and attracted wide popular attention.

Consequently, the history of nineteenth-century Troy and Cohoes is of more than merely local relevance or antiquarian interest. The contrasting histories of the two illuminate the *process* of social transformation which resulted in American industrial society. By the mid-1850s the Industrial Revolution had proceeded apace, and while its date varies for each region and industry, the first phase was ending in the North Atlantic states. The permanence of the new industrial regime had been established in the antebellum years. There were urban markets, transportation facilities, available technologies, and a reserve labor force.

Between 1840 and 1860 the United States achieved a rapid and sustained economic growth.[16] Its population increased 85 percent, buoyed particularly by extensive Irish and German immigration between 1845 and 1854. Newcomers from Ireland settled mostly in the north and east, swelling the cities there. The shortage of skilled labor, especially in comparison with England, had encouraged the search for new technologies and the development of a capital-intensive economy. Simultaneously, the largely unskilled Irish immigrants provided an abundant supply of cheap labor. Together, abundant unskilled labor and advanced technology would help

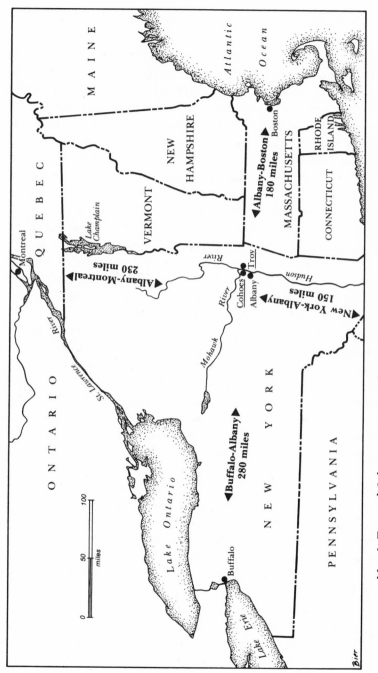

MAP 1. Troy and Cohoes region. Note both cities' relationship to rural New England, French Canada, coastal urban centers, and major waterways.

catapult American industrial production into a position of world leadership by 1900.[17]

By the mid-1850s most major manufacturing industries in Troy and Cohoes had been transformed by technology. The Cohoes textile industry had been almost completely mechanized; a dramatic ninefold increase in the number of spindles per cotton mill between 1815 and 1860 suggests the dimensions of this technological achievement.[18] Though full mechanization in other industries lagged somewhat behind such developments in the cotton industry, the technology for full-scale factory production had been introduced into many major manufacturing areas by 1870. In Troy a horseshoe machine revolutionized the Burden Iron Works in 1846. Ten years later, in England, the Bessemer process had been developed; Troy manufacturers soon purchased the patent rights. And within the next decade, like the more familiar case of shoe manufacturing, the shirt-and-collar industry would be transformed from an independent cottage industry to large-scale factory production.[19]

In addition, substantial foreign investment entered the United States from 1851 to 1857, at a rate comparable to that of the 1830s.[20] Output also rose. In the 1850s, for instance, cotton textile production increased 77 percent, pig iron and railroad iron production increased 54 percent and 100 percent respectively, and the output of engines and machinery rose 66 percent.[21] By the Civil War, then, industrialization was well under way, and the problems connected with *becoming* industrialized lay behind the nation.[22]

By the mid-1880s, when this study ends, Troy and Cohoes had developed many of the characteristics of a mature industrial society.[23] The main criterion for such a society—about half the population living in cities—had been met in the North Atlantic states: 51.8 percent of the people in this region were urban dwellers in 1890.[24] Most urban workers were no longer new to industry, having lived in cities and worked in factories for two or three generations. Immigration continued, of course, but newcomers now entered a more settled industrial world. Work rhythms and factory discipline could still be dislocating and, in fact, were still contested. But, to many longtime residents, the regime was familiar and relatively entrenched.

Industrial capitalism also underwent a fundamental change during this period. An emergent monopoly capitalism began to dominate the local political economy. Before the war, as a leading historian of American industrialization described it, "competition was usually preserved and monopoly avoided by the sheer elasticity of the market."[25] By the 1890s, however, rival companies were amalgamated in industry after industry and city after city.[26] In Cohoes, for example, rival cotton mills had become concentrated in a single large cotton manufacturing company, the Harmony Mills; and the iron mills of Troy were combined in one vast rolling mill, the Troy Iron and Steel Company. While the stove industry had not gone through such a process, workers labored in increasingly large foundries and one company, the Clinton works, had come to dominate the city's stove industry.[27] Finally, the horizontal integration of competing companies—some of which had previously expanded vertically—heralded the development of what would later prove to be an important new economic and social sector: white-collar managerial bureaucracies. (The full emergence of this sector, however, would not take place until the twentieth century.)

The mid-1880s are a convenient juncture in another respect. Adaptation and acculturation had begun for the Irish, English, and German immigrants who arrived during the early and mid-nineteenth century. Associations and institutions reflect the changing ethnic and class alliances. With the important exception of substantial numbers of French Canadians who settled in Cohoes in the 1870s, this study concludes before immigrants from Eastern and Southern Europe arrived and renewed the process of adaptation and struggle.

Moreover, as noted above, there are good reasons for studying Cohoes and Troy together. Immigrants from England and Ireland came early to each city and soon dominated both the cotton and iron industries. Furthermore, these cities are only two miles apart, which permitted occasional interaction between their inhabitants. Indeed, Troy's ironworkers helped organize and sustain the Cohoes cotton workers during the industrial crises of this period.

More important, however, were the differences between the cities and the situations confronting their respective workforces. Cohoes was a textile village of 8,800 people in 1860 that quickly became a one-company town. Between two and twenty wool knit-goods factories employed several thousand workers and made Cohoes the nation's largest producer of wool knit goods during the immediate postbellum years. But it was the cotton manufacture of

the Harmony Mills which made Cohoes a company town. By the end
of the Civil War, Harmony Mills had absorbed all of Cohoes's cotton
mills and workers. As in Troy's iron industry, many of the operatives
were Irish immigrants, and they had entered the mills in large numbers prior to the war. But Cohoes differed from Troy in two important particulars: a new immigrant labor force (of French Canadians)
arrived in the 1870s, and cotton and woolen workers were largely
women and girls.

To continue this study in contrasts, Troy's population grew from
39,235 in 1860 to 56,757 in 1880. It was a much more complex city
than Cohoes, with two major industries: the iron mills and foundries, and the shirt and collar industry. The latter employed women,
while the ironworks only hired men and boys. Several large iron
mills and foundries (and a growing shirt, collar, and laundry industry) dominated Troy's social and industrial life. Three large iron and
steelworks (each with 500-2,000 employees), and numerous but relatively small stove foundries (50-200 employees) existed there, and
they were to provide the focus for worker protest. Moreover, as
noted, in the twenty years after the Civil War, Troy possessed one of
the nation's strongest and best-organized labor movements. Troy's
iron molders flourished until the 1873–77 depression, when the
concerted efforts of local iron founders combined to thwart their organization and power. In response, the protracted period of violence
which erupted—the so-called reign of terror—contrasted with
Cohoes's relative quiescence in the 1870s.

The central concern of this study is the contrasting situations and
behavioral patterns of iron and cotton workers in post–Civil War
Troy and Cohoes. These neighboring industrial cities had emerged
very differently from the war. Troy became a "worker city," and
Cohoes a "company town." The difference encapsulated by these
terms produced different responses from their respective workforces. But, while this study points toward the eruption of lengthy
strikes and violence, first in Troy and later in Cohoes, a description
of the distinct patterns of order and disorder in each considers the
specific circumstances as well as the broader historical process
within which the strikes developed. This monograph, then, is a historical anatomy of emerging protest. It examines worker adaptation
in two industrial capitalist societies maturing between 1855 and

1884, and describes how specific forces and institutions affected the timing, stages, origins, and character of protest therein.

Local history tends to emphasize the unique in each situation, and ultimately what we have is simply a history of Troy and Cohoes. A comparison of these cities cannot provide a definite model for worker protest, for, as Marc Bloch warned, the comparative method "is not capable of solving everything."[28] Rather, as another scholar has observed, a comparative *perspective* "reduces our bias by presenting us with alternative systems of values and world views, and by imparting to us a sense of the richness and variety of human experience; *it provides us not with rules, but with insights.*"[29] Although the comparison of two cities as different as Troy and Cohoes can only begin to clarify the *cluster of causal agents underlying different behavior patterns*, such a comparative perspective does enable us to study the contrasting ways in which specific social and economic variables may influence the distinct timing and patterns of protest in each city. Only when other American cities have been similarly studied will it become possible for historians to compare American and European protest patterns.

Cohoes typified the company town; Troy was the larger, more diverse city. Cohoes had mostly female cotton workers and a complex ethnic and social community; Troy's male ironworkers and their community provide a contrasting but no less intricate configuration. Finally, and most importantly, the cotton and iron industries differed in two significant ways. First, the cotton industry was mechanized early (in contrast with the iron industry), and technological innovations continually intervened in the working lives of cotton hands in these years. Second, and it must be emphasized, railroad growth led the Industrial Revolution. Overproduction of rails, and the fact that stoves (consumer goods with a relatively high durability) had been the major iron commodity in the 1860s, meant that the 1873–77 depression especially affected the iron industry.[30] Protest must be examined in the context of these specific conditions.

Of course, neither Troy nor Cohoes can tell the whole story of urban industrial protest; no one or two cities can. Yet both were major manufacturing centers, and the large modern factory came quickly to each. Moreover, immigrants dominated the working class of each city in its early period of significant growth. So we can examine the ways in which radical technological and social change, a fluid but discernible class structure, and immigrant life affected working-class protest in these two urban areas. Likewise, we can study the reverse process: the extent to which the conditions of working-class life interacted with particular technological changes and conditioned behavior. Most importantly, though, the 1882 Harmony Mills strike and the organization and protest associated with the Troy iron molders have been significant but heretofore neglected chapters of America's social and labor history.

This study seeks to combine several different traditions in labor historiography. First, an analysis of the origins of protest in Troy and Cohoes includes the older trade union history. However, it also considers the broader class experience that informs trade union activity, such as non-union labor, family life, working and living conditions, popular attitudes and values, and the political and economic structure of the city. Unfortunately, the paucity of some local sources—a problem endemic to community studies—thwarts a full examination of all these areas, making the discussion of such topics as religion more speculative than one might like. Second, this monograph attempts to synthesize the "new" and "old" social history, combining the use of elementary descriptive statistics with literary and narrative accounts.[31] But this is not simply another quantitative inquiry into social mobility or family structure; rather, it is a social history of adaptation and of protest and repression within two communities. Third, this study is located in two adjacent cities, but its larger context is that of a maturing industrial society. To begin to understand working-class behavior, historians must place the above-noted processes in a specific historical context: we must be city-specific, industry-specific, and skill-specific. Here, then, are two specific situations: ironworkers in a burgeoning city with a diversified economy and with extended industrial violence, and cotton workers in a company town in which protest did not develop until the 1880s. Each city's unique economic and social structure dominated urban working-class life over a half-century, and each sharpened the protest patterns of its workforce.

This monograph tries to demonstrate how specificity and differences associated with each city and its workforce constitute a neglected framework for understanding working-class behavior. It also urges a reconsideration of one of the enduring interpretations of America's history; namely, that the Civil War ended sectional disputes and prompted a resurgent nationalism.[32] I will argue that localism, and not the triumphant nation, continued to dominate the day-to-day concerns and behavior of most Americans and to structure much of postwar history. To be sure, a new national awareness was developing, but this study will suggest that, at least for the increasing numbers of urban, working-class Americans, the local community constituted the main arena of intellectual, social, and political life. Increasingly protest occurred in an urban economy beset both by national economic pressures and by a growing dependence on national political authorities, but a narrowly privatized and local vision also persisted within large segments of the working class. On the national level, in addition to the direct involvement of many workers in the Civil War (Troy molders, for example, enlisted en masse), local Troy and Cohoes labor engaged in or responded to national and international movements and ideas throughout the period, including the Cooperative Movement, Greenback Movement, Land and Labor Leagues, Eight-Hour Movement, and the development of citywide Trades' Assemblies and the Knights of Labor. Workers also joined national trade unions, and incoming aid was a valued and important asset. But, to repeat, though local worker activities were built in the context of these national and international currents, the immediate situation and the personal needs and experiences of workers still tended to dominate.

The traditions and expectations which immigrants brought to America, as well as the impact of the specific situation encountered here, contributed to this immediacy. Even for immigrants the hegemonic culture worked some of its magic. Many newcomers enlisted in the fight for the Union and swore allegiance to their adopted homeland. They were immersed in such nationally celebrated beliefs as upward social mobility, the melting pot, and the moral virtue of the independent, self-sufficient yeoman—propositions which tended to obscure the reality of social class in America. But daily life was a struggle to survive and achieve, and for many urban workers and their families the immediate context for that struggle extended simply from the home to the community and factory—and, finally, to the city.

The struggle between capital and labor to determine the shape of the new factory environment is a major theme of postwar America. Ironically, the old, established farm families and rising industrial entrepreneurs began to lose control of the very towns the latter had helped change. New immigrant working-class communities established themselves and reshaped the priorities and institutions of the urban environment in their own image. However, this transition did not take place unopposed, and the contest for control provided the major focus for the energy and concern of city dwellers. In Cohoes and Troy the struggle was resolved by national forces which only the manufacturers seemed able to harness, mostly because, as the power brokers, they found the options available under industrial capitalism working in their favor. When the discipline of unruly workers was at issue, they turned to state and federal courts or troops if local authorities failed them. As a last resort, they risked losing their older markets and their capital investments by moving to newer markets and cheaper sources of labor in the South or West, leaving behind a factory shell and a shocked workforce. This last tactic would be repeated at other times.[33] New immigrant groups would have to fight these battles in a somewhat different context, but the elements in the process would be much the same: arrival, adaptation, struggle, and protest.

We can begin by identifying the social and economic characteristics of these communities. Such a complicated task requires a complicated strategy. The contrasting urban structures and histories demand separate consideration, for the most part; yet the ethnic elements of one city also lived in the other, and many of the economic and social conditions were regional. Therefore this volume's middle chapters, on attitudes and social conditions, consider the workers of both cities together.

Part I consists of successive chapters describing the structure of each city. There is further background on the major industries, their founders and labor force, and the effect of technological developments. This discussion sets the stage for the larger theme, the ways in which census data permit our reconstruction of the ethnic and class configurations which shaped working-class behavior. The focus in Part II shifts to the process of adaptation in these cities, in order to locate the postwar protest in the context of changing living and working conditions. Chapter 3 describes the early industrial history of both cities, leading up to the 1866 molder lockout, the region's first collective protest of major significance. That chapter traces the organized beginnings of the largely immigrant workforces of each city, the differing results, and the attempt to shape an urban order suitable to their social and political priorities. Chapters 4 and 5, which remain city-specific, industry-specific, and skill-specific, describe conditions under which workers settled, and how their experience and settlement provided the groundwork for protest. Part III presents a chronological discussion of urban working-class protest in the 1870s and 1880s. This section focuses on trade union activity, but places the violence in the context of worker and manufacturer competition to control the workplace. This violence ultimately involved the mayor's office, the police, the courts, and the support of the iron and cotton-worker ethnic communities. We have looked at Cohoes from 1855 to 1884, but have restricted our study of Troy to four unusually intense and dramatic periods—1855 to 1860, 1864 to 1866, 1873 to 1877, and 1880 to 1884—years during which American industrial society matured.

NOTES

1. *Troy Daily Times*, December 29, 1880.
2. U.S. Census Office, Tenth Census, 1880, *Statistics of the Population*, MS for Rensselaer County, N.Y. Campbell either married a woman many years his junior or had remarried: his wife, Anna, was listed as twenty-nine years old in 1880 (Campbell was sixty), while his eldest child was fifteen years old. He also had five other children, aged fourteen, eleven, eight, six, and four.
3. Most of the biographical information on Dugald Campbell's life is pieced together from references in the *Iron Molders' International Journal*, 1864–84, *Troy Daily Times*, 1873–77 and 1880–85, and *Cohoes Daily News*, 1880–84.
4. *Iron Molders' International Journal*, September, 1866.
5. Ibid., December, 1866.
6. *Troy City Directory*, 1869.
7. *Iron Molders' International Journal*, February 1874.
8. *Cohoes Daily News*, February 29, August 24, September 20, November 8, 1882. I have no evidence of Campbell's views on the Woman Question; he recognized their particularly exploited economic position and worked to unionize them.
9. *Iron Molders' International Journal*, April, 1874. Campbell puts this epitaph in quotes but does not attribute its authorship to anyone else. Angus McLaren, however, has uncovered this ditty in a Malthusian pamphlet by W. J. Douse, *The True Remedy for Poverty* (27th ed., Nottingham, 1895), p. 43, with the word "pauper" instead of "molder."
10. Neil Smelser, *Social Change in the Industrial Revolution* (London, 1959); and Michael Anderson, *Family Structure in Nineteenth-Century Lancashire* (Cambridge, 1971). Melvyn Dubofsky kindly forced me to develop the argument in this section.
11. Edward Shorter and Charles Tilly, *Strikes in France, 1830–1968* (Cambridge, 1974), p. 47.
12. Ibid., pp. 255–67.
13. Ibid., pp. 288–90. They also have a third category, "metropolitan," for cities such as Paris. New York or Philadelphia would be American equivalents.

14. Robert Vogel, Chairman of the Department of Science and Technology, Smithsonian Institution, in an address to the Institute on Industrial Archeology, Rensselaer Polytechnic Institute, Troy, June 1974.

15. See, e.g., John R. Commons and associates, *History of Labor in the United States* (New York, 1918–35), II, 48–56; Joseph G. Rayback, *A History of American Labor* (New York, 1959), p. 107; and Philip S. Foner, *History of the Labor Movement in the United States* (New York, 1947), I.

16. Douglas C. North, *The Economic Growth of the United States, 1790–1860* (New York, 1966), v and *passim*.

17. H. J. Habakkuk, *American and British Technology in the Nineteenth Century: The Search for Labor-Saving Inventions* (Cambridge, 1962), pp. 124–28.

18. Victor S. Clark, *History of Manufacturers in the United States* (New York, 1929), I, 450–53.

19. Peter Temin, *Iron and Steel in Nineteenth-Century America: An Economic Inquiry* (Cambridge, Mass., 1964); Samuel Rezneck, "Office Building 1881, Burden Iron Company, Troy: Historical Information," in *A Report of the Mohawk-Hudson Area Survey*, comp. Robert M. Vogel (Washington, 1973), pp. 73–94; and Alan Dawley and Paul Faler, "Working-Class Culture and Politics in the Industrial Revolution, 1820–1890," paper delivered at the American Historical Association convention, Chicago, December 28, 1974.

20. North, *Economic Growth*, Tables II–VIII, p. 238.

21. Eighth Census, 1860, *Manufactures in the United States*, Introduction, cited in North, *Economic Growth*, p. 168.

22. North, *Economic Growth*, pp. 165–76.

23. Peter N. Stearns, *European Society in Upheaval: Social History since 1740* (New York, 1975), pp. 179–81.

24. Eleventh Census, 1890, *Report on the Population of the United States*, I, p. lxviii.

25. Thomas C. Cochran and William Miller, *The Age of Enterprise: A Social History of Industrial America* (New York, rev. ed., 1961 [1942]), p. 61.

26. Ibid., chs. 7 and 9.

27. See ch. 1 and Table 1.2.

28. Marc Bloch, "Toward a Comparative History of European Societies" [1925], in *Enterprise and Secular Change*, ed. Frederick C. Lane and Jelle C. Riemersma (Homewood, Ill., 1953), p. 495. William Sewell generously provided me with this reference. See his article, "Marc Bloch and the Logic of Comparative History," *History and Theory* 6, no. 2 (1967): 208–18. Credit for much of the current interest in comparative social history must be given to the article by Peter N. Stearns, "National Character and European Labor History," *Journal of Social History* 4, no. 2 (Winter 1970):95–124.

29. Sewell, "Marc Bloch," p. 218. Emphasis mine.

30. Clark, *History of Manufactures*, II, 1860–93, pp. 280, 355–57, 403–17; Rendig Fels, *American Business Cycles, 1865–1897* (Chapel Hill, N.C., 1959); Paul F. McGouldrick, *New England Textiles in the Nineteenth Century: Profits and Investment* (Cambridge, Mass., 1968); and S. B. Saul, *The Myth of the Great Depression* (London, 1969). Prof. Sidney Ratner kindly directed me through this literature.

31. I have commented elsewhere at greater length on the need to use statistics with non-quantitative sources. See Daniel J. Walkowitz, "Statistics and the Writing of Working-Class Culture: A Statistical Portrait of the Iron Workers in Troy, New York, 1860–1880," *Labor History* 15, no. 3 (Summer 1974):416–60.

32. Robert H. Wiebe, *The Search for Order, 1877–1920* (New York, 1967), has earlier challenged this conventional view and described nineteenth-century America as a "society of island communities." This study builds on Wiebe's fine work, but focuses more on the social class dynamic in local situations in a somewhat earlier period.

33. See Herbert G. Gutman, "Work, Culture, and Society in Industrializing America, 1815–1919," *American Historical Review* 78, no. 3 (June 1973):531–88.

PART I

Social and Economic Structure

Quite a party went up to modern Ilium to attend the opening of the Free Reading Room and Library, opened under the auspices of the Trades' Assembly. We found the Hall completely filled, and an Editor addressing them. . . .
We found a well-filled library, and on file several daily and weekly papers, including the *Review*. Take this Reading Room and their Union Store, with the way they generally do business there, and they are justly entitled to the name of the Banner City.

—Anonymous letter to the editor, *Fincher's Trade Review*, July 29, 1865

But most of all to admire is the substantial houses either of wood or brick for the employees of Harmony Company. Everything is so home-like.

—*Cohoes Cataract*, June 20, 1868

CHAPTER 1

Worker City: Troy and the Ironworker Community

TROY WAS SITUATED on a narrow plateau along the east bank of the Hudson at the confluence of the Mohawk River. It was formed in 1789, more than a century after the old Dutch city of Albany some seven miles to the south. Unlike many other American cities, two industries shaped its growth: the shirt-and-collar industry, and the iron industry. Still called the "Collar City," Troy today is a mere shadow of its former self. Only one shirt factory remains, and the iron industry is gone. In the mid-nineteenth century, however, the small market and dock town was rapidly transformed into a mature industrial city; its two industries dominated a bustling urban economy in which men labored in iron mills and foundries and women stitched, ironed, and finished shirts and collars in large factories.[1]

Industrialization created new jobs, and they attracted many of the Irish immigrants then arriving in the United States. Moreover, Troy's numerous foundries and mills offered work to both men and women. Compared to New England textile towns, this diversified economy provided relatively open employment, as well as more fluid social and political opportunities. Census data suggest such opportunities by outlining Troy's social and economic structure.

For a fuller understanding of the city's ironworkers, we must look at the individual workers—particular molders and puddlers, for instance—and, by using city directories and narrative sources, some description of working-class leadership will be possible in later chapters. Meanwhile, in addition to offering important information about Troy's social and economic structure, these data provide a crucial link between the narrative of labor events and the social context in

19

which they took place. The census enables us to identify the social characteristics of the ironworkers: their ethnic background, age, property holdings, residential patterns, occupation, and household structure. With such data labor history can begin to evolve into social history. For example, we can inquire whether a group of workers who struck at a certain time were, in the aggregate, significantly older or younger, more or less likely to be married (i.e., "settled"), or more often Irish or English than workers in the same trade at another time. Such information opens an important comparative dimension: the study of those periods or situations in which protest does and does not occur. Even quite simple descriptive statistics can provide the groundwork for studies in social history.

Analysis of Troy's social and economic structure, its diverse economy and developing iron industry suggests the alternatives offered to urban labor. The industry itself provided good job opportunities in many mills and foundries, and no single firm dominated the city's economic, social, or political life. The census reveals three general developments: increasingly, between 1860 and 1880, the Irish became predominant within the iron industry; they experienced considerable mobility into skilled positions; and some obtained property. These achievements of Irish ironworkers contrasted favorably with the pre-immigration poverty which they or their parents had recently experienced.

Economic Development

Troy was geographically well situated for rapid growth. The region was rich in natural resources, with mountain streams generating power for the mills. The adjoining canal and river network provided cheap and convenient transportation for raw materials and for the distribution of finished products to other markets. Troy serviced northern New England and, after 1825, served as the embarkation port for points west and north on the Erie and Champlain canals respectively. Finally, the city was near those mineral deposits so necessary to iron manufacture: dark magnetic ore from the mines of the Lake Champlain region; limestone for flux and ample quantities of molding sand from the Hudson Valley; coal from the anthracite regions of northeast Pennsylvania; pig iron for the foundries from Vermont and Pennsylvania, from Columbia and Dutchess counties

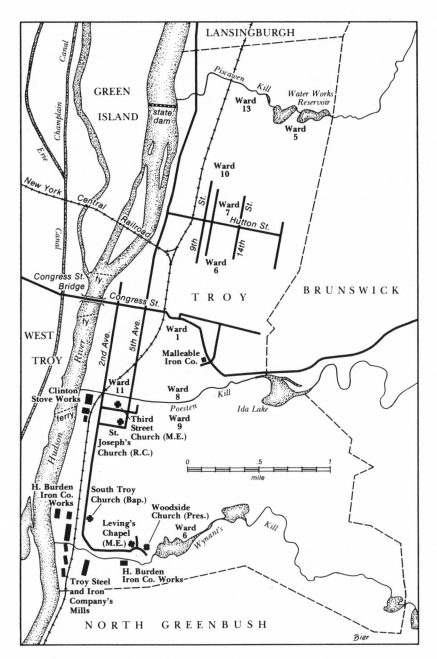

MAP 2. Late Nineteenth Century Troy

in the Hudson Valley, and from Clinton and Essex counties in the Adirondacks.[2]

In the 1870s, the iron and the shirt-and-collar industries not only paced Troy's growth but shaped it in special ways, so that the city's social structure reflected the presence of these enterprises. For instance, employment opportunities for women in the collar and shirt factories made for a more balanced sex ratio than in nearby Cohoes, where a single cotton mill dominated the city and depended so heavily on women workers as to upset the male-female balance.[3] In addition, these industries attracted a substantial workforce. Troy counted 39,235 residents in 1860 and 56,747 twenty years later (Table 1.1).[4]

Immigrants and their children were in the majority, with three out of every five falling into this category in 1860. The flow of foreign born increased over the next two decades, so that by 1880 immigrants and their children comprised nearly two out of every three residents. Troy's iron industry absorbed more than its share of these newcomers. Some 2,000 men, almost one of every six Troy males over the age of fourteen, worked in an iron mill or foundry in 1860; twenty years later the figure had climbed to 4,500, and the ratio was now 1:4. The industry's share of the labor force had outpaced the city's population growth, and within particular immigrant groups this ratio rose even higher. Among the Irish, for example, who made up the largest number of workers in 1880, about three of every eight males were employed in the iron industry. The ratio of Scottish and English ironworkers was slightly higher, and that of the Canadians, Germans, and native-born Americans lower. Troy's small black population was systematically excluded from the industry.[5]

What, then, of the iron industry itself? Not surprisingly, it had modest beginnings, but expanding markets and the direction provided by several entrepreneurs and inventors caused the industry to grow steadily. The Civil War brought in orders for horseshoes and iron plate which greatly stimulated Troy's iron manufacture. The small mills of the first half of the century began to amalgamate after hostilities ended, and work became concentrated in a few large mills and foundries.

Troy's local historian has described how the Albany Rolling and Slitting Mill opened on the lower falls of Wynants Kill in 1807. Two

TABLE 1.1. Troy Population Statistics, 1860 and 1880

	1860	1880	Change (%)
Total population	39,237	56,747	+44.6
Non-white	611	577	− 5.6
Foreign born	13,461	16,938	+25.8
Native born	25,774	39,809	+54.5
Foreign extraction[a]	23,000 (est.)[b]	36,000 (est.)[b]	+56.5
Percent of total	59% (est.)	64% (est.)	+ 8.5
Males 15 and over	12,018 (est.)	18,884(est.)	+57.1

[a] "Foreign extraction" refers to immigrants and those with a foreign father.
[b] Estimates based on Rensselaer County figures for 1860, New York State figures for 1880.

years later a similar mill built by "other capitalists" started on the upper falls.[6] These were small works, and nothing much is known of them. By contrast, in a fifteen-year period after the Civil War, two newcomers to Troy developed their respective enterprises into multi-million-dollar businesses. One was Erastus Corning, an Albany entrepreneur, and the other a Scottish immigrant inventor named Henry Burden.

In 1826 Corning purchased the lower mill. He renamed it the Albany Iron Works in 1838, and had expanded it into a major Troy industry by the outbreak of the Civil War. With the assistance of a Vermont-born iron manufacturer, John F. Winslow, he operated a mill which employed 500 men and boys in the manufacture of bar and sheet iron. (Under their direction, the iron plates for the *Monitor* were made.) Renamed the Erastus Corning Company in 1867, it merged in 1875 with the Rensselaer Iron Company and Bessemer Steel Works of John A. Griswold & Company (Griswold being the other prominent Troy ironmaster) to form the gigantic Albany and Rensselaer Iron and Steel Company. Another operation, the Rensselaer Iron Works, had emerged in 1854 from the Troy Vulcan Company (1846) rolling mill. By 1860 the mill (controlled in a partnership by Griswold and Corning and their sons) employed 350 men and boys in the manufacture of bar and sheet iron. Lastly, the Bessemer Steel Works started in 1863 when three Troy entrepreneurs—Winslow, Griswold, and Alexander L. Holley—bought the American patent of the Bessemer process. (On February 16, 1865, iron was converted to steel for the first time in Troy.) After an extensive fire nearly destroyed the works in 1868, John A. Griswold & Company became owners. By 1880, with the merger of all three operations—the Albany Iron Works, the Rensselaer Iron Works, and the Bessemer Steel Works—the new Albany and Rensselaer Iron and Steel Company employed at least 1,500 men. It was incorporated as the Troy Iron and Steel Company in 1885 and capitalized at $2,500,000.[7]

Henry Burden's achievement was no less remarkable. The small mill begun in 1809, ten years before his arrival, had become the Troy Iron and Nail factory by 1813. In 1822 Burden, an engineer and inventor, was appointed superintendent there. During the next twenty-five years he held patents on a wrought iron nail-and-spike machine for railroad ties (1841), the rotary concentric squeezer (1840) which (substituting for the large hammer) converted balls of puddled iron into blooms, a horseshoe machine (1843), and many refinements on these and other machines. Finally, in 1848, he assumed control of the mill. During the Civil War his 370 employees produced horseshoes in great numbers for the Union Army.[8] The mill expanded rapidly and acquired forty-five acres along the Hudson. When Burden's two surviving sons incorporated the Burden Iron Company in 1881, the plant employed over 1,000 men and boys in the production of bolts, rivets, spikes, and wrought iron bars ("Burden's Best").[9]

Such developments meant that a large number of Troy ironworkers labored in mills of considerable size owned by local capitalists. By 1880 several of the iron mills had merged and, by contemporary standards, all had become vast enterprises. New businesses started, but the trend was toward larger operations. The three iron mills had become uniformly large, averaging 882 workers, with a sizeable unskilled workforce.[10] Two of the mills, however—the Burden Iron Company and the Troy Iron and Steel Company—employed more than 96 percent of all the Troy iron millhands. Similarly, work in the foundries increasingly concentrated in larger plants. In 1880 eighteen of the twenty-two foundries still employed less than one hundred men, most of whom were skilled stove-molders, mounters, and pattern-makers; however, the concentration of Troy foundry ownership in the next five years dramatically changed that picture. Foundries amalgamated rapidly and by 1885 work was concentrated in only seven shops. The largest—the Clinton Foundry—easily absorbed the foundry workforce, growing at an incredible rate. As late as 1880 it employed only 550 workers (one out of every four Troy foundry hands); by 1885 there were 1,200 (better than half of Troy's foundry workforce). Consequently, molders—skilled workers who organized more easily than the unskilled—concentrated until the early 1880s in relatively small foundries, which facilitated greater worker organization and protest among them than among iron-workers.

In sum, better than four out of every five employees worked in mills and foundries that employed at least a hundred men in both census years. Ownership concentrated, though, on a few large shops which employed an increasing share of the labor force. In addition, several hundred worked in smaller foundries or in iron-related in-dustries.[11] The entire city depended on the iron industry, especially on a few large mills. Consequently, when the iron industry suffered through a depression or strike, the entire city was immediately in-volved. The size of a mill tells us one thing, but the kind of manage-ment which workers confronted is also important. Hence, before examining Troy's ironworkers more closely, we must briefly look at the lives of those entrepreneurs who guided the industry and struc-tured much of the city's industrial life.

The Troy Ironmasters

Troy industrialists were readily distinguishable from the immigrant men and women who worked in their factories. As in other American cities at this time, they were mostly native born and Protestants. Their fathers were born in the United States (in 82 out of 104 in-stances), and by 1880 these native-born Americans accounted for almost half the entrepreneurs (54 out of 111), though native-born Protestants constituted less than one-third of the local population.[12] Except for Henry Burden, all the ironmasters seem to have been na-tive born. Aspiring immigrant capitalists like Edward Murphy, Jr., and Edmund Fitzgerald, both of whom later became part of Troy's ruling elite, started businesses such as breweries that had less estab-lished local competition and required less initial capital outlay.

Two entrepreneurial sectors existed within the iron industry: a group of small founders, and a smaller group of powerful financiers. Many of those with small works may have begun, like Jospeh Foxell, as molders who started independent operations with limited capital. As a union molder, Foxell participated in the lockout of 1866, but in 1875 he co-owned and operated Foxell and Jones' Foundry, with

about twenty-five molders. These small foundries were encounter-
ing increasing financial difficulty in their competition with the few
expanding larger works. Especially after 1880, most seem to have
disappeared upon the deaths of their owners, or to have become
amalgamated into the ever-expanding Clinton Foundry. Specific
reasons for this attrition remain unknown, but we may surmise that a
substantial cause lies in Troy's turbulent labor history and the
achievements of the molders' union. Perhaps, too, the sons of these
small founders began to prefer more stable non-industrial occupations. Some firms undoubtedly moved to new places, as did Philips
and Clark's Foundry when it was threatened in 1884. In addition,
according to a union molder who complained to a state legislative
committee in 1883, other founders established shops in prisons with
convict labor.[13] But most founders do not appear to have left, or
used cheap labor, or gone bankrupt. Rather, they sold out. The sons
of the first generation of owners rarely stayed with the iron industry;
however, they often remained in the city, holding prestigious financial and philanthropic posts.[14]

As the number of small foundries declined and the iron mills expanded and amalgamated, power concentrated in the hands of six
men and their families: four mill owners, Henry Burden, Erastus
Corning, John Griswold, and John Winslow; and the co-owners of
the Clinton Foundry, Joseph W. Fuller and Joseph M. Warren.
With the exception of Burden, these men did not remain involved in
the daily routine of shop production. Most were businessmen and
financiers who (like Corning) invested capital in Troy's mills, or (like
Winslow, Fuller, Warren, and Griswold) used the wealth amassed
from their operations as a springboard to influential political and
financial positions. Much of Corning's fortune actually came from
railroads, and he was the first president of the New York Central.
Winslow was president of Troy's Rensselaer Polytechnic Institute in
the mid-1860s, and he later headed the Poughkeepsie and Eastern
Railroad. Fuller became president of Troy's United National Bank,
and Warren became first vice-president of the Troy Savings Bank. In
addition, each of these men wielded considerable political
influence. Before the Civil War, Warren and Griswold were Troy
mayors, Corning was mayor of Albany, and both Griswold and Corning subsequently became congressmen. Only Burden remained rel-

atively uninvolved in such political and financial dealings, instead focusing his talents on operating and expanding his plant, and on inventions for the iron and steamship industry.[15]

In addition, these entrepreneurs evidently came to Troy with the advantages of higher education, political connections, or economic contacts, and they or their sons often improved their social status through marriage with other manufacturing families. Burden had been trained in engineering at the University of Edinburgh and arrived in America "bearing letters from the American minister at London to Stephan van Rensselaer and Senators Benson and Calhoun." Griswold's father had been a member of the New York legislature, and as a teenager the son entered the hardware house of Hart, Lesley & Warren of Troy. Griswold later secured his social position by marrying Hart's daughter. Winslow came from an old colonial family and was educated at select schools in Albany until he entered a commercial house as a nineteen-year-old clerk. And Corning, also the descendant of an established colonial family, "served his apprenticeship in business as a clerk in the [Troy] hardware store of his uncle, Benjamin Smith."[16]

In mid-century, by the time these men had established themselves, they were of course much more than ironmasters. Together with the smaller iron manufacturers, other industrialists, and established merchants, they comprised Troy's elite. Wealthy and "respectable," they served on the boards of directors of financial and charitable institutions, periodically uniting to found a benevolent association or to provide some social service for the city. As just one example, an association was formed in 1859 in order to demonstrate the feasibility of using steam apparatus for fire-fighting. Its members included Warren and Fuller, while N. B. Starbuck of Starbuck's Foundry was captain of the engine. Moreover, long after they or their fathers had left the iron industry, names familiar to the history of Troy's iron manufacture still filled the lists of local bank directors.[17]

Troy industrialists also lived near one another in one of two almost classic settings: in the aristocratic surroundings of a brownstone mansion near the business district on Washington Square, or in the semi-feudal ambience of a brick mansion which stood atop the hillside dominating their industrial serfs. In order to see the Burdens, for example, an ironworker had to look heavenward, up the hill.

Census listings for the Burden family in 1860 and 1880 provide a sense of how one successful ironmaster and his kin lived during these turbulent decades. By 1860 Burden's wife had died, and he lived with two of his sons and his daughter Jessie. The eldest son, William, dwelt in another house on the estate with his wife and two children. The combined households reported $85,500 in the bank, and Henry Burden listed real estate holdings worth $96,000. The eight Burdens had eleven servants to tend to their needs: one housekeeper, one chambermaid, one cook, two waitresses, two coachmen, and four other servants. By 1880 the surviving Burden sons, I. Townsend and James, had married and had three and four children respectively. The eleven Burdens in these two nuclear families now had between them seventeen servants, two of whom were married with two small children of their own. The Burden family had weathered the two decades very well.

Troy's ironmasters generally comprised a select group of native-born American manufacturers who came to their positions with all the advantages nineteenth-century America could provide, and who became larger owners and entrepreneurs. The handful of entrepreneurs who owned the large mills where most ironworkers labored were largely industrialists and financiers and were not primarily engaged in day-to-day shop activities. Before the Civil War they held important local political positions, but afterward their place in city government was taken by a rising generation of Irish politicians with working-class connections. Their factories and wealth continued to expand, however; and together with the rising professional class of lawyers, physicians, accountants, and clerks, and the growing group of shirt-and-collar manufacturers, these mill owners established a formidable interlocking directorate of financial power and social prestige. They were affected by several developments: the loss of local political authority meant increasing reliance upon state and national authorities; the diversification and expansion of their economic holdings gave them alternative financial resources during strikes in the iron industry; and the departure from Troy of men like Corning and Winslow and their sons, and the amalgamation of their interests in the Troy Iron and Steel Company, further removed owners from the problems of labor and tended to intensify these men's focus on rates of profit.

The Workforce in 1860

As the above suggests, Troy's ironworker community did not develop in a social vacuum. After the Civil War, industrialization as well as the demands of the highly competitive profit system forced extensive and rapid changes in the conditions of labor and in the social order. The iron industry had a uniquely elaborate occupational hierarchy which remained relatively untouched by technology during this period. Jobs ranged from among the most skilled labor in American industry (molders and puddlers in particular) to middle-level jobs of various sorts, to menial, unskilled work. Constantly changing market conditions and a growing concentration of ownership affected the entire workforce. Corporate amalgamation meant that workers found themselves dealing with evolving management bureaucracies in an increasingly non-competitive local labor market. At the same time, developing western markets were more cheaply served by newer midwestern foundries located near the vast Pennsylvania and Ohio bituminous coal fields. These factories did not have to convert old anthracite furnaces to burn the coke used in steel production, and they often had a less-developed union movement to confront. Such advantages handicapped Troy foundrymen and ironmasters, forcing those who wanted to maintain existing profit levels to further intensify labor: to seek lower wages, a more rationalized workforce, and higher production quotas.

Troy workers resisted these changes. The era between 1860 and 1880 was not simply the age of enterprise; it was also the age of resistance. Entrepreneurs struggled to gain control of burgeoning markets, while labor fought for control over work conditions, wages, and the political and social institutions of the city. Greater attention to the origins and nature of this fight follows in later chapters; suffice it to say now that violence and disorder characterized this period and touched the ironworkers. Skilled labor, molders and puddlers in particular, led the resistance.[18] Consequently, while we study the whole ironworker community, we pay special attention to the ethnic characteristics and occupational mobility of these skilled workers during these two decades.

Who were Troy's ironworkers? The 1860 federal population census discloses that immigrant Irishmen had a central role even *before* the Civil War. (See Table 1.2.) Studies of the antebellum Irish have reinforced the traditional image of "Paddy" working as domestic

TABLE 1.2. Selected Ironworkers and Ethnicity, 1860 (Raw totals, and percentage of the total in the trade)

Ironworker's birthplace: / Father's birthplace		Population (1)b 25,774	Managerial (2) 85	Laborer (3)c 77	Molder (4) 209	Puddler (5) 31	Heater/Roller (6) 60	Stove-mounter (7) 44	Pattern-maker (8) 53	Machinist (9) 188	Totals (Columns 3–9) (10) 622
U.S.A.	N		82	47	152	19	43	42	53	169	525
	%	37.8	78.8	18.0	31.2	11.5	25.9	58.3	71.6	57.0	33.9
Ireland	N		8	174	266	66	92	18	10	55	747
	%	46.0	7.6	66.6	54.7	40.0	55.4	25.0	13.5	18.5	46.9
England	N		5	16	19	62	22	7	4	32	162
	%	5.4	4.8	6.1	3.9	37.5	13.2	8.7	5.4	11.8	10.2
Canada	N		2	16	21	12	4	5	4	12	74
	%	4.1	1.9	6.1	4.3	7.2	2.4	6.9	5.4	4.4	4.6
Scotland	N		4	5	18	3	3	0	1	17	47
	%	2.6	3.8	1.9	3.7	1.8	1.8	0	1.3	6.3	3.0
Germany	N		3	3	10	0	4	4	2	9	32
	%	4.1	2.9	1.1	2.0	0	2.4	5.5	2.7	3.3	2.0
Other	N		0	0	0	3	0	1	0	2	6
	%	0.2	0	0	0	1.8	0	1.4	0	0.8	0.4
Total	N	39,235	104	261	486	165	166	72	74	296	1,593

a For a more complete breakdown of all the ironworkers, see Daniel J. Walkowitz, "Working-Class Culture" (Ph.D. dissertation).
b The ethnic breakdown is based upon a 5 percent sample population of every twentieth person listed on the 1860 manuscript census tract.
c This total is low; it does not include men listed as "laborer" unless "in iron mill" was specified.

help or as a day laborer in the streets and ditches of urban American cities.[19] Oscar Handlin, for example, has written that Boston's Irish, unlike the city's other new immigrant groups, "remained unneeded and unabsorbed . . . and had the service occupation almost entirely to themselves. . . . Even the Negroes, who stood closest to the Irish in occupational experience, fared better than they."[20] Troy, an inland manufacturing center, suggests differently. Indeed, as others have noted, in its factories, as everywhere in urban America, the Irish formed a pool of "cheap, unskilled labor."[21] However, while the Irish made up the bulk of unskilled day laborers and service workers of Troy, they were also much more than ditch-diggers and coachmen.

Troy's Irish filled vital roles, both skilled and unskilled, in the expanding iron industry and had secured their foothold by 1860. Not all of them worked in factories, to be sure, but the typical ironworker in 1860 was Irish. Moreover, in each of the three largest skilled trades—molders, puddlers, and heaters and rollers—they constituted the largest number of workers. Among the unskilled, the Irish constituted two-thirds of the laborers and 73.6 percent of the service workers; among the skilled trades, they constituted 54.7 percent of the molders, 40 percent of the puddlers, and 55.4 percent of the heaters and rollers. Considering that most had lived in Troy, and perhaps in the United States, little more than a decade, these skilled jobs represented a considerable improvement over subsistence tenant farming in rural Ireland or low-paid work as day laborers.

Except for the boiler-makers, whose occupation was closely related to that of the puddlers, native-born labor filled most of the other skilled iron trades. American-born workers held an especially high percentage of pattern-makers' jobs in the foundries (71.6 percent) and occupied 39 of 61 places as nailors and spikers in Burden's nail factory. In the latter trade, Canadians made a strong showing, with 45 percent of the small sample: there were 13 Canadian nailors in 1860. Such evidence suggests that ethnocentricity, concern with status and security, and prior skills may have channeled those of similar national origins into different trades at a given time. In any case, workers tended to congregate in a particular ethnic group once a trade opened to that group.

The degree to which the various trades were "open" to those of different national origins in 1860 and 1880 is suggested by Table 1.3.

(If an ethnic group had a proportion of workers in a trade equal to the proportion of that group in the population, it will have a base figure of 100 in the table.) In 1860, while 78.8 and 3.8 percent of the managerial positions (manufacturers, stove dealers, firemen, and superintendents) were held by native-born Americans and Scotsmen respectively (Table 1.2), the relative concentrations of both Americans and Scots were well above average, 208 and 146 respectively (Table 1.3).[22] The Irish constituted the largest block of unskilled workers. English and Canadian immigrants were also above average in that category.

In the skilled trades, the ethnic occupational pattern reflected the large blocs of immigrants who already populated the industry. The Irish had relative concentrations close to or above the base figure in each of the three major trades, and the American-born exceeded 100 in all the others. English and Scottish immigrants, undoubtedly with some previous experience in the industry in Great Britain, and even the Canadians, although few in number, had a relatively easier

TABLE 1.3. Relative Concentration of Selected Ironworkers, 1860 and 1880 (Proportion among gainful workers in all occupations = 100)

Birthplace of ironworker's father	Managerial	Laborer	Molder	Puddler	Heater/ Roller	Stove- mounter	Pattern- maker	Machinist
1860								
U.S.A.	208	48	83	30	69	154	189	151
Ireland	17	145	119	87	120	54	29	40
England	89	113	72	694	244	161	100	219
Canada	46	149	105	176	59	168	132	107
Scotland	146	73	142	69	69	0	50	242
Germany	71	27	49	0	59	134	66	80
1880								
U.S.A.	140	35	58	7	18	91	133	120
Ireland	34	134	133	170	158	101	41	49
England	297	175	125	170	205	90	215	295
Canada	66	94	52	84	31	185	140	68
Scotland	380	333	233	60	60	0	140	607
Germany	38	56	64	6	20	86	216	105

time than the Irish in gaining entrance to all the skilled trades. Finally, some figures are especially significant. There were fewer English than Irish puddlers, but the former's concentration was an extraordinarily high 694. In addition, while the samples are somewhat scanty relative to other immigrant groups, the Irish were relatively unrepresented in two skilled trades, stove-mounters and pattern-makers.

Immigrants, especially the Irish, had gained easy access to the iron industry by 1860. The well-organized and militant unions of molders, puddlers, and rollers were probably dominated by Irish workers. First-generation immigrants constituted the bulk of these ethnic groups, further suggesting that newcomers entered the iron mills without difficulty. Of the ironworkers, only ninety-seven native-born (slightly more than 6 percent) had immigrant fathers;[23] of the ninety-seven, seventy-five were of Irish origin, and forty-nine of those were molders.

Irishmen entered Troy's iron industry soon after their arrival. Some, like Cohoes's Joseph Delehanty, had worked in English factories before coming to America. Others, like Patrick Kelly, who molded stoves in Troy as early as 1845, were pre-famine immigrants. Though it is impossible to trace them back to their Irish communities, a growing number were peasants who had fled famine. For them, the sudden adjustment to urban society must have been tremendous.[24] Writing thirty years later, Troy's local historian gives some sense of the early experience of the immigrants, of their arrival in poverty and illness, with cities like Troy inadequately prepared to help them:

> In consequence of the famine in Ireland at this time, many of the emigrants reached America in a starving condition. The ship fever . . . prevailed to an alarming extent in Troy among those of the inhabitants with whom they were at first allowed to mingle. The city authorities were compelled to erect temporary sheds as hospitals for this class of people, and to isolate them until the fever abated. Sometimes there were as many as two hundred sick persons in these rude buildings.[25]

In spite of such difficult circumstances, Irish immigrants continued to pour into this country, especially between 1845 and 1848; they made up the backbone of the skilled and unskilled labor forces which built the iron industry. They constituted a powerful working-class bloc and, like their Scottish neighbors, were able to secure jobs as skilled molders for their sons, friends, and neighbors. The Yankee and his son, in contrast, felt compelled to look elsewhere for employment.

The history of puddling and molding and the labor process involved therein may help to account for the early presence of Irish immigrants. Both were relatively new trades, and hence newcomers did not displace old artisan craftsmen. Those occupations expanded rapidly at a time when skilled labor was in short supply; their expansion coincided with the immigration of the Irish and English to these cities; and they entailed hard physical labor under intense heat and dangerous conditions. A final connection can also be suggested: nativist sentiment in the 1850s—anti-immigrant, but especially anti-Irish and anti-Catholic Know-Nothing stereotypes of "brutish" immigrants—perhaps made employers view Irishmen as a natural labor source for the brutal mill labor.

The use of coke as a fuel, replacing charcoal, stimulated production of wrought iron and cast iron products. This discovery and a series of related technological developments in the 1840s and 1850s made possible the emergence of puddling and molding as new industrial trades.[25] The puddlers controlled the vital middle stage in wrought iron production. Iron ore and coke had been burned in the blast furnace to create an alloy of iron and carbon called pig iron. By constant stirring in the puddling furnace, the carbon was expelled from the pig iron to produce wrought iron. The ingots would then be reheated and shaped in the rolling mill. The work of the puddler was both difficult and skillful. He operated the iron through ports in a furnace wall by agitating small batches of the molten pig iron over the flames on the end of a pole until the metal purified. He worked a ten-hour day, or as long as it took to complete six heats of metal—a ton per day. The temperature in this inferno of the puddling forge was well over 100° F., and the weight of the molten metal was such that the work had to be done in stints. But wages were high—three or four times those of a laborer—and these "aristocrats" of the iron mills also hired and paid their own crews of helpers, which gave them the status and power of subcontractors.[27]

Technological developments stimulated similar growth in the cast iron industry. Molding had deep pre-industrial roots, but the use of coke created a stronger, less brittle cast iron, and the development of the cupola to remelt the pig iron enabled foundries to expand enormously. Although molder operations had not changed appreciably, the cast iron industry offered many new job opportunities by mid-century.[28] But the molder's work was difficult and required a four- to seven-year apprenticeship. Sand or loam of the exact proper consistency and wetness had to be prepared; the wood or cast iron patterns (prepared by the pattern-maker) had to be filled with sand and "rammed" strenuously to make a mold; the mold had to be "rapped" carefully to remove the pattern without breaking the mold; and the mold had to be "poured" quickly but evenly.[29] A mistake at any stage could render the mold unusable and entail the loss of several days' labor. Not only was working with molten iron strenuous and exacting, it was also debilitating and dangerous. Still, high wages and status—like that of the puddler—attracted the immigrant worker. The molder also hired his own helper. In addition, both groups punctuated their hard day's work with breaks for beer and ale. Such traditions, and control over their pace, constituted an important and valued part of these men's work experience. But, in turn, the shortage of skilled labor, and the strenuous work involved, made English and Irish immigrants appear to be a logical and attractive source of labor for Troy ironmasters.

The Workforce in 1880

Some of the changes in the demographics of Troy ironworkers between 1860 and 1880 are reflected in the two census tracts. A more precise analysis, requiring the difficult and time-consuming tracing of the 1860 population, lies beyond the broader scope of this inquiry. Nonetheless, aggregate 1880 data indicate that English, Canadian, and German workers constituted a relatively larger share of the population, while the percentage of the native-born Americans and Irish declined. The latter figures reinforce the 1860 picture and demonstrate the continued Irish domination of the expanding iron industry. (See Tables 1.3 and 1.4.) Whereas 6.1 percent of the ironworkers in 1860 had been the sons of immigrants, 34.1 percent of all ironworkers in 1880 were in that same category. But the percentage of these immigrant sons who were of Irish parentage remained stable, at 77.3 percent. In total, six out of every ten ironworkers in 1880 were of Irish extraction. Undoubtedly many of them had not been

TABLE 1.4. Selected Ironworkers and Ethnicity, 1880 (Raw totals, and percentage of the total in the trade)

		Population	Managerial	Laborer	Molder	Puddler	Heater Roller Rougher	Stove-mounter	Pattern-maker	Machinist	Totals (Columns 3–9)
Ironworker's Birthplace: U.S.A.		(1)ᵃ 39,809	(2) 87	(3) 730	(4) 497	(5) 12	(6) 82	(7) 148	(8) 86	(9) 182	(10) 1837
Father's birthplace											
U.S.A.	N		54	169	153	5	13	58	58	108	564
	%	31.8	48.6	11.2	18.5	2.3	5.8	29.0	42.3	38.1	16.7
Ireland	N		19	936	511	166	171	94	26	65	1969
	%	46.4	15.7	62.4	61.9	79.0	73.3	47.0	18.9	22.9	58.2
England	N		22	161	63	22	28	11	18	51	354
	%	6.1	18.1	10.7	7.6	10.4	12.5	5.5	13.1	18.0	10.5
Canada	N		5	88	27	11	4	23	12	12	177
	%	6.2	4.1	5.8	3.2	5.2	1.9	11.5	8.7	4.2	5.3
Scotland	N		7	75	29	2	2	0	3	26	137
	%	1.5	5.7	5.0	3.5	0.9	0.9	0	2.1	9.1	4.0
Germany	N		3	55	34	1	3	11	19	19	142
	%	6.4	2.4	3.6	4.1	0.4	1.3	5.5	13.8	6.7	4.2
Other	N		1	23	8	3	3	3	1	2	43
	%	1.6	0.8	1.5	0.9	1.4	2.3	1.5	0.7	0.7	1.3
Total	N	56,747	111	1,507	825	210	224	200	137	283	3,386

ᵃ The ethnic breakdown is based upon a 4 percent sample population of every twenty-fifth person listed on the 1880 manuscript census tract.

working in 1860. For instance, a surprising number of Troy policemen had once been molders.[30] Some skilled ironworkers have dual
listings in various census tracts and city directories. Some (Dugald
Campbell, for example) molded stoves in a local foundry in the late
1860s while simultaneously operating another business (in
Campbell's case, a saloon or grocery). Finally, there is the problem
of great geographic mobility. Several historians have found that
close to half the population left town during a typical decade in the
mid-nineteenth century; such a rate was discovered, for example,
among unskilled laborers in Newburyport, Massachusetts.[31] Death
accounts for some absences, but most people probably left for better
jobs elsewhere. Though the substantive record of their lives must
remain untold here, aggregate data on those who stayed or now lived
in the city is impressive.

The Irish, by their sheer numbers, overwhelmed other ethnic
groups in the major iron trades. By 1880 the percentage of skilled
Irish workers had risen in every iron trade and had increased with
particular significance among the molders and the puddlers, as well
as among the rollers, roughers, and heaters. Figures for native-born
American molders remained constant, while those for Irish molders
doubled. The number of English puddlers dropped to one-third of
its 1860 total, while the Irish total increased to a point where they to-
tally dominated the trade. The number of American-born heaters,
rollers, and roughers declined to less than a third of its 1860 total,
while the Irish total almost doubled. Even among stove-mounters,
an occupation which had been dominated by the native-born in
1860, the Irish were ascendant. Of the skilled iron and iron-related
trades, only the pattern-makers, engineers, and machinists contained predominantly non-Irish ethnic groups.[32]

Although Troy's Irish comprised the largest and most powerful
bloc of iron workers in 1880, those of Scottish and English extraction
had the highest relative concentrations within the industry. (Table
1.3.) The British and Irish had doubled over the twenty-year period,
and the new immigrants found easy access to the iron industry at all
levels. On the other hand, those of German, Canadian, or American
origins fared worse.[33] Between 1860 and 1880 it was the Irish who
became established and secure in the iron mills and foundries. But
just what did the high proportion of Irish workers signify?[34] And
how did employment patterns in the iron industry compare with

those for other Troy trades? These questions require study of Irish experiences and expectations.

Social status and occupational mobility are related but distinct measures of social position. Although historians have suggested that the high proportion of Irish workers by 1880 coincided with a decline in the status of iron labor, that may not have been entirely true in Troy.[35] For the Irish, Troy's largest ethnic group (40 percent of the population), jobs in the iron industry still afforded some measure of both status and achievement.

The relative concentration figures for other Troy occupations suggest that being a skilled ironworker held less status for the English immigrant or the native-born American, but was the mark of a successful Irishman. The high concentration of a certain ethnic group in a specific trade did not necessarily reflect the decline of that trade, or a technologically related decline in the skill involved in that trade, or the failure of an ethnic group to gain jobs in one trade rather than another, though each of these may be factors. Shared values and ethnic and family cohesiveness attracted men to certain trades. High relative concentration figures reflect how different ethnic groups entered trades at different rates. There were German cigarmakers (658), Canadian carpenters (396), English carpenters (243), and Irish policemen (215) in Troy. Each ethnic/occupational group took pride in their group's ability and their place in Troy's economy. Since many Irishmen came to the United States without factory skills, they did much of the hard manual labor; yet the fact remains that they quickly filled most of the skilled iron trades. Certain jobs in the industry were hot, dirty, and unpleasant, but increasing numbers of Irish workers received relatively high incomes, gained some stature, and stayed. Some sense of the status accorded molders may be seen from their position in Troy's 1858 Independence Day procession. Invited to participate, the new union resolved "as an expression of their patriotism" to "join *en masse* in the procession." Four hundred molders assembled, grouped by foundries into about twenty wagons, dressed in their "uniforms" of black coats, black pants, and glazed caps, and "with implements of their trade and samples of their manufacture." The parade was divided into three sections, with military bands, local politicians, veterans, firemen, and tradesmen comprising the first two sections. The molders were given a place of honor at the head of the third division.[36]

Native-born workers might not have wished to associate with a particular trade any longer, especially if it was dominated by a particular ethnic group. But Irish-Americans still found stove-molding to be a well-paid and satisfying, albeit exhausting, experience. They were artisans who had completed lengthy apprenticeships and had a distinctive work routine that continued to allow them to regulate their own pace. They were also doing highly skilled work involving intricate patterns. In the mid-1870s, for example, molders at the Clinton Foundry produced about two hundred different models from more than sixty patterns. Their stoves were sold throughout the world, in such distant countries as Holland, Italy, Turkey, China, and Japan.[37] It was in the context of this sense of accomplishment that union militancy, strikes, protest, and even violence emerged after 1870, at the same time that manufacturers tried to lower wages, destroy the unions, and impress controls (such as time cards) on skilled workers. A closer look at certain skilled and unskilled ironworkers during this period discloses varying degrees of achievement. This part of their job experience may provide clues to the attitudes, values, and lifestyle that influenced their social behavior.

Mobility: Age and Job Opportunities

An analysis of ethnic origins in the different iron trades permits a tentative assessment of occupational opportunities within the iron industry. Data on the marital status, age, and property holdings of unskilled and skilled workers disclose that skilled work in Troy's mills and foundries provided a base for organization, stability, and a sense of achievement in the worker community. Opportunities for iron work awaited immigrants and their sons, and vacancies created by war deaths and the labor demands of expanding industries seem to have hastened the movement of young men into the industry.

Not surprisingly, the vast majority of the unskilled in 1860 were single, propertyless young men. Unskilled mill, furnace, and foundry hands contained the lowest percentage of married men in the industry (47.4 percent) and had the lowest percentage of workers with real estate holdings (7.7 percent). In 1880 the mills attracted even larger numbers of youthful and single unskilled men. Whereas no one under fifteen was listed as working in the iron industry in 1860, 8.3 percent of the unskilled ironworkers were fourteen and younger by 1880. One employee was only nine years old. In contrast, however, the percentage of unskilled workers between the ages of fifteen and nineteen had declined since 1860, from 27.7 to 17.4 percent.

A survey of skilled trades both in and outside the iron industry suggests a reason for the changes. All skilled trades reflected a similar drop in the number and/or percentage of employed men between the ages of fifteen and nineteen;[38] hence the change probably resulted from the delayed impact of the Civil War, rather than from worsening conditions that forced families to send young boys into the mills, or from a change in attitudes of young men toward these trades. Those who were fifteen to nineteen years old in 1880 were born during the war, and employment figures of 1880 parallel a low wartime birth rate and a postwar population explosion. The great demand for ironworkers and the relatively scarce supply of older teenagers required that the unskilled workforce be buttressed with the large crop of postwar babies.

Industrial expansion and the demographic consequences of the war also increased the opportunities for skilled labor, but the lucrative wages for such work always made these jobs most attractive within the working-class community. Once trained at the craft, skilled workers would be hard pressed to find more remunerative work. Not surprisingly, then, a large number of skilled workers, especially molders, were in their twenties in 1860.[39] By 1880 they appear to have become attached to their trade. John J. Grace and Darius Potter, for instance, were both young molders in the 1860s who remained to lead their compatriots two decades later.[40]

But molding stoves was strenuous work, and men like Dugald Campbell retired as they got older to become, for example, policemen or saloon owners. While Troy's molders had almost doubled in numbers by 1880, young Irishmen continued to grab the greatest share of the additional well-paid jobs. Many of the molders had remained in the trade during the 1860s and 1870s, providing continuity and familiarity within the workplace and the union. But opportunities kept opening up in the industry, and there was also a youthful group of molders in 1880. In 1860 there had been only 30 molders (6.2 percent) in their forties, whereas in 1880 there were 182 (22.1 percent). Meanwhile, though their share of the jobs had decreased, the number of molders in their twenties had actually increased slightly, from 266 in 1860 to 280 in 1880.

Regular skilled employment offered many families the opportunity to acquire some property. Although Troy's Irish immigrants did not generally arrive with adequate funds to purchase property, this possibility would be meaningful for immigrants who could remember a history of English rent-racking and land shortages. As Troy's skilled workers grew older, they were more likely to have acquired property. While the percentage of skilled workers owning property was considerably lower than that of the managerial class, the percentage was above that of the generally unskilled millhands. The meager 9.3 percent of the molder property-holders nearly tripled in those trades conspicuous for their lack of Irish workers (such as nailors and spikers, and pattern-makers). When the Irish entered a trade in great numbers, however, they acquired property at a higher rate than other nationalities. For example, the percentage of Irish molders with real estate (10.2 percent) was almost double that of the native molders (5.9 percent). This stronger showing for the Irish conforms to Thernstrom's findings in Newburyport.[41] Property obviously had priority for the Irish; equally important, significant numbers of them were able to realize this desire.

Finally, almost all the propertied were married. In addition, as immigrants settled into the community, the percentage of skilled married workers increased in the iron mills and furnaces, from 55.3 percent in 1860 to 61.5 percent in 1880. Job opportunities translated into family responsibilities. Such material changes in their lives gave ironworkers and their families additional priorities, obligations, and resources—all of which had to be considered before, for instance, supporting a strike action.

Thus we have the Troy ironworkers. Largely immigrants and Irish between 1860 and 1880, they managed to secure positions throughout the iron industry. The typical unskilled Troy ironworker in 1860 was probably much like Michael Maloney, a laborer who boarded behind the docks near the Albany Iron Works. He remained a bachelor until thirty, owned no property, and lived in one of Troy's south wards. Nor was Patrick Sullivan, the typical skilled ironworker, much different. Also Irish, he was most likely a molder in his twenties who had recently married an Irish girl. His family might live in a rented house near the mill or foundry in which he was employed; Sullivan, a molder, resided near Eddy, Corse and Company's foundry with his family. In 1880 not much had changed, except that the ironworker was even more likely to be of Irish extraction. The unskilled worker was now more likely to be single and younger, and the average skilled worker was more likely to be a molder, married, and twenty years older than his 1860 counterpart. James Turner and his family illustrate how the Irish "made it" into skilled work.

The James Turner Family

Like many other Irishmen and women, sixty-year-old James Turner and his forty-year-old wife, Mary, had emigrated with their four sons around 1850.[42] In 1860 they lived on one floor of a two-story brick row house above the Albany Iron Works. They probably paid rent to the iron company or to one of the local landlords, such as Thomas Hopkins, an Englishman with some $20,000 in real estate holdings, who lived a few blocks away. Like other ironworker families, one need scarcely add, the Turners were less affluent than ironmaster families like the Burdens. By 1860 they had been able to save only about fifty dollars. Now, with the Civil War imminent, and with the recurrent problems of inflation and depression, it was crucial that the sons find early employment in the mills in order for the family to gain some security—money for food and possibly for some land, which had been so precious back in Ireland. The youngest son, twelve-year-old Michael, and a daughter, now eight, who had been born in the United States, attended school, awaiting that time when they would enter the iron and collar mills respectively. Meanwhile, every morning before 6:00 A.M. Mr. Turner and his three older sons, aged fifteen, eighteen, and twenty, left for another long day in the iron mills. Mrs. Turner kept house while Turner and their two younger boys worked six-day weeks as unskilled iron millhands; the eldest was already a skilled roller. After eleven or twelve hours of hot, hard work, which at times dragged on for fourteen hours, the men returned home for dinner. For this sixty-six to seventy-two-hour work week, each unskilled Turner received perhaps four dollars, and the skilled eldest son earned perhaps as much as twelve

dollars. These wages had to tide them over during strikes and the
four winter months when the mills usually shut down. Such figures
compared with weekly wages of about four dollars paid to unskilled
female shirt-and-collar workers.[43] Finally, on Sundays the family
traveled to the nearest church (Presbyterian or Catholic)[44] in the
center of the city to receive spiritual instruction, see their compatriots, and consider their lot in this world and the next.

If this portrait seems to suggest a restricted existence, it is because
the long mill hours left little time for recreation. What activities
people did have *were* important to them. Life revolved around the
church and ethnic associations: Sunday school and church picnics,
fraternal organizations and nationalist groups such as the Fenians
and the Clan na Gael. Masonic clubs, fire brigades, baseball clubs,
and even ethnic politics were also an integral part of the culture of
the working class, just as they were for the socially prominent. This
cultural aspect is an important supplement to the portrait drawn
from statistical data and will be described later.

In 1880 only the eldest son, William Turner, was listed as living in
Troy. This solitary listing is not unusual, given the problems of tracing people in the census, the relatively high worker mortality, and
the considerable geographic mobility over a twenty-year period.
William married an Irish woman and moved to the same brick row
above Troy's ironworks, a few doors from his parents. They had
the first of many children in that year. Meanwhile, all three younger
brothers followed his route; by 1866 they had become skilled rollers.
By 1870 the family had reorganized—the father died, his wife followed a few years later, the younger sons apparently left Troy, and
the two older boys, William and John, now family men, had become
heaters in the mill. Both families still lived above the ironworks.
John had died by 1880 and his widow still resided on the same street;
William and his family lived a few blocks away. Their oldest son, now
twenty, had also been a heater for some years, but now worked as a
clerk in a saloon. His sixteen-year-old sister worked in a collar shop;
his fifteen and fourteen-year-old brothers labored in the iron mills;
four brothers, ages five to twelve, attended school; and their mother
stayed at home with the two little boys. Between 1860 and 1880
ironworkers like the Turners had made modest gains in the mills.
Though their conditions and lifestyle did not change dramatically,

the family had remained intact. Food, clothing, and shelter had been provided, and the sons had gained training and skilled employment in the iron industry.

The Turner family tells us something of the Irish immigrants in Troy's ironworks. By 1860 they already dominated this industry and would continue to do so over the next twenty years, gaining the lion's share of the skilled molder and puddler jobs in particular. Skilled, and even unskilled labor in the mills provided greater security for food, clothing, and shelter than did Irish peasant life, or the meager day-laborer wages of many fellow Irish-Americans. One central fact cannot be overlooked: in a purely material sense, the position of the typical Irish ironworker improved rather than declined in this period. Irishmen gained a firm foothold in the iron industry, and that industry fulfilled certain expectations of the skilled laborer.

Between 1860 and 1880 the Troy economy expanded steadily and dramatically, and jobs, both skilled and unskilled, opened for the new, largely Irish, immigrant workforce. A relatively young, ambitious group of molders won well-paying jobs for themselves and relatives in the foundries. Although few molders duplicated Joseph Foxell's achievement and successfully opened their own foundries, such personal accomplishments nevertheless demonstrated for others that the American success story was alive and well. The fuller dimensions of that story and its pervasiveness (or lack of it) for the entire working class await analysis in later chapters. Everyone could observe the achievements of molders and puddlers, however, and the perception of success widely informed working-class convictions of an open American society. Finally, these immigrant ironworkers gained their jobs and some property during a period of increasing amalgamation and concentration of capital in the iron industry. Iron production itself, however, remained largely untouched by technological change, and ironmasters had to seek alternative means to increase efficiency and maintain a competitive profit margin. How their demands clashed with the ironworkers' quest for security and modest successes is part of the historical emergence of Troy's immigrant American working class. That that emergence varied with a different set of circumstances is evident when we turn to Cohoes.

NOTES

1. Arthur James Weise, *Troy's One Hundred Years, 1789–1889* (Troy, 1891), pp. 407–15, counts twenty-two shirt and collar factories in Troy in 1890. He states these factories employed over 7,000 Trojan girls and women and an additional 7,000 from neighboring towns.

2. Rezneck, "Office Building," p. 82; Margaret Burden Proudfit, *Henry Burden: His Life* (Troy, 1904), pp. 70–77; and John G. Waite and Diana S. Waite, *Industrial Archeology in Troy, Waterford, Cohoes, Green Island, and Watervliet* (Troy, 1973), p. 4.

3. Troy's sex distribution reflected the slightly larger percentage of women nationally. Females comprised 53.9 percent of the population in Cohoes in 1860. In contrast, Troy's two industries nicely balanced one another: women comprised 51.8 percent and 50.7 percent of the Troy population in 1860 and 1880 respectively.

4. There had been fewer than 20,000 in 1840, and fewer than 5,000 in 1820. (Tenth Census, 1880, *Census Reports, Tenth Census, June 1, 1880*, Vol. 1, pt. 2, *Statistics of the Population*.) Unless otherwise noted, data for all tables have been compiled from federal MS census schedules for 1860 and 1880. These schedules are available in the MS collection of the New York State Education Library in Albany. Eighth Census, 1860, *Population of the United States in 1860*; Tenth Census, 1880, *Statistics of the Population*, and *Manufactures in the United States in 1880*.

5. These are not precise figures. The Irish estimate is based on the percentage of ironworkers of Irish extraction (estimated at 59.5%), compared to the percentage of Troy's population that was of Irish extraction (estimated at 40.4%) in 1880. I have estimated the number of Irish ironworkers because the totals in the manufacturing census conflict with the figures compiled from the MS population census. The discrepancy is much larger in 1860 and is due to several factors. Some trades are "mixed": engineers and machinists, for instance, worked both in and outside the iron mills. Many workers were listed by the 1860 census-takers simply as "laborers." Some workers probably lived outside the city limits. (These and other problems involved with using these statistical materials are detailed in a series of essays edited by Seymour Martin Lipset and Richard Hofstadter, *Sociology and History: Methods* [New York, 1968].) The plight of Troy's blacks, however, is clear: during these years of tremendous industrial expansion, while Troy's population increased 45 percent, the number of blacks (and mulattoes) declined almost 9 percent. According to both census tracts, only one black person was employed in the iron mills; blacks filled service positions or migrated elsewhere.

6. Weise, *Troy's One Hundred Years*, p. 264.

7. The employment figures are estimated from ibid., and from Ninth Census, 1870, *Manufactures in the United States in 1870*. The manuscript Tenth Census, 1880, *Manufactures*, was incomplete for Rensselaer County.

8. Henry Burden's achievements are nicely detailed in Rezneck, "Office Building 1881," pp. 73–82. Someone in the South evidently had planned to steal one of Burden's machines and erect a horseshoe factory in Atlanta, but that plan was aborted by Sherman's march.

9. See *Burden Iron* (Troy, 1920) advertising pamphlet published by the Burden Iron Company; Weise, *Troy's One Hundred Years*; Eighth Census, 1860, *Manufactures*; Ninth Census, 1870, *Manufactures*; and Tenth Census, 1880, *Manufactures*.

10. The Malleable Iron Company, a relatively new firm, had enlarged its workforce from 8 to 140 between 1860 and 1880, but it still lowered the average considerably.

11. Much of my data on Troy, and an extended discussion of its meaning, can be found in Walkowitz, "Statistics and the Writing of Working-Class Culture."

12. See Frances W. Gregory and Irene D. Neu, "The American Industrial Elite," in *Men in Business: Essays on the Historical Role of the Entrepreneur*, ed. William Miller (Cambridge, Mass., 1952), pp. 193–211.

13. *Troy Daily Times*, March 1, 1883, January 23 and March 24, 1884.

14. Arthur James Weise, *The City of Troy and Its Vicinity* (Troy, 1886), pp. 281–86.

15. See *Dictionary of American Biography*, 20 vols. (New York, 1930), for biographical sketches of Corning, Burden, Griswold, and Winslow. See also Weise, *Troy's One*

46 WORKER CITY, COMPANY TOWN

Hundred Years; and Irene D. Neu, *Erastus Corning, Merchant and Financier, 1794–1872* (Ithaca, N.Y., 1960).

16. *Dictionary of American Biography*, vols. 3, 4, 8, 20.

17. Arthur J. Weise, *History of the City of Troy* (Troy, 1876), p. 223. See the frequent listing of such names as Ingram, Eddy, Tibbits, Burdett, Fales, Burden, Fuller, and Warren in the advertisements for banks in any volume of the *Troy City Directory*, 1870–85, or in the appendices to Weise's *City of Troy* or *Troy's One Hundred Years*.

18. Molders cast molten pig-iron into ranges, stoves, bells, etc. In puddling, carbon was removed from pig iron to make wrought iron by heating the iron to a molten state, while the roller operated a pair or series of grooved rolls to make shapes of uniform cross-section. The heater put some of the carbon back into the iron by reheating wrought iron with charcoal to make steel. Each of these processes had to be completed while the metal was molten; each type of worker was engaged in a hot, dangerous, and delicate craft. See Temin, *Iron and Steel in Nineteenth Century America*, pp. 17–18, 125–26.

19. See Oscar Handlin, *Boston's Immigrants, 1790–1865: A Study in Acculturation* (Cambridge, Mass., 1941), pp. 61–75; Thomas N. Brown, *Irish-American Nationalism: 1870–1890* (Philadelphia, 1966), pp. 18–19; William V. Shannon, *The American Irish* (New York, 1963), pp. 28, 95; and Carl Wittke, *The Irish in America* (Baton Rouge, 1956).

20. Handlin, *Boston's Immigrants*, pp. 61–75.

21. Brown, *Irish-American Nationalism*, p. 18, describes Troy's Irish in these words.

22. The Scottish were the Burdens; in this case, a highly successful and powerful foursome in Troy.

23. See Table 1.2, column 10. The difference between first two rows of figures in Table 1.2 represents the small number of second-generation immigrants, American-born children of immigrant fathers, who worked in the iron factories in 1860.

24. New York State, Census Office, *The 1855 New York State Census of Population*, lists each person's birthplace (by country, state, or New York county) and the number of years he or she has lived in Troy. While I have not systematically tabulated this data, and while some people may have resided in port cities en route to Troy, the records make it overwhelmingly clear that most of the Irish in Troy left Ireland after the potato famine. See, e.g., this pattern in Cohoes (Table 2.1).

25. Weise, *History of the City of Troy*, p. 204.

26. Before the mid-1840s puddling and shaping had been combined, in the forge, with the laborious work of a hammer. The transition to separate rolling and puddling mills required the development of the reverberatory furnace, with a low internal wall to prevent the fuel from contaminating the metal. In addition, iron bottoms were introduced to minimize loss from spillage, while double puddling furnaces were developed to increase output. See Temin, *Iron and Steel in Nineteenth-Century America*, pp. 100–106, for elaboration of these and other developments in the rolling mill.

27. David Brody, *Steelworkers in America: The Nonunion Era* (Cambridge, Mass., 1960), pp. 8–52.

28. H. J. Fyrth and Henry Collins, *The Foundry Workers: A Trade Union History* (Manchester, 1959), pp. 1–15.

29. *Practical Iron Founding* (London, 1889). Raphael Samuels kindly provided me with information from his work in progress on mechanization in nineteenth-century trades.

30. See biographical sketches of Troy policemen in Frederic T. Cardoze, *History of the Police Department of Troy, N.Y. from 1786 to 1902* (Troy, 1902). For further discussion, see ch. 5.

31. Thernstrom, *Poverty and Progress*, p. 85. See also Anderson, *Family Structure in Nineteenth-Century Lancashire*, pp. 40–41.

32. The Irish constituted 33.7 percent of the engineers, but eleven of the thirteen men listed as firemen in the ironworks were Irish. Although these firemen are usually combined with the engineers, they clearly had different ethnic patterns.

33. Immigrants from Great Britain assumed managerial posts and became skilled machinists, engineers, molders, boiler-makers, and pattern-makers. Interestingly, the English also had one of the highest increases in relative concentration in the unskilled posi-

tions. Although those of German, Canadian, or American origins fared worse, all three groups had near- or above-average relative concentrations in two stove-related trades: mounters and pattern-makers. The Germans had a particularly high concentration of pattern-makers, a skill that may have involved the sort of woodwork training that many had received in their native Germany. In fact, the Irish were the only major immigrant group to have a below-average concentration of pattern-makers. Lastly, men of American extraction had slightly above-average concentrations in managerial positions and as engineers and machinists; and engineers of Canadian extraction and machinists of German extraction were slightly above average in their relative concentrations.

34. Edward P. Hutchinson, *Immigrants and Their Children, 1850–1950* (New York, 1956), pp. 103–4, lists the relative concentrations of immigrant iron and steel operators in 1880; for men born in Ireland the figure is 278, and for men born in Great Britain it is 315. These figures compare well with those for Troy's foreign-born Irish (175) and British (278).

35. See Handlin, *Boston's Immigrants*, pp. 72–84. Handlin focuses on 1830 to 1865, and while I think his argument is fundamentally correct, it defines status with a contemporary middle-class bias against manual labor, both skilled and unskilled. The native-born American minority may well have disdained work in the iron mills, but the views of the immigrant majority are less clear.

36. *Troy Daily Times*, June 15–July 5, 1858; "Minutes," Iron Molders' International Union No. 2, June 1858.

37. *Troy Daily Times*, October 15, 1875.

38. The number of workers below twenty years of age is in ratio to the total employed in the following two representative industries:

	1860	1880
Machinists	43/296	25/283
Puddlers	6/165	1/211

39. Of the molders, 54.7 percent were in their twenties in 1860. Among the other active iron unions, 46.6 percent of the puddlers and 47.1 percent of the rollers were also in their twenties. Cf. stove-mounters (33%), pattern-makers (31.1%), and nailors (22.5%).

40. Grace later became president of the molders' union, and Potter, a union molder as early as 1858, testified on behalf of the union before a state commission on convict labor in 1883 (*Troy Daily Times*, March 1, 1883). See chs. 6 and 7.

41. Thernstrom, *Poverty and Progress*, ch. 5, theorized that the Irish put their children to work in the factories earlier than other ethnic groups in order to save enough money to buy a house. To these transplanted peasants, a home, food, and shelter—rather than education—provided stability, security, and status. More recently, Michael Katz, among others, has suggested that the Irish chose the factory rather than the school only because Catholic parochial education was not available. This does not negate the higher rate of Irish property-holding, however.

42. The biography of the Turner family is reconstructed from Eighth Census, 1860, *Population*; Tenth Census, 1880, *Population*; and *Troy City Directory* (annual), 1860–80.

43. Eighth Census, 1860, *Manufactures*. Generally the ironworkers were unemployed, however, during four months of the year.

44. Without consulting and correlating local church records, there is no way to tell if the Turner family was Orange (Scotch Presbyterian) or Green (Catholic). For the period under consideration, the overwhelming majority of the city's Irish were Catholic.

CHAPTER 2

Company Town: Cohoes and
the Cotton-Worker Community

THE DEVELOPMENT OF the Cohoes cotton industry paralleled that of Troy's iron industry. Both types of enterprise were well established and expanding by the mid-1850s; each greatly contributed to the transition of its respective urban area to an industrial center with a permanent factory workforce. But while the processes of industrialization were similar, there were significant differences in the two communities' social structures.

Cohoes was a one-industry village, one-third the size of Troy. Although small knitting mills proliferated in the lower part of the town, one large cotton manufacturer, the Harmony Mills, dominated by the end of the Civil War. Physically, the Harmony Mills overlooked Cohoes from a hill on the north end of town. Economically, it employed approximately one out of every four residents, regardless of age. Socially, it was paternalistically involved in the lives of the workers and their families. Politically, its management and directors were part of an interlocking directorate with the privately owned Cohoes Water Company. (They controlled the vital water power in the city with their complex of canals.)

Textile mills also employed a workforce different from that in the iron industry. Most textile workers were women and children, usually laboring for lower wages than male ironworkers and only during a particular stage in their lives: from adolescence until they bore children (in the case of females), or until they were strong and skillful enough to find a better-paying job (in the case of males). Moreover, New England's textile industry, besides employing large numbers of Irish immigrants, received an infusion of French-Canadian im-

48

migrants in the 1870s. Cohoes, in contrast to Troy, contained two substantial ethnic groups, the Irish and the French Canadians. This development raises a question for later study: how do ethnic newcomers confront, challenge, and adapt in an industrial community dominated by an earlier, more settled group? This portrait of Cohoes's social and economic structure emphasizes its special character and enables us to begin to understand the absence of sustained protest by the cotton workers before 1880.

Textile Village

About two miles upstream from Troy, the Mohawk River spills down a splendid cataract into the Hudson. Throughout the seventeenth and eighteenth centuries, travelers and young lovers from the Albany area knew the falls as a wild, romantic spot dangerous to voyagers and canoeing Indians.[1] These falls lay in the northern part of the township of Watervliet, the first township formed in Albany County from the west district of the Manor of Renssalaerwyck.[2] Early in the nineteenth century, a manufacturing village bearing the Indian name "Gahoose," meaning variously "a canoe falling" or "parting of the waters," grew up on the south bank of the Mohawk.[3] One of America's earliest cotton factories, the Cohoes Manufacturing Company, started there in 1811 but burned down in 1829. By 1830 the settlement had expanded to approximately twenty houses. Thrifty and prosperous Dutch farmer families—the Lansings, Fondas, Clutes, and Schuylers—now made room for new entrepreneurs. The Champlain Canal had been completed in 1823, and the Erie Canal soon thereafter. The developing canal network began to attract men for whom the falls meant water power. In 1826 one of them, Canvass White, an engineer on the Erie Canal construction, persuaded the patroon and principle landlord in the area, Stephen van Rensselaer, and a New York City capitalist, Peter Remsen, to finance a hydraulic company at the site. For one dollar van Rensselaer turned over his water rights on the Mohawk to the Cohoes Company, and in 1831 it put a small wooden dam across the Mohawk above the falls and began operation. Thus the company controlled the water rights and owned most of the village land.[4] In that same year an Albany storekeeper named Egbert Egberts, "the father of the knitting business in this country,"[5] hired an ingenious cabinetmaker's helper named Timothy Bailey to devise a power knitting

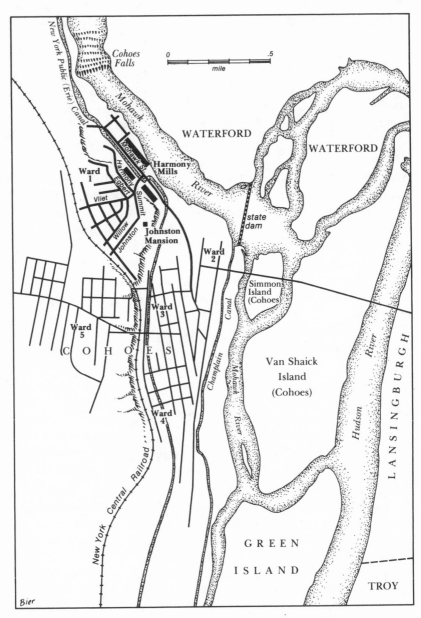

MAP 3. Cohoes, ca. 1880; Harmony Hill, Ward One

machine. In 1832 he financed Joshua and Timothy Bailey in establishing Cohoes's first knit factory to run with power looms. Four years later Peter Harmony, a wealthy Spanish gentleman, founded the Harmony Manufacturing Company with a group of New York capitalists. Among the first stockholders were Stephen van Rensselaer, Peter Remsen, and Hugh White (Canvass's brother).[6] When their cotton mill opened in 1837, 250 hands—one out of every four Cohoes residents—worked for Peter Harmony's new cotton company.

This first mill was built on the south bank of the Mohawk River, on a hill overlooking the quiet hamlet. It cost $72,000 and contained 3,000 spindles. Its workers, in 1837, produced 1,500,000 yards of print cloth. Alongside the mill, three brick tenements, each two stories high with a basement, were constructed at a cost of $3,000 each.[7] These tenements were the prototypes of some 800 brick houses eventually erected in the Harmony Hill community. Still occupied today, they are an impressive testimony to good workmanship and the fine materials used. However, the company's early financial record was less noteworthy. Except for 1838, the company lost money every year until 1850;[8] during this period of absentee management, it changed hands several times. Finally, owing to a series of floating debts, the sheriff sold the Harmony Manufacturing Company at a forced sale to two cotton manufacturers, Thomas Garner of New York City and Alfred Wild of Kinderhook, New York. They had purchased the mill at the suggestion of Robert Johnston, an inventive mule-spinner with extraordinary foresight. Johnston was immediately installed as superintendent, and under his leadership the renamed Harmony Mills began its meteoric expansion. Cohoes had become a textile center.

Social and Economic Development

From its opening the Harmony Mills dominated Cohoes, but that company's growth was paralleled by the expansion of Cohoes's knit goods industry. While this industry generally flourished, most factories did not greatly expand in size. The number of knit goods mills increased from eight in 1860 to seventeen in 1876, but the four largest mills still employed 200–400 hands.[9] In contrast, while the four cotton mills averaged 388 workers in 1860, the Harmony Mills employed all 4,808 of Cohoes's cotton workers in 1880. Together, the woolen and cotton mills shaped Cohoes's social structure by attracting a predominantly female and immigrant workforce.

Since textile mills employed mostly women, the community's sex ratio was unbalanced. Females comprised 53.9 percent and 55.2 percent of all Cohoes residents in 1860 and 1880 respectively; naturally, the percentage of adult women was even higher. Moreover, as the mills expanded, so did the share of jobs for women. In this respect Cohoes differed from the national pattern, where, according to Edith Abbott, "the tendency" was "toward a decrease in the proportion of women employed in the [cotton] mills."[10] Women's employment in America's cotton mills dropped from 62 to 57 percent between 1860 and 1880,[11] while the percentage of women in Cohoes's cotton mills increased from 60.6 to 67.4 percent. Although figures are unavailable for 1880, the percentage of women woolen millhands in 1860 was even higher (78 percent). But women continued to receive lower wages than men for the same work, and the better-paid jobs—such as those of mule-spinners—remained closed to them. Women, it was conventionally argued, did not have the strength to operate the mules; furthermore, their dresses would get caught in the machinery. In addition, the spinners were the best-organized textile workers, and they were sure to oppose the introduction of lower-paid females into the trade. Nonetheless, rather than leaving the industry, Cohoes women continued to find substantial and increasing textile employment in less-skilled positions throughout the Gilded Age.

Cohoes's population increased dramatically between the 1830s and 1880. The city had only 1,850 residents in 1840, but 8,800 in 1860 and 19,416 in 1880. As in Troy, immigrants and their children accounted for most of this increase. The native-born population had migrated into Cohoes from neighboring New York counties or from predominantly rural New England areas. Only 4 of the 111 native-born families who had settled there between 1845 and 1855 came from other states, and only 23 more already lived in Albany County. Fully 77 percent of the substantial number of Irish immigrant families arrived after 1845, mostly, one suspects, after the famine. (See Table 2.1.)

And this was but the beginning. Immigrants continued to pour

TABLE 2.1. In-Migration to Albany County, 1855, for the Fourth Election District (Cohoes, Watervliet)[a]

Years in county	Father's birthplace				
	Ireland	England	Scotland	Canada	U.S.A.
0–5	48.7 (%)	64 (%)	71 (%)	50 (%)	30.9 (%)
6–10	28.2	27	14	22	26.3
11–15	11.8	4.5	—	22	11.9
16–20	7.8	4.5	14	5.5	12.4
21+	3.5	—	—	—	18.5
N	255	22	14	18	194

SOURCE: New York State, 1855 Census, *Population of New York State in 1855*, for Albany County.

[a] Cohoes was part of two election districts. This district seems to have encompassed more of the Irish families.

into these cities in succeeding decades. The 1880 Cohoes census counted only 339 more native-born residents than in 1860, while over 10,000 more immigrants and their children had settled there. A similar dramatic increase was reflected in other statistics. The foreign-born and their children made up 69.8 percent of Cohoes's 1860 population, but 79.4 in 1880.[12] Furthermore, unlike Troy, where the Irish constituted by far the largest ethnic group of new residents, nearly 40 percent of Cohoes's newcomers were French Canadians. (See Table 2.2.) The town's social structure differed from Troy's in two ways. First, prior to the Civil War, the Irish predominated in both cities, and their communities grew during the next decades. But in Cohoes the postwar period witnessed a huge influx of French Canadians. Second, Cohoes had a preponderance of adolescent and adult women who comprised a majority of the factory workforce. These differences influenced the emergence of social protest in each city.

Industrial expansion, especially that of the Harmony Mills, kept pace with urban growth and met the demand for jobs. Cohoes's population increased 2.2 times between 1860 and 1880, but the number of cotton workers increased 3.1 times. While approximately one out of every four townsfolk worked as a cotton hand in 1860 (1:4.2), the ratio had risen to almost one out of every three in 1880 (1:3.2). However, since the woolen mills had not expanded greatly,

TABLE 2.2. Cohoes Population by Ethnicity, 1860 and 1880

Father's birthplace	1860 (%)	1880[a] (%)
U.S.A.	30.2	22.1
Ireland	47.8	38.3
French Canada	7.7	24.0
England	9.0	8.5
Scotland	3.7	2.8
Germany	1.0	3.3
Other	0.7	1.0
N	8,800	19,416

[a] The ethnic breakdown for 1880 is based upon a 10 percent sample population of every tenth person listed on Cohoes's 1880 manuscript census.

the percentages of men, women, and children employed in *both* the woolen and cotton mills remained about the same: in 1860 and again in 1880 almost half of all teenagers and adults worked in textile mills (1:2.1). The ratio, however, varied considerably for women, for particular ethnic groups, and among age groups. The Irish, for example, constituted the major group of millhands in 1860; one out of every three adults and adolescents who worked in the mills was Irish. The ratio of Scottish, English, and French-Canadian immigrant workers was slightly higher, but that for native-born Americans was lower (2:9). The percentage of millhands, furthermore, generally dropped as the women grew older. While 81.9 percent of all Irish girls between fifteen and nineteen worked in Cohoes's textile mills in 1860, only 47.7 percent of those in their twenties did so. Other differences can be noted, but what matters here is that the textile industry, and particularly the cotton mills, paced Cohoes's growth, stimulated the development of a new French-Canadian community, and provided considerable employment for female laborers, especially those at a particular stage in their early adult life.[13]

Finally, other aspects in the economic history of Cohoes, including textile production methods and technological developments, shaped the wool and cotton industries differently and affected work conditions in textiles generally. Cohoes's knit goods factories were quite unlike the cotton mills. The woolen mills specialized in consumer knit goods, while the cotton mills mass-produced cloth. Although production increased in both industries, Harmony Mills' cotton production well exceeded the combined output of all the woolen mills by 1880. But business had not stagnated in either industry; rather, an increase in technological efficiency and industrial output had substantially increased all textile production. (In contrast, while developing technology in steel would ultimately restructure the entire process of iron production, iron mills and foundries remained largely unmechanized during this period. Skilled ironworkers were not displaced in numbers until the late 1880s.[14]) The textile industry had been almost fully mechanized by mid-century, increasingly reducing even formerly skilled weavers and spinners to semi-skilled machine operatives. Moreover, textile innovations constantly modified and placed stress on the various jobs. New power looms and machines that simplified and accelerated the various processes dramatically affected work conditions. For instance, when the power loom was introduced, a single weaver tended one loom that ran 80-100 picks per minute; by 1850 she tended four looms with 600 picks per minute; by 1895 she could operate eight looms with 1,500 picks per minute.[15] Similarly, spinning frames were gradually replaced by the spinning mule, and in the 1870s a new machine, the slasher, sized the yarn that had previously been done by the well-paid female dressers.[16] Each of these changes reduced the mill labor force, modified the workload, and affected the place of women in the industry.[17] These technological changes allowed textile manufacturers to cut their labor force and total wage bill while vastly increasing production. Between 1853 and 1876 technological changes tripled the output of each wool millhand and doubled that of the average cotton millhand. (See Table 2.3.)

In sum, although production climbed in all textile manufacturing, it increased more rapidly in Cohoes's cotton mills than in the knit goods mills, with the Harmony Mills, under Robert Johnston's supervision, leading the way. A brief look at Johnston and his managerial associates illuminates the way in which a political, social, and financial elite controlled Cohoes until 1882.

The Managerial Elite

Robert Johnston was born in Dalston-Carlisle, England, on February 2, 1807. At the age of seven he began work in Northumberland cotton mills, becoming an expert mule-spinner. In 1833 he emigrated to the United States. Johnston settled in Providence, Rhode

TABLE 2.3. Per Capita Production in Cohoes Woolen and Cotton Mills

	1853	1876
Woolen:		
Dry goods		
produced	45,000	444,000
Workforce	750	2,379
Average	60 doz./hand	190 doz./hand
Cotton:		
Yards produced	7,542,000	80,000,000
Workforce	800	4,000
Average	9,427.5 yds./hand	20,000 yds./hand

SOURCE: Masten, History of Cohoes, pp. 119, 243–44.

Island, and, while employed by the Providence Steam Mills, gained a name for himself by demonstrating what was thought to be impossible: the spinning of warp on mules. Moving to Valatia, New York, he took charge of the local cotton mill (owned by Nathan Wild, the father of one of the purchasers of the Harmony Mills) and spun the first *mousseline de laine* (a worsted fabric) ever produced in this country. He was also the friend and co-worker of Samuel Slater, considered to be the father of American cotton spinning.[18]

Under Johnston's direction, the Harmony Mills flourished. The Mills incorporated in 1853 and an annex, built in that same year, almost doubled its size. The company's expansion over the next fifteen years seemed boundless. In 1857 it erected No. 2 Mill, employing an additional 500 hands. It also acquired an additional seventy acres for more tenements. In 1859 it purchased the two Ogden Mills that were begun in the mid-1840s, and promptly expanded their capacity. Six years later it acquired the Strong Mill (built in 1846), thereby gaining a local monopoly. Stimulated by the government demand for cotton goods during the war, the company built further additions and improved its mills between 1860 and 1865. The pace of construction quickened further after the war with two major building projects: an addition to No. 2 Mill which doubled its capacity to 48,000 spindles; and erection of the mammoth No. 3 Mill (the so-called Mastodon Mill, named for the skeleton of the prehistoric elephant found during its construction). This latter plant became the "model cotton producing plant in this country."[19] Frequently visited by cotton capitalists from across the nation and abroad, this mill alone contained 130,000 spindles, 2,700 looms, and over seven miles of gas and water pipes.[20] Robert Johnston's son, David, had entered the mill office in 1850 at the age of sixteen and, replacing his father, served as supervisor during these years of expansion. In 1866, as a reward for his leadership, the corporation gave him a share in the company. His father, meanwhile, remained general manager. Wild sold out to Garner for $950,000 a year later, and by the late 1860s Garner and Company controlled Harmony Mills. The operation included 203,000 spindles, "more than were operated by any other single firm or corporation in the United States in any one locality." In addition, the 3,100 employees received an annual payroll of almost a million dollars. Finally, when an addition was built on the No. 3 Mill in 1872, the Mastodon Mill, now 1,185 feet long, 75 feet wide, and five stories high, became the country's largest complete cotton mill.[21]

By 1872, the physical expansion of the Harmony Mills plant had been essentially completed. Garner, the principal owner, remained in New York City, leaving day-to-day operation to the Johnstons— Robert as general manager, and David as superintendent. They had directed the consolidation and expansion of Cohoes's cotton mills, as well as the lives of an entire community—the Harmony Hill village. For thirty-nine years David Johnston served as superintendent of the Harmony Union Sabbath School, a non-denominational institution maintained by the Cohoes company. This Sunday School, organized in 1853, met regularly in the mill rooms. The company also extended its involvement beyond the realm of moral and spiritual instruction. It rented some 800 tenement houses to its employees, housed unmarried workers in five large boardinghouses, and ran a company store. Such institutions and practices suggest the extent to which company paternalism was involved in the cotton-worker community.

Management's political and social positions further suggest the interlocking character of Cohoes's political and financial power. William E. Thorn, the Harmony agent and treasurer from 1867 to 1910, illustrates how the textile manufacturers were knit into an interlocking directorate. The son-in-law of Commodore Cornelius Vanderbilt and the nephew of Thomas Garner, Thorn received a law degree from Columbia College. In 1867 he became the executor and trustee of Garner's estate and the guardian of Garner's three

daughters, all of whom became titled heiresses—the Marquess de
Bretevil, Lady Gordon Cumming, and the Countess de Miltke.
After moving to Cohoes in 1867, Thorn served on the board of
directors of the Cohoes Company. He was also secretary and treasurer of the Cohoes Gas Light Company (controlled by the Garner
interest), director and first president of the Manufacturers' Bank of
Cohoes, and instrumental in organizing the Cohoes Mechanics'
Savings Bank. Thorn was elected mayor of Cohoes in 1878 and 1880,
and he served as a Republican presidential elector in 1892.[22] Other
textile manufacturers held virtually every major political and financial post in the city. Egbert Egberts and his nephew, Charles H.
Adams, were the most prominent of a group of about twenty knit
goods manufacturers, all but one of whom appear to have been
native-born.[23] Through the scrupulous control of Cohoes's banking
machinery they translated their virtual domestic monopoly on
machine-knit shirts and drawers into the city's largest personal
fortunes.[24] Egberts founded the city's first bank, the National Bank
of Cohoes, and at his death the presidency passed on to Adams.
Charles H. Adams also served as an assemblyman and state senator,
and in 1873 he was elected to the House of Representatives. Robert
Johnston was president of the Mechanics' Savings Bank, and another
prominent Cohoes iron and knit goods manufacturer, Henry D.
Fuller, filled the presidency of the city's fourth bank, the Cohoes
Savings Institution. Fuller, Adams, and David Johnston frequently
served either as president of the village, mayor of the city, or in some
appointed official capacity, and when they were unavailable,
another mill official was usually elected to office.

The key point, however, is that this network of political and
financial connections among the business elite affected the
working-class community in social as well as economic affairs. Harmony Mills' paternalism remains most obvious, but all of these
powerful corporations shaped Cohoes's growth by their social regulation. For instance, in 1846 the Cohoes Company, the privately
owned utility, allowed a local machinist, Samuel H. Baldwin, to rent
the land for his store. The rental provided an annual $104 fee for
power—100 square inches of water from a twenty-foot fall—with a
typical proviso: no tavern could be built on the land without a license
from them, "nor a public house or entertainment nor any livery
stable, nor sell any spirituous liquors of any kind in any shop, or

other building." By 1877 the company owned, operated, and leased water power from an elaborate canal network—ten canals on six different levels, each with a twenty-foot drop. With or without explicit regulations on the usage, this water-power monopoly wielded considerable influence.[25] Throughout this dynamic industrial period in Cohoes's history, the manufacturers who founded, directed, and eventually monopolized the growth of the cotton and woolen mills also controlled the public utilities, guided the financial institutions, held the political reins, and dominated much else in the life of the Harmony Hill community.

In contrast to this rapid industrial growth at an early period, uncertain economic conditions marked the years after 1872. Only 24,000 spindles were added to the Harmony Mills between 1872 and 1887, an increase of less than 10 percent. Notwithstanding this relative stagnation, Harmony, as compared to any of the woolen mills, had expanded tremendously since 1853. The typical knit goods employee actually worked in a smaller factory in 1876 than in 1860;[26] by 1880, in contrast, Harmony had acquired all of Cohoes's cotton mills, and its operatives now worked for an enormous company with nearly 5,000 employees.

The Textile Workers in 1860

Who were the workers in these mills? How did they confront the enormous financial, political, and social power of this interlocking group of industrial barons? Unfortunately, deficiencies in the federal manuscript population censuses for 1860 and 1880 give us only limited answers. Distinctions between wool and cotton hands in Cohoes were not made in 1860; skilled workers were infrequently noted in each census, and an undercount of perhaps 25 percent was probable.[27] Still, the 1860 manufacturing census reported that 3,210 Cohoesiers, 48.3 percent of those aged ten and over, worked in textile manufacturing, 1,550 of them in the cotton mills. In 1880 manufacturers put the number of textile operatives at approximately 7,750, of whom 4,808 worked for Harmony Mills. This latter figure was 50.9 percent of the total population aged ten and over. Such numbers demonstrate the extent to which Cohoes's ethnic communities depended on the textile mills. However, the manuscript population schedules enumerated only 1,889 Cohoes textile workers in 1860, and only 3,284 cotton hands in 1880. In both census years the large majority of those not enumerated appear to have been women and young girls.[28] Some of the "missing" lived in neighboring villages, while others probably did not appear for the same psychological, linguistic, and social reasons that still plague census- and poll-takers.[29] Thus data based upon the manuscript population census schedules provide only a partial indication of those women and young girls who were working in the Harmony Mills. A good many more than those recorded in the census were probably involved.

The average Cohoes textile worker was not native-born.[30] Factory life had become primarily an immigrant experience by 1860, when more than half of the employees were either Irish immigrants or their children. Only a quarter were native-born Americans, while English and French-Canadian hands each constituted less than a tenth. The typical cotton hand had a dual social and cultural identity: this worker was both Irish and female (Table 2.4). Moreover, the Harmony Mills cotton operative was most likely an unskilled and unmarried woman between the ages of fifteen and twenty-five. Four out of every five Irishwomen between the ages of fifteen and nineteen worked in the mills in 1860 (Table 2.5).

Among other ethnic groups, fewer women and young men were employed, but they also followed a common pattern: children entered the mills in their early teens and often departed in their twenties. Interesting variations reflected the options open to male workers—namely, ethnic preferences, and skills learned previously by many English workers. Teenage girls were more likely to work in the mills than teenage boys, for males had attractive alternatives that held out the promise of higher wages and an improved living standard. They might help with construction work, become apprentices to artisan brickmakers or molders, or find work at Daniel Simmons's axe factory. Similarly, while English teenagers worked in the mills, they did so much less frequently than the Irish, French Canadians, or native-born Americans.

After marriage, most men and women seem to have left the mills. Women probably departed to raise children, though some may have periodically returned to work. (According to local residents, in the early twentieth century the Harmony Mills even ran a day-care center.[31]) Others perhaps engaged in traditional forms of unreported part-time employment as washerwomen or needlewomen to

TABLE 2.4. Factory (Textile) Workers Aged Ten and Over and Ethnicity, 1860

		Male	Female	Total	Percent of population (ten and over)	Factory workers (%)
Cotton workers	N	610	940	1,550		
(manufacturing census)	%	39.4	60.2		23.3	
Textile workers	₊N	778	1,103	1,881		
(ten and over)[a]	%	41.4	58.6		28.3	
Ethnicity:						
Native-born American	N	197	293	490		
	%	40.2	59.8		22.8	26.0
Irish	N	377	617	994		
	%	37.9	62.1		31.6	52.8
English	N	101	74	175		
	%	57.7	42.3		30.0	9.3
French Canadian	N	50	74	124		
	%	40.3	59.7		26.2	6.5
Scottish	N	39	35	74		
	%	52.7	47.3		30.9	3.9
Other	N	14	10	24		
	%	58.3	41.7		—	1.5

SOURCE: Manuscript 8th Census, 1860, *Population*.
[a] Six boys and two girls under ten were enumerated as well.

supplement the family income. Men from most ethnic groups sought more permanent and better-paid employment outside the mills. Englishmen were the exception, working in the mills in great numbers; while most other males in their early twenties chose employment outside the textile industry, close to half the Englishmen between the ages of twenty and forty did not. Usually married, like James Frost, they worked as relatively well-paid spinners, weavers, carders, and the like. Frost himself was a twister.

The fathers of many cotton mill workers found other jobs, but it is important to remember that Harmony Mills employed entire families of workers. Furthermore, one-quarter of the cotton-worker families were headed by widows. Some native-born fathers entered trades or businesses outside the textile factory, and even fewer Irish and French-Canadian fathers became unskilled day laborers on the Erie and Champlain canal network, or perhaps were near their children as factory maintenance workers (Table 2.6).

TABLE 2.5. Number and Percentage of Cohoes Men and Women of an Age and Ethnic Group Employed as Factory (Textile) Workers, 1860

Ethnicity		10–14	15–19	20–29	30–39	40+
				Age		
Females						
American	N	8	107	134	27	17
	%	5.4	57.2	34.8	13.3	6.9
Irish	N	44	299	210	38	26
	%	14.7	81.9	47.7	13.7	6.2
English	N	6	29	22	12	5
	%	11.5	50.8	31.8	21.8	9.2
French Canadian	N	5	47	18	4	0
	%	11.1	77.0	26.0	12.1	0
Males						
American	N	7	81	68	25	16
	%	6.4	50.3	24.9	13.7	7.4
Irish	N	46	186	84	33	28
	%	16.4	67.6	29.4	18.1	8.8
English	N	2	15	36	35	13
	%	3.6	40.5	52.1	44.3	23.6
French Canadian	N	4	18	16	6	6
	%	7.8	58.0	27.1	25.0	10.7

As in Troy's iron mills, immigrant Irish families had found work for their children in the Harmony Mills even before the Civil War. While the Irish clearly dominated the mills, they were joined there by a sizable number of native-born workers. Other ethnic groups also moved into textiles in numbers equal to their share of Cohoes's population (Table 2.5). Finally, the mills did not draw mothers away from their families. Women ceased work after they married and began raising families, although later their children worked. (See Table 2.5.[32]) The additional income, especially from unmarried daughters, could be put to good use. It enabled the family to gain property—that small measure of the security Ireland had not afforded. As in Troy, only a few Cohoes families headed by Irish cotton workers accumulated property. Eleven percent of these Irishmen over the age of twenty owned property in 1860, compared to only 5.9 percent of the Englishmen and 1.8 percent of the Americans.[33]

Cohoes differed from the early New England textile towns. In place of the celebrated apple-cheeked, native-born farm girl who

TABLE 2.6. Number and Percentage of Cohoes Men of an Age and Ethnic Group
Employed as Laborers, 1860

Ethnicity		Age				
		15–19	20–29	30–39	40–49	50+
American	N	4	9	7	5	7
	%	2.5	3.3	3.8	4.5	4.4
Irish	N	16	49	61	95	72
	%	5.8	17.2	33.5	54.3	54.5
English	N	0	0	3	0	1
	%	0	0	3.8	0	4.8
French Canadian	N	2	5	5	10	11
	%	6.5	8.5	20.8	30.3	50.0

came to her new city "boarding school" as a factory hand in the 1820s
and 1830s, young immigrant Irish women dominated
the Cohoes cotton mills in 1860. By this time weaving remained the
only skilled or semi-skilled trade in which women still found ready
employment: slightly more than half of Cohoes's weavers in 1860
were women. The number of more skilled workers noted in the
census leaves much to be desired, but while the English filled
skilled positions in the mills considerably in excess of their relatively
small numbers, Irishmen and women held skilled as well as unskilled positions (Table 2.7). Significantly, like Joseph Delehanty, an
organizer of the 1882 Harmony Mills strike, a few had prior experience in English textile mills before emigrating to America. As in
Troy, Irishmen did more than dig ditches and lay railroad track, and
Irishwomen worked in other than domestic services.[34] While the
relative concentration of female English weavers was six times that
of the Irish, Irishwomen in Civil War Cohoes held as many semi-
skilled weavers posts as did native-born and English workers.
Native-born Americans still held about a quarter of the jobs, but by
1860 Cohoes's cotton mills had become largely Irish "institutions."

The Cotton Workers in 1880

Between 1860 and 1880 the most dramatic change in the Harmony
Mills labor force involved the introduction of French Canadians.
The Mastodon Mill had been built between 1866 and 1872, and
thousands of additional workers had been needed. The Quebec area

TABLE 2.7. Percentage and Relative Concentration of Selected Cohoes Workers by Ethnicity, 1860

Percentage

	Unskilled								Skilled				
	Managerial[a]	Clerical[a]	Laborer[a]	Service[b]	Factory (textile) worker — Male	Factory (textile) worker — Female	Weaver — Male	Weaver — Female	Spinner[a]	Dresser[a] Carder	Seamstress Milliner Dressmaker[b]	Carpenter[a]	Machinist[a]
U.S.A.	70.4	54.5	8.8	17.5	25.3	26.5	2.4	32.6	16.6	46.1	53.3	52.7	38.1
Ireland	13.1	24.6	80.3	77.7	48.4	55.9	36.6	32.6	25.0	7.6	21.6	23.1	27.0
England	8.1	7.7	1.0	0	12.9	6.7	46.3	32.6	50.0	30.7	5.0	8.3	17.5
French Canada	0	0	9.1	1.8	6.4	6.7	0	0	0	7.6	3.3	11.1	0
Scotland	6.5	6.4	0.2	1.8	5.0	3.1	12.2	2.1	8.3	7.6	1.6	2.8	11.1

Relative Concentration
(Proportion among gainful workers in all occupations = 100)

	Managerial[a]	Clerical[a]	Laborer[a]	Service[b]	Factory (textile) worker — Male	Factory (textile) worker — Female	Weaver — Male	Weaver — Female	Spinner[a]	Dresser[a] Carder	Seamstress Milliner Dressmaker[b]	Carpenter[a]	Machinist[a]
U.S.A.	222	172	28	55	80	84	8	103	52	145	168	166	120
Ireland	29	55	178	159	107	114	81	67	55	17	44	51	60
England	82	78	10	0	130	86	468	418	505	310	64	84	177
French Canada	0	0	123	26	86	97	0	0	0	103	48	150	0
Scotland	171	168	5	55	132	94	318	64	218	200	48	74	292
N	61	77	372	108	778	1,103	41	46	12	13	60	108	63

[a] All males.
[b] All females.

was a logical place for recruiting family labor:[35] English investors had been slow to introduce agricultural technology to rural Canada, and competition from midwestern American farms had led to distress among the inhabitants of Quebec province. Furthermore, during the 1873 depression many workers in the stagnant shipbuilding and timber trades fled southward looking for work.[36] Textile towns like Cohoes offered abundant positions, and, from the manufacturer's perspective, French-Canadian women and children provided a large pool of cheap labor. Consequently, while one out of every four unskilled textile workers in Cohoes in 1860 had been native-born, and less than one in ten was of French-Canadian origin, by 1880 the percentages were virtually reversed. The Harmony Mills workforce had doubled, but the number of American-born hands was almost half its 1860 figure, dropping 42 percent. (Compare Tables 2.4 and 2.8.) The 124 French-Canadian textile workers counted in 1860 had increased ninefold, to 1,109, in the cotton mills alone. Almost half the workers were still Irish, but better than one-third of the unskilled cotton hands were of French-Canadian ancestry. Young people with names such as Derocher, La Pine, Hebert, Archimbeault, and Generaux now filled the mills; native-born and English workers now each comprised less than one-tenth of the total.

Notwithstanding the influx of large numbers of "cheap" French-Canadian laborers who found Harmony Hill to be an attractive workplace (see relative concentration figures in Table 2.9), the Irish obtained additional employment in the mills. It is true that almost all teenage members of a family had to labor for subsistence wages, and that everyone in the community depended heavily on company paternalism. The work patterns of the William Devine and Belina La Morey families suggest as much. Devine, an Irish laborer, lived on the Hill with his wife and six children. Mrs. Devine stayed at home with the three youngest offspring, while each of the three older ones—girls aged nine, ten, and fourteen—worked in the mills for about 50 cents a day. Belina La Morey, a widow from Canada who lived a few blocks away, depended on the income that her three oldest children—a ten-year-old daughter, and two sons, aged seventeen and twelve—brought home from the mills. Mrs. La Morey remained at home with her little boy. Money was tight, but the

TABLE 2.8. Cotton Workers Aged Ten and Over and Ethnicity, 1880

		Male	Female	Total	Percent of population (ten and over)[b]	Cotton workers (%)
Manufacturing census	N	1,568	3,240	4,808		
	%	32.6	67.4		31.6	
Cotton workers	N	1,280	1,964	3,244		
(Ten and over)[a]	%	39.5	60.5		21.3	
Ethnicity:						
Native-born American	N	136	148	284		
	%	47.9	52.1		9.1	8.8
Irish	N	514	958	1,472		
	%	34.9	65.1		26.8	45.4
English	N	151	111	262		
	%	57.6	42.4		19.2	8.1
French Canadian	N	435	674	1,109		
	%	39.2	60.8		24.6	34.2
Scottish	N	20	33	53	c	
	%	37.7	62.3			1.6
German	N	23	30	53	c	
	%	43.4	56.6			1.6
Other	N	1	10	11	c	
	%	9.1	90.9			0.3

SOURCE: Manuscript 10th Census, 1880, *Population*.
[a] 16 boys and 24 girls under ten were enumerated as well.
[b] Estimated, using data for Albany County in 1880.
[c] Unavailable.

Harmony Mills offered steady employment, solid brick housing, and a steady though meager income. Like their Irish neighbors, the French Canadians had found the bases for building a new home. Although each ethnic group had distinct work patterns which reflected its cultural origins, there were similarities among them. Two out of every three cotton workers in 1880 were female. The Irish and French-Canadians maintained this ratio; in contrast, the numbers of native-born men and women were almost even, and, as in 1860, English males outnumbered English female millhands. Native-born Americans had started to leave the mills: the 1860 figure of 22.8 percent of the native-born aged ten and over had dropped to 9.1 percent by 1880. Otherwise, among each of the three large immigrant groups—Irish, French Canadians, and English— the percentage of cotton workers remained about one out of every four or five "adults" (Tables 2.4 and 2.8). Finally, as in 1860, the

English continued to show a distinctive work pattern. The average English cotton hand was a married man who was older than his Irish, French-Canadian, or native-born counterparts.

The typical unskilled cotton hand in 1880 was probably a young and unmarried Irish or French-Canadian woman. Conversely, the Irish or French-Canadian girl growing up in Cohoes probably once worked, or would shortly work, in the Harmony Mills. She started work at an earlier age in 1880 than she would have in 1860, especially if she was of French-Canadian extraction.[37]

Half of the workers were less than twenty years of age in both census years, but the percentage of those under fifteen tripled between 1860 and 1880 (from 7.4 percent of the workforce to 24.1 percent). While the rise was more marked among boys than among girls, both greatly increased, and children from every ethnic group were involved. The average age for all workers remained fairly constant, at about twenty, although the average for women *did* vary with ethnicity. Two out of every three female French-Canadian cotton workers were *under* twenty, while the same proportion of Englishwomen were *over* twenty. These figures suggest different attitudes toward the child's role in the family, as well as varying birth rates among the ethnic groups.[38] Fewer Englishwomen and children worked. Remaining at home, perhaps with some unreported work to supplement the family income, Englishwomen kept their daughters at home or in school. Their decision had various motivations: the desire to educate or to protect their daughters was one; cultural animosities (the fear of lost status through association with the mostly Irish and French-Canadian cotton workers) was another.

Anti-Catholic prejudice certainly existed; Cohoes's Catholic church, for example, was vandalized as early as 1855.[39] During the mid-1850s the American "Know-Nothing party" won local elections promising, in the alleged words of one party leader, not to allow "them 'furriners' " to "elbow Americans out of the factories."[40] Such appeals further stigmatized factory labor for some ethnic elements. For the Irish and French-Canadians, however, there was more to be gained than lost by working in the mills. Families were large.[41] True, children worked the exhausting seventy-two-hour week at absurdly low salaries; but this meager income enabled their mothers to stay at home with their youngest offspring. Cohoes Police Sergeant Mathew B. Smith agreed with the cotton workers who testified, before the 1882 New York state legislative committee investigating child labor, that parents lived off the labor of their children. Smith, however, mistook this for exploitation, rather than financial necessity, and incorrectly attributed it to paternal laziness. "You find these old fellows," he claimed, "lying around the streets smoking pipes and at noon going with five or six pails of dinner for their children in the mills."[42] Charles Denn, an overseer in the Harmony Mills spinning room, contradicted this view. He knew of only one father among the parents of working children who did not work himself, and Denn stated that the man in question could "not get work."[43] Denn's view was generally confirmed by census listings of employed fathers, and it supported the testimony of thirteen Harmony Hill families interviewed by the committee: without child labor these families usually could not remain out of debt.[44] Finally, the mills also offered the prospect of some modest occupational mobility for Irish youth; achievement therefore related to the family fortunes. Many Irish workers appear to have become skilled weavers and spinners as early as 1860, and by 1880 they filled a majority of the more skilled cotton mill positions. Irishwomen comprised 72.9 percent of the female weavers, and their sons and husbands fared equally well. Skilled Irishmen constituted 60 percent of the spinners and 54.5 percent of the dressers, carders, and loom harness makers in 1880 (Table 2.9).

Status and Immigrant Expectations

The experience of individual workers varied, but, viewed collectively, the new generation of Irish workers had made some gains by 1880. The hours were long and the work among the whirling machines was dangerous, but the Irish family nonetheless procured work for as many children and fellow immigrants as might turn up.[45] In Cohoes, where good company housing was provided, a few even translated earned income into small property-holdings. In this way, the history of Cohoes's working-class Irish and French Canadians suggests the need to reconsider what success or failure may have meant to the nineteenth-century working class.[46]

To measure the workers' sense of achievement, we need to consider their goals and aspirations, in addition to knowing their wages and occupational advances. Then the impact of technology, economic pressures, and social attitudes toward women can be

TABLE 2.9. Percentage and Relative Concentration of Selected Cohoes Workers by Ethnicity, 1880

Percentage [a]

	Managerial (textiles)	Unskilled cotton workers		Weaver		Spinner	Dresser Carder Loom-maker	Total	Carpenter	Machinist	Painter
		Male	Female	Male	Female						
U.S.A.	69.6	10.6	7.5	11.1	2.0	0	9.0	4.6	24.2	38.7	33.3
Ireland	4.3	40.2	48.8	44.4	72.9	60.0	54.5	63.4	31.4	22.5	33.3
England	26.1	11.8	5.7	11.1	14.5	33.3	22.7	19.3	28.5	14.5	24.2
French Canada	0	34.0	34.3	0	4.1	0	4.5	2.8	7.1	12.9	3.0

Relative Concentration [a]
(Proportion among gainful workers in all occupations = 100)

	Managerial (textiles)	Unskilled cotton workers		Weaver		Spinner	Dresser Carder Loom-maker	Total	Carpenter	Machinist	Painter
		Male	Female	Male	Female						
U.S.A.	315	48	34	50	9	0	41	21	110	175	151
Ireland	11	105	127	116	190	157	142	166	82	59	87
England	307	139	67	131	171	391	267	227	335	171	285
French Canada	0	142	143	0	17	0	19	12	30	54	13
N	23	1,280	1,964	9	48	30	22	109	70[b]	62[b]	33[b]

[a] Unless otherwise indicated, all enumerated were male.
[b] Ward 1, Districts 1 and 2 only (Harmony Hill). These were most likely to be people employed by the Harmony Mills to maintain the mills and tenement houses.

assessed. Given her conditions, could not, for example, the Cohoes cotton worker share the Troy iron molder's expectations? Might not newly arrived millhands share the same social dream—of finding ample and steady employment in the mills, maintaining a tenement home, and developing community fellowship? Cohoes's Irish and French Canadians found full employment in the Harmony Mills, and the former, over two decades, increasingly dominated the skilled crafts. Life was not easy, as a survey of social conditions will make clear, but, unlike many other factories, the Harmony Mills provided regular employment throughout depression of the 1870s. It also maintained some unusually well-constructed brick tenements for its employees. Living and working conditions may indeed have been arduous, but compared to the low wages and inferior housing in most English manufacturing districts, and relative to the conditions that impelled immigrants to leave Ireland or Quebec, it is easy to understand the workers' willingness to defend this small but, for them, not insignificant improvement in their lives.[47]

The Patrick Dillon Family

Patrick Dillon and his family are a representative cotton-worker family.[48] Dillon probably left Ireland with his wife, Ellen, and their six children during the potato famine. They arrived in New York around 1850, added three more children during the decade, and, at the outbreak of the Civil War, lived in a four-room company tenement at 4 Willow Street, in the heart of the Harmony Hill community. The Dillons managed to save approximately three hundred dollars, but it had not been easy: four members of the family worked full time. Every morning before six o'clock the forty-five-year-old head of the household left for work as a day laborer. His two eldest sons, Michael and William, twenty and eighteen respectively, answered the six o'clock chime of the Harmony Mills bell. Patrick, the sixteen-year-old son, joined his father as a day laborer. Perhaps they worked on one of the canal or railroad labor gangs involved in area construction; they may also have worked for the Harmony Mills, building new tenements or enlarging the newly acquired Ogden Mills. Meanwhile, Mrs. Dillon was occupied at home. Matthew, age fourteen, and the twelve-year-old twin girls did not yet work, and only the six-year-old boy attended school. The baby had only just celebrated her first birthday and must have required considerable attention; so, too, a three-year-old daughter. In addition, Mrs. Dillon was pregnant again.

The men came home for lunch on their forty-minute noon break and then returned to the mills. At half past six the closing bell rang. For these twelve hours of work an adult common laborer received seventy-five cents, while a skilled mule-spinner received up to twice that. Women and especially children who labored in the mills received considerably less: a "back boy," for example, received thirty cents for his twelve-hour day.[49]

Work in the mills was steady, and each of the two unskilled Dillon boys employed there probably earned an annual wage of about $225. Day laborers worked less regularly, and many spent whole months unemployed; thus the senior Dillon and the sixteen year-old may have earned an annual wage of $150 each. Therefore, the estimated Dillon family income in 1860 was about $750. When the monthly payday arrived in the mills, the tenement house rent—of $5–7—was deducted. What remained had to feed, clothe, and entertain the family.

Patrick Dillon died late in the 1860s, but his widow continued to maintain the family home. Finally, in 1875, she moved to Orchard Street, a few blocks away, where she worked occasionally as a dressmaker. Of her children, Patrick, Jr., died suddenly in 1870 at the age of twenty-six, shortly after his marriage, and James died on September 15, 1874, at the age of nineteen—both from undisclosed causes. Michael and Matthew reappear periodically in the city directories as millhands. Michael lived with the family for a few years in the mid-seventies, only to disappear from the directory completely in 1879; Matthew, though moving almost yearly, remained on the Hill, and thus near the family. Although listed each year in the directory as a "spinner," he does not appear in the 1880 census schedule. By 1880, the older girls had probably married. The rest of the Dillons still lived in their old mill house, and William, the second-eldest son twenty years earlier, had become its head.

William Dillon had married an Irish-born woman, Elizabeth, soon after the Civil War. In 1866 their son, Patrick III, was born, followed two years later by a daughter, Hannah. His father's death, coupled with that of his elder brother, Patrick, Jr., thrust considerable obligations upon William's shoulders. His job in the mill now had to support not only his own family of four, but also his widowed mother and her four children, none of whom yet worked. Family economics required that the widow open her small house to another Irish family—John Kahal, his wife, and two children—and to an Irish boarder. Both of the male boarders worked in the mills, and the additional income helped sustain the family.

By 1880, the family once again maintained itself without boarders. William Dillon's first wife having died, he married another Irish-woman, also named Elizabeth, who was fifteen years his junior and only nine years older than his fifteen-year-old son, Patrick.[50] William no longer worked for the mill. Since 1871 he had operated a "saloon" in the old homestead, most likely on the ground level, with the family moving upstairs. Elizabeth stayed at home to take care of their three-year-old nephew, John, possibly the son of one of her husband's dead brothers or sisters. Finally, William's three youngest sisters, now nineteen, twenty, and twenty-two years old, together with Patrick, worked in the Harmony Mills, much as the family had done for the past two decades. There had been many deaths in the Dillon family over the years, most of them at relatively young ages, but those who remained had secured a place within the community.

Mill work, meanwhile, had hardly changed. The pace had been sped up, but hours had been slightly reduced. More children and more French Canadians now labored there, and the opening bell now rang a half-hour later—at six-thirty in the morning—and a half-hour earlier at the end of the day—at six in the evening. Lunch had been extended ten more minutes to fifty minutes, the result of a strike victory that spring. Daily wages had dropped back from their 1867–75 high to the 1864 levels. A common laborer now received $1.12½, a skilled spinner $1.75, and a back boy $0.42.

The mills continued to play a central part in the family life of the Dillons. The old Willow Street tenement remained a focus for the family, and the mills continuously employed the teenagers and adults. Indeed, in 1880 five of the seven family members worked, four of them in the mills. Cotton operatives struck for a month, but each of the four Dillons probably earned about $325 for the year regardless. With income from the saloon, the family's 1880 income may have exceeded $1,500. Five years later the Dillons evidently felt secure enough to permit twenty-year-old Patrick—whose grand-father had arrived in America almost forty years earlier—to leave the mills and return to school. As a "student," he acquired the considerable occupational and social status traditionally afforded to the educated. Though, for many of his relatives, mobility had been only from the mills to the grave, young Patrick had achieved an avenue to status which both he and the dominant culture could celebrate.

Like those of the Turner family in Troy, the Dillon family's experiences extended beyond the factory and were fuller and richer than this industrial portrait suggests. On Cohoes's Harmony Hill, Irish and French-Canadian cotton workers like the Dillons established a diverse community life, a complete network of ethnic, religious, social, and political associations. Chapter 5 will detail the role such associations played in the lives of these millhands and their community.

Certain things about Cohoes's social life, however, may be immediately summarized.[51] Irish workers dominated the mills even before the Civil War; French Canadians entered them in the 1870s, and the native-born were displaced. Both ethnic groups came in search of economic improvement, and both gained some modest occupational security for themselves and their offspring. Between 1860 and the early 1870s, workers like Patrick Dillon had achieved a secure position within the mill community, and they managed to maintain that position throughout the protracted economic depression that followed. There were openings for semi-skilled and skilled workers, and a few Irish families even managed to become property holders. Some of Cohoes's Irish had prior industrial experience in English textile mills, but many, if not most, of the cotton workers had been uprooted from rural societies and directly transplanted into the midst of the American Industrial Revolution. In contrast to memories of famine or inferior English housing and wages, the ever-present specter of poverty, constantly changing technology, and the work experience in these monster mills, they could appreciate the meager but regular employment and perhaps coherent aspects of community life.[52]

The iron and cotton industries went through a similar industrial transformation between 1855 and 1885. Both industries expanded rapidly and amalgamated; their production increasingly concentrated in a few large factories (or, in the case of Cohoes, in one company), and their owners constantly sought ways to rationalize, discipline, or control the workforce. In addition, the mid-1870s were marked by a prolonged depression that placed stress on both industries. There were, however, important differences in the social makeup of these two cities, and in the respective industrial workforce of each. Troy's diversified economy and working class were dominated by the Irish; Cohoes's Harmony Hill community contained two distinct ethnic groups when the French Canadians arrived in the 1870s. Ironworkers comprised a permanent workforce; not so with young women and children who supplied most of the labor in the textile mills. Young men did not normally work in the textile mills after adolescence, and women worked intermittently after they began to bear children. So there were important differences in the workforces in each industry and in the ways in which technology affected them. One central similarity remains: both the iron and cotton industries expanded tremendously in these years, and workers found jobs readily available. Some, even immigrants, obtained skilled positions and (especially within the iron industry) a little property.

These two tendencies of the era, however, increasingly conflicted. Modest worker achievements facilitated integration of the immigrant family and community; on the other hand, industrial amalgamation and concentration placed constraints on these achievements. Each development must be seen in the context of the other. Identifying the participants in this historical drama through the use of statistical data only provides a framework for larger questions about social behavior. Whatever relative or actual achievements these urban workers experienced must still be placed in the broader context of the political and industrial problems they confronted, and the social conditions in which they lived and organized.

NOTES

1. The poet Thomas Moore immortalized the romance of the mighty falls in thirty-four lines of verse written after a visit to Cohoes in 1804. The poem, entitled "Lines Written at the Cohoes or Falls of the Mohawk River," included these lines:

> From the rise of morn till set of sun
> I've seen the mighty Mohawk run . . .
> Oh, may my falls be bright as thine!
> May heaven's forgiving rainbow shine
> upon the mist that circles me.
> As soft as now it hangs o'er thee!

2. Kilian van Rensselaer, a pearl merchant and director of the Dutch West Indies Company, was authorized as patroon to purchase most of the land in the upper Hudson Valley from the Indians in 1630. The estate was later subdivided among the different settlers. Most of Cohoes stands on land originally included in the West District of the Manor of Rensselaerwyck. The East District included the present site of Troy.

3. For much of the material used in this paragraph on Cohoes's early history, I am indebted to Arthur H. Masten, *The History of Cohoes, New York* (Albany, 1877), and George Rodgers Howell and Jonathan Tenney, *History of the County of Albany, N.Y., from 1609 to 1886* (New York, 1886).

4. Samuel Rezneck, "Cohoes: The Historical Background, 1811–1918," in *A Report of the Mohawk-Hudson Area Survey*, comp. Robert M. Vogel (Washington, 1973), pp. 121–23.

5. Howell and Tenney, *County of Albany*, p. 956.

6. Rezneck, "Cohoes," p. 123.

7. Edward Joseph Clark, "An Economic History of the Harmony Mills of Cohoes, New York" (Master's thesis, Siena College, 1952).

8. Howell and Tenney, *County of Albany*, p. 952.

9. Tenth Census, 1880, *Manufactures*, the section of the manuscript for Albany County, was missing in the State Education Library in Albany. An advertisement by the Harmony Mills in *The Troy Directory* for 1880 supplied the number of cotton workers employed. The woolen mill figures for 1876 appear in Masten, *History of Cohoes*, p. 244.

10. Edith Abbott, *Women in Industry: A Study of American Economic History* (New York, 1910), p. 99.

11. Ibid., p. 102.

12. Tenth Census, 1880, *Population*. Unless otherwise noted, data for tables have been compiled from federal manuscript census schedules for 1860 and 1880. These schedules are available in the manuscript collection of the New York State Education Library in Albany. Eighth Census, 1860, *Population* and *Manufactures*; Tenth Census, 1880, *Population* and *Manufactures*.

13. Additional supporting data for this chapter are available in Daniel J. Walkowitz, "Working Class Women in the Gilded Age: Factory, Family, and Community Life among Cohoes, New York, Cotton Workers, 1860–1880," *Journal of Social History* 5, no. 4 (Summer 1977):464–90.

14. Temin, *Iron and Steel in Nineteenth Century America*, pp. 206, 218.

15. Abbott, *Women in Industry*, p. 95.

16. Ibid., pp. 92–99.

17. Abbott (ibid.), Elizabeth F. Baker (*Technology and Woman's Work* [New York, 1964]), and Carroll D. Wright (quoted in Baker) all attribute the decreasing number of female workers to new technology.

18. Clark, *History of Manufacturers*, pp. 18–19; Masten, *History of Cohoes*, p. 112.

19. Clark, *History of Manufacturers*, p. 24.

20. Ibid.

21. Ibid., pp. 24–30.

22. James H. Manning, *New York State Men* (Albany, 1911), cited in Clark, *History of Manufacturers*, p. 32.

23. Alfred LeRoy, a French Canadian, opened the Globe Mill in 1872; see the federal MS population censuses for Albany County in 1860 and 1880. See also Masten, *History of Cohoes*, p. 244, for biographical information. More information about the social origins of these lesser manufacturers was unavailable.

24. Charles H. Adams, quoted in Masten, *History of Cohoes*, p. 78.

25. Rezneck, "Cohoes," pp. 123–25.

26. The average mill employed 140 hands in 1880, compared to 207.5 in 1860.

27. In 1860 all textile workers were simply described as "works in factory." According to both contemporary newspaper accounts and reports by manufacturers, the total number of "factory" or cotton workers enumerated was only 75 percent of the total employed.

28. In the case of the Eighth Census, 1860, *Population*, the number of male workers

should be increased by 25 percent, while the number of women actually employed in the mills should be *more than doubled*. In Tenth Census, 1880, *Population*, the same trend is found. (Cf. number of male and female workers Tables 2.1 and 2.6.) The possibility remains that the manufacturers were inflating their figures. While this may be partially true, the particularly large discrepancy among women workers suggests that other factors were also at work.

29. French Canadians are frequently described in the census as unable to read or write. Many of these people undoubtedly spoke French and were literate, but the census enumerator listed anyone who did not read English as functionally illiterate. Because of state regulations and social pressure against child labor, it also seems likely that many young children who worked in the mills were not enumerated as doing so. The manufacturer would hardly be interested in exposing the extensive use of child labor, and families would not want to risk losing the income from such labor.

30. Unless otherwise indicated, the father's place of birth is used to define ethnicity. A native-born American is someone whose *father* was born in the United States.

31. Anonymous street interview with Harmony Hill resident by the author, Cohoes, June 1974.

32. Data from 1880 note the same pattern. Only about one-tenth of the women workers in both 1860 and 1880 were over thirty years old.

33. The population studied included 145 Irishmen, 109 Englishmen, and 109 men whose fathers were born in America. The French-Canadian number was too small to be meaningful.

34. See Handlin, *Boston's Immigrants*, pp. 61–75; Brown, *Irish-American Nationalism*, pp. 18–19; Shannon, *The American Irish*, pp. 28, 95; and Carl Wittke, *The Irish in America*.

35. *Cohoes Cataract* reported that the Harmony Mills advertised in the Montreal-Quebec region and had agents there periodically in the 1870s.

36. Hugh Mason Wade, *The French Canadians* (Toronto, 1968), I, 333–36, and *The French-Canadian Outlook* (New York, 1946), pp. 84–90.

37. Only 6.6 percent of the female workers and 8.5 percent of the male workers were under fifteen years old in 1860. By 1880 these percentages had risen to 19.7 and 29.9. About two out of every three French-Canadian females who worked in both census years were under twenty, however, though their percentage of all female workers under fifteen climbed from 6.4 percent in 1860 to 27.3 percent in 1880.

38. The birth rate can be approximated using the survival rate of children under ten. For Cohoes in 1860 this rate is: native-born Americans, 209 per thousand population; English, 263; Irish, 277; French Canadians, 308.

39. *Cohoes Cataract*, May 12, 1855. Since only a chalice and several ornaments of small value were taken, the intent was thought to be desecration, not plunder.

40. Ibid., April 19, 1856.

41. Some sense of this is evident in the statistic that the first 250 families enumerated on Harmony Hill in 1880 averaged 2.79 cotton workers each; the average among French-Canadian families was 3.63. It should be remembered that, in most such families, neither parent worked in the mills: usually the father was a day laborer and the mother was at home.

42. New York, Bureau of Statistics of Labor, *Second Annual Report, 1884*, Legislative Assembly Document no. 26 (1882), "Establishing the Fact of the Existence of Child Labor in the State," pp. 64–66.

43. Charles Denn to the New York Legislative Committee, ibid., p. 79.

44. Ibid., pp. 111–20.

45. In 1880 four or five people worked in the average Irish or French-Canadian household on Harmony Hill; in contrast, only two or three people worked in the average English or American cotton-worker household. These figures are reflected, too, in the average number of cotton workers in each family. (See Table 4.5.)

46. Stephan Thernstrom reopened the mobility debate in 1964 in *Poverty and Progress*. Warner's Yankee City Series, written in the climate of the Great Depression, argued that

for most people, especially the immigrant working class, America had not been the land of opportunity with ready mobility into the world of affluence. Study of the new nineteenth-century industrial elite confirmed this view: almost all were white Anglo-Saxon Protestant sons educated with all the advantages that society could offer. See Gregory and Neu, "The American Industrial Elite," in Miller, ed., *Men in Business*, pp. 193–211. Thernstrom's original response to this in *Poverty and Progress* was clarified in various articles. See, e.g., his "Working-Class Social Mobility in Industrial America," in *Essays in Theory and History: An Approach to the Social Sciences*, ed. Melvin Richter (Cambridge, Mass., 1970), pp. 221–38. Thernstrom discovered limited mobility, but, as I do, he emphasized that this must be measured against a worker's perception of his mobility.

47. John Foster, *Class Struggle and the Industrial Revolution* (London, 1974), pp. 91–98, Appendix one, demonstrates the substantial level of poverty in English industrial towns at mid-century. Only 15 percent of working-class families would have escaped a period of poverty during their lives.

48. The biographical sketch of Patrick Dillon and his family is based upon the original federal MS census schedules for Albany County, Eighth Census, 1860, *Population*; Ninth Census, 1870, *Population*; and Tenth Census, 1880, *Statistics of Wages*, pp. 361–63. See also *Troy Directory*; Masten, *History of Cohoes*.

49. Caroline F. Ware, *The Early New England Cotton Manufacture* (Boston, 1931), pp. 244 and *passim*, presents a picture of the wage structure in New England cotton towns that is sensitive to the dependence of the employee on meager wages, to the ways in which the workers' salaries were tied to their total social condition through rent and store pay, and to the reduced wages of women and children.

50. This fifteen-year age difference between William Dillon and his second wife reflected the usual pattern. When widowers remarried, there was almost always a larger age gap with the second wife than with the first. This suggests the poor odds against a widow remarrying. For an extended discussion of this problem, see William J. Goode, *World Revolution and Family Patterns* (New York, 1963), pp. 318–19.

51. United States, Immigration Commission, *Reports*, 1910, Vol. 10, pt. 3, *Immigrants in Industries*, p. 47, states that the Irish came to Cohoes "during the period 1870–1880" and were "partially displaced by the French-Canadians . . . [who] first entered the city in the early part of the period 1880–1890, at the time of the expansion of the cotton industry." We now know that none of this is accurate.

52. See chs. 5 and 6 for a more detailed discussion of the ambiguous way in which paternalism affected the Harmony Hill community.

PART II

Adaptation and Organization

You know that workingmen do not have much time to think about anything else than how best to keep hunger, nakedness, and cold from becoming members of his family. . . . If the [National Labor Union] Convention will adopt . . . a plan . . . in less than ten years every member of our Union will be a capitalist, and independent of strikes, lock-outs, and all such expensive entertainments.

> —Letter to the Editor of the *Iron Molders' International Journal*, May, 1868, from a member of Troy Local No. 2

The Trades' Assembly has got to be quite an institution here. They had a pic-nic sometime since, as you were informed by Mr. Sylvis, who was here for the avowed purpose of starting a library and reading room for workingmen. They had the pic-nic, raised the funds, but we have no library yet, but all in good time. They are now engaged in starting a Cooperative store. God bless the movement. I understand that they have also organized a Union of the Tailoresses; another good move. . . .

I tell you, Mr. Editor, "things are working", there is nothing like Union. . . .

> —Lazy Ned to the Editor, *Fincher's Trade Review*, October 15, 1864

CHAPTER 3

Workers Organize, 1855–66

IN THE IMMEDIATE antebellum years, and from 1864 to the 1867 recession, a relatively new and largely immigrant Irish and English workforce began to establish itself within the Troy iron-worker and Cohoes cotton-worker communities. Until the Civil War iron- and cotton-worker patterns of industrial organization and protest were similar. Workers began to organize industrially, socially, and politically, and each group supported brief strikes for higher wages. The issues were local, and they were settled locally. By the end of the war, however, Harmony Mills had completed its takeover of Cohoes's cotton industry, buying out its three competitors of earlier years and transforming Cohoes into a "company town." Its new Mastodon Mill cast a long shadow over the political and industrial life of the city.

In contrast, Troy had developed a more complex structure, with a more volatile pattern of protest. If Cohoes emerged from the war as a "company town," Troy came out as a much more economically diverse "worker city." Not only had its thriving iron foundries expanded and iron mills begun to amalgamate after 1865; in addition, its shirt and collar and laundry businesses were also developing, soon to share the industrial stage with Troy's renowned iron trade. Moreover, led by the iron molders' union, the city's working class had built an effective trade union movement and political base and had begun to assert its views. Troy molders had initiated a similar effort in Cohoes, but with less success. By the time of the 1866 molder lockout, the contrasts between both cities were apparent and instructive.

Cohoes cotton workers, mostly women and children, settled into company housing and found regular and abundant, though poorly paid, employment; they would not strike, in spite of the long hours and low pay. In Troy, by contrast, approximately 800 well-paid, highly skilled, adult male and mostly Irish iron molders resisted the 1866 lockout. Their action, in behalf of union molders across the country, was integrated by a national association of iron founders. Much of Troy's labor protest in the 1870s retains the character of small-scale violence, pitting communal groups against representatives of those holding power. But the protest surrounding this lockout is also significant in the transition to more "modern" action, for a specialized association—a union—arose. It had well-defined objectives, was organized for economic protest, and recognized the importance of national interests.[1] The lockout began as a defensive protest, in that the molders fought to preserve their union. Most impressive, however, was the positive shape it ultimately took: the union established a producers' cooperative as an alternative to employer control.

Since so much in the histories of both cities is comparable, this chapter considers them together, and then describes the 1866 molder lockout. The intention is to provide background to postwar developments, and to place workers within this emerging social context.

UNIONIZATION

Nineteenth-century accounts characterize Cohoes workers as well-behaved, content, and benign. Relative to laborers in neighboring cities such as Troy, they had been fortunate. The *Cohoes Cataract* observed: "It is a noticeable fact that Cohoes thus far has never suffered from the strikes that have brought untold misery and want in many portions of the country."[2] A local historian, Arthur H. Masten, agreed: "We have none of those long continued strikes which have caused so much distress elsewhere and the degree of suffering among the poorer classes has thus far been much less than in neighboring cities."[3] Cohoes's social history certainly had not been as tumultuous as Troy's in the preceding decade, but Masten, writing in 1876, could hardly have foreseen the suffering and distress produced by the lengthy strikes in 1880 and 1882.

Prior to 1866, however, the labor histories of Troy and Cohoes had not been very different. Male ironworkers and male and female cotton operatives had organized unions and waged strikes in both cities. Before the mid-1850s, worker associations had been short lived and limited in scope and ambition. For instance, as early as 1842 the "workmen" struck the Harmony Manufacturing Company, protesting a 20 percent wage reduction.[4] The next strike indicates that these "workmen" were probably women, but the price of their protest may have been their jobs. In September, 1849, the Ogden Mill operatives struck against a 15 percent reduction. One enthusiastic letter-writer to the *New York Weekly Tribune* championed the support of the "fair sex." America, the New World and the land of free, would not oppress its womenfolk! That was an Old World trick: "Noble girls! They have taken the right course, and may that spirit prevail wherever the iron rod of oppression is lifted. May they show that though England can grind down the poor operative into dust, and make the fair sex worse than Africa's slave, it can not be done in America."[5] But work resumed three weeks later, when the mill's agent threatened to bring in outside labor to replace these striking women. The panic of 1857 renewed the efforts by Troy and Cohoes workers to rescind wage cuts. Since the last major depression in 1837, the country had progressed far along the road to industrialization. Now labor reacted with a new intensity to this more fully encompassing industrial environment, and worker organization and protest grew in size and durability.

During the 1857 depression, nearly all the Cohoes wool knitting mills shut down. About 1,500 workers (a third of the city's workforce) found themselves unemployed. In addition, the town's three cotton manufacturers enforced time and wage reductions: the Harmony Mills ran at half to three-quarters time and cut wages 10 percent; the Ogden Mill (sold two years later to Harmony Mills) operated at half-time; and the Strong Mill (sold to Harmony in 1865) ran at three-quarters time.[6] The depression had disabled almost the entire Cohoes working-class community.

After the October, 1857, work reduction, Harmony Mills closed its doors, throwing about 1,000 operatives (one-eighth of the city's population) out of work. The company hoped this action would reduce the supply of cotton cloth, which in turn might increase the demand sufficiently to raise prices to a more profitable level. Two weeks later, the mills reopened half-time. Management, finding this operation a "ruinous sacrifice," instead proposed full employment at reduced wages. On December 18 it posted a notice that wages would be reduced 25 percent until further notice; in return, the company maintained full production. Displeased, the operatives sent a delegation of one overseer from each department to speak to Alfred Wild, the company agent. He claimed that the alternative was to close down, and suggested that wages might be advanced by March 1, or as soon as business improved.[7] Assured that the reduction was temporary, the operatives agreed to return to work.

That winter a Relief Committee for the Poor maintained a soup house and bread line in Cohoes.[8] Hard-pressed to sustain their families, the workers "hoped against hope" that the wages would be restored by March 1.[9] In mid-February Harmony Mills "settled" a rumored strike by discharging two or three employees.[10] Then, in late February, "matters transpired" which convinced the workers that there would be no increase. Instead, they had reason to believe that the company was distributing its wage schedule to other manufacturers, as the Operative Committee stated, "for ought we know, for the purpose of making these reduced prices the general prices throughout the country."[11] Disappointed and incensed, the workers sent a Committee of Ladies to meet with Wild. The committee, composed of weavers, told him the workers would strike in four days if the 25 percent reduction was not rescinded. Returning on the next morning, as requested, they were told that the company had planned only one week before to increase their wages by 10 percent on April 1.[12] To the cotton workers, however, this explanation was unsatisfactory, for, according to the public statement, "a change of goods" had accompanied the 25 percent wage reduction. (They were paid piece rates, and the length of the cloth was probably increased.) This change, they argued, actually made the wage cut "equivalent to full 33 percent on the weaving department, acknowledged so by employees."[13] The 10 percent increase offered on the reduced rates, therefore, only made up about 8 percent on the old rates. So, led by the overseer and weavers, 800 of the 1,000 Harmony Mills employees went out on strike.[14]

The strike lasted three weeks. During the first week, the approximately 300 Ogden Mill operatives joined the strike, but they then returned to work with the promise of an increase "as times improve." The Harmony Mills workers persevered, however, convinced that their situation required special action. Several of the Cohoes mills paid higher wages for less work than the Harmony

Mills. In fact, the Strong Mill, a smaller and supposedly less efficient enterprise, ran half-time but had not cut wages. To the strikers, then, two company attitudes were clear: management thought that "one meal per day is sufficient for that child who works twelve hours, because his or her parents are poor," and "not content because their profits do not show the same high figures now as when times are good, [they] adopted this course to reduce the pay for labor, and by doing so be enabled to make as much money now as heretofore."[15] Insufficiently paid but sufficiently angered, the cotton workers— again, mostly women and children—sustained their strike until Wild offered a 12 ½ percent advance on the present wages. In effect, the advance was closer to 10 percent at the old standard. The operatives, with some dissension, voted to accept the offer. Consequently, after three weeks the Harmony Mills cotton workers had won slightly more than a 2 percent increase over the original offer. This small raise had a larger symbolic significance: for the first time in Cohoes's history, workers had collectively forced the town's largest and most powerful corporation to raise their wages. Moreover, this time no one was discharged.

Other workers took notice. The axe makers of Cohoes struck in April and gained back their pre-Panic wages.[16] Three months later, the Harmony Mills weavers struck again to have their wages fully restored. During this walkout, men, women, and children from the mills marched in procession to band music; they carried a long pole with a loaf of bread stuck on top, symbolically presenting supper to those who had "sneaked back to their work without obtaining their rights."[17] This strike ended unsuccessfully after a week, but not before violence erupted. The deputy sheriff and his force policed the mill grounds, at company request, to protect those who were disposed to work. Two unnamed men were arrested and marched off toward the jail, but on the way, as they passed the Strong Mill, a party of cotton workers rescued them. One member of the rescue party, John Cain, was himself arrested subsequently. A week later he was joined by a discharged striker, Thomas Dunn, taken into custody for brandishing a knife at the Harmony Mills manager.[18] Finally, the Strong Mill weavers struck for higher wages in early August. Little, however, is known of this walkout.[19]

Stimulated by the success of the Harmony Mills strike of March, 1858, Cohoes workers began to organize and to press for a decent

standard of living. These workers preferred shorter hours to reduced wages, for they realized that the issue was more than
money—it was the regulation of the marketplace. Furthermore, in
their conflict with the police, they illustrated the ways in which
working-class living conditions and labor protest contained both
political and industrial dimensions.

Cohoes textile workers did not, however, sustain their organizations. Most of the workforce consisted of young men and women; the
latter assumed a traditionally passive role. A Committee of Ladies
met with agent Wild, but older men spoke publicly for those on
strike.[20] Few of the female operatives expected to work in the mills
past adolescence; hence, their working conditions were only a temporary problem.

Meanwhile, Troy workers organized at the same time, but for
more complex reasons. The city's stove and machinery molders, as
well as the puddlers (who were largely immigrants and mostly
Irish by 1858), expected the status of the skilled workers. But the
expectations of this skilled workforce had been frustrated outside
the factories. Their contribution to the industrial well-being of the
city was not esteemed by Troy's political leaders; furthermore,
through groups such as the Know-Nothings, these same politicians
tried to downgrade the workers' place in society. In addition to
ethnic and class prejudice, depressed economic conditions also
thwarted expectations. As in Cohoes, reduced wages, considerable
unemployment, and increased poverty attended the price decline in
the winter of 1857. Under these conditions the Troy ironworkers
began to organize.

The iron molders' union lasted through the entire period, always
remaining at the center of the area's worker movement. Born in the
wake of the widespread wage reductions and hardships that accompanied the 1857 depression, the union rapidly gained local and
national prominence. After Philadelphia's iron molders organized in
the mid-1850s, they issued a call for national unionization, and the
Troy molders were the first to respond. On April 28, 1858, Iron
Molders' International Union No. 2 of Troy formed with six members. Their first meeting was held at Druids Hall "for the purpose if
possible to enhance the position of the Molders and likewise to
maintain and if necessary to raise the prices [wages] and for all other
purposes deemed expedient by them."[21] Nine days and two meet-

ings later, the union had grown to fifty-one and elected its first president, Simon F. Mann.[22] Within a year it claimed nearly 300 members from the Troy region, developed an intricate body of customs, rules, and regulations, sustained strikes in several local foundries, and stimulated the formation of a molders' union in Albany. Beginning primarily among the largest group, Clinton Foundry workers, the local included dues-paying representatives from thirteen stove foundries in the Troy vicinity by 1860.

Throughout the next twenty-odd years, the iron molders' union, primarily stove and range molders during much of the period, remained one of the strongest and most militant unions locally and nationally.[23] The Troy local provided substantial political and financial aid to the Iron Molders' International Union in the 1860s, when the International led the struggle for national unionization. It also remained in the forefront of the developing labor movement in Troy itself. Strikes occurred regularly, and new unions formed in iron-related trades as well as outside the industry. Molders sparked and supported such movements, but with the exception of two unsuccessful attempts (by Troy puddlers and unskilled iron millhands) to resist wage reductions owing to the 1857 depression, Troy's fledgling labor movement remained quiescent until the molders asserted themselves in the spring of 1859.[24]

The molders were concerned with four issues at this time: an undesirable foreman, low wages, the use of helpers at molders' work, and "obnoxious contracts" which stipulated that workers had "no right in action to recover damage for any insult or injury" inflicted by management.[25] The history of their protest provides a case study of early craft union behavior. The union began to contemplate action at its first meeting of 1859. Two weeks later it resolved to oppose the use of helpers in all cases, except "to shake out flasks and to cut up sand." A month after that, members resolved to strike on March 1, rather than accept a wage reduction. Upon learning that the foundries would not reopen early in March as usual, they postponed the work stoppage indefinitely. Two weeks later, they resolved not to sign any contracts when the spring season began.[26] The foundries finally opened in mid-March at the previous fall's reduced rates, and Clinton and Washington foundry molders walked out.

During the next month, 105 molders joined the union. The issue had become not just wages, but the union's existence, the conditions of industrial life, and control of the workshop. *Troy Daily Whig* editorials railed against the molders' association as a tyrannical combination.[27] The union, however, had a different view. When molders complained of unfair contracts and when the union sought to limit the role and number of apprentices, ironmasters threatened an essential corporate prerogative—their access to a cheap alternate workforce. But the manufacturers conceded after only two and a half weeks, and the strikers returned to work, secure in the knowledge that the union had survived intact and had won wide support from Troy's other molders. As part of the strike settlement at the Clinton Foundry, ironmasters agreed to replace the objectionable foreman with a member of the union's own relief committee.[28] The molders had not gained a wage increase, but they had won considerable power within the iron industry.

The molders' union flexed its muscles over the next few years. While puddlers lost a three-week strike for higher wages in May, 1859,[29] molders began to regulate the foundry workforce. During the next year their union extended its influence over the number and training of apprentices, and the union shop's executive committee gained acceptance of uniform wages for a given type of job in all the city foundries.[30] By the spring of 1860, the Troy local, with more than 400 members, had become the nation's largest.

The coming of the war brought change in union fortunes. In March, 1861, the Washington Foundry proposed to implement a helper system. In so doing, it again attacked the center of the union's power: its ability to control the workforce and, consequently, to affect prices and production. The union voted to strike the shops involved on March 22. During the next five months a series of events, related and unrelated to the work stoppage, virtually destroyed the union. First, the strike and the Civil War began at about the same time, and a "goodly number" of molders were among the first of Troy's young men to enlist.[31] Suffering from a substantial loss of membership, the union urged new tactics and more formal organization. Members enforced secrecy in union meetings; the leadership urged them to use all lawful means to keep men from work during the strike; and any member found talking to a boss would be expelled.[32] The membership voted to allow apprentices to join the union, and $64.20 was allotted to provide transportation home for the "scabs" hired by foundry proprietors to replace the striking molders.[33] Second, in response, management had taken the offensive. Some foundries hired non-union molders; one posted a notice requiring employees to sign a pledge not to join any union;[34] and the union found itself obliged to hire an Albany lawyer (at a cost of $250) to defend its membership before a Troy grand jury. Union members had been charged with conspiracy—of forming a secret and unfair combination.[35] Unfortunately, little is known of what transpired in court, but the union largely disbanded after the judicial proceedings ended.

Between September, 1861, and February, 1862, with many of its members off at war, the union only met three times. Then, at the urging of the Albany local (originally begun with assistance from the Troy molders), the Troy molders' union revived. For the next two years the Troy local concentrated on rebuilding its strength. It implemented new and more elaborate rituals to cement the brotherhood and insure secrecy; it again brought the membership up to 400; and it prepared to organize the city's workingmen and to reassert its power.

In Cohoes, cotton workers also mobilized, but their action was generally abortive. The Harmony Mills experienced some economic difficulty due to the Civil War's impact on the cotton market; during the early 1860s the mills operated at three-quarters time or less, and the operatives' wages were not restored to their pre-Panic level until November, 1862. Woolen spinners established an association during this period, and they even struck briefly against one knitting mill in May, 1863, with the issue being maintenance of a closed shop.[36] Cotton workers did not act until later that year. Harmony Mills wages had not kept pace with the steadily increasing wartime cost of living, and diminished wages from part-time work were insufficient. On a Monday morning in November, 1863, the weavers, who worked at the time "but ten hours per day," demanded a wage increase. They resumed work after being assured that their demand would be considered. Later that week they learned that the high price of cotton prevented an advance. The majority then refused to work and marched to the Ogden Mill, where other operatives joined them. All the workers met on the cricket field to discuss the situation, but they reached no decision. After a week some operatives, concluding that the company could not be moved from its position, returned to work. By Tuesday the rest had followed, and the only Harmony Mills "strike" between 1858 and 1880 had ended.[37]

Working-class organization and union activities in Troy and Cohoes had only begun. Several major strikes were won between 1864 and 1866; equally important, labor succeeded in building a union movement sensitive to wages and factory conditions, as well as to the social and political environment of the working class. Skilled male knit wool spinners who worked in Cohoes's many small factories led in organizing the textile workers, though they could never fully mobilize the almost 3,000 now employed by the Harmony Mills cotton monopoly. In contrast, while Troy molders initiated or enthusiastically supported all the activities in both cities, only in Troy were they really successful.

Early in February, 1864, the Troy iron molders' union informed the region's foundry masters that they wanted a 15 percent wage increase on March 1. Only one manufacturer was prepared to yield; the others refused to increase wages more than 10 percent. On March 3 the molders struck, emerging two weeks later with the 15 percent increase.[38] Other strikes followed and generally were also successful. For example, the Cohoes Woolen Spinners' Association fought a five-week lockout by the knit goods manufacturers and won a 25 percent increase. Five hundred Trojans, "mostly molders" according to the *Troy Daily Press*, traveled to Cohoes to demonstrate their support for the woolen workers. At a rally held in downtown Cohoes, three to four thousand workmen cheered as Henry Rockefeller, president of Iron Molders' International Union No. 2, donated $200 in union funds to support these Cohoes strikers.[39] In June the Cohoes molders, members of the Troy local, struck to prevent their foundry from violating the union's apprentice regulation.[40]

A series of strikes in 1864 also found Troy's ironworkers playing a prominent part. Again, while the struggles often focused on wages, the underlying issue was working conditions. In February the collar laundresses of Troy—one of the first unionized associations of female workers in the United States—struck and won a 25 percent increase. Once more the molders were there to lend moral and material support to the women. According to the *Troy Daily Times*, "a prominent member of the Molders' Union . . . pledged that body to extend aid to . . . [any] sewing girls who should be thrown out of work as long as a dollar was left in the treasury of the Association."[41] In May and June a series of strikes crippled iron production, and the familiar pattern was repeated. Although they had not yet formed a permanent organization, skilled workers—this time, puddlers—led the way. Again, issues involving wages and work discipline provoked the labor force. No details of the settlement are available, but when Burden's nail factory hired an ex-puddler whom the other puddlers found "obnoxious," the workers halted production for almost seven weeks.[42] Later, the puddlers at Winslow's Albany Iron Works struck for four weeks and won a wage increase of one dollar per ton (a ton was one day's work); the new rate was six dollars per ton, with a helper being paid about one-third of that sum. When this strike ended, puddlers at Corning's Rensselaer Iron Works demanded and received a similar raise.[43] Finally, in brief skirmishes during these same months, Burden's teamsters demanded, were denied, and subsequently gained a wage hike, and the laborers at his old mill gained a "one shilling" per day wage increase (they had demanded three) after walking off their jobs.[44]

Troy and Cohoes labor did not restrict itself to strike actions. Under the leadership of the molders, a regional trades' assembly formed in June, 1864, with fourteen participating local unions. Among those involved were the Cohoes Woolen Spinners' Association No. 1 (whose delegate served as the first vice-president of the assembly) and three of Troy's iron industry unions: Stove Mounters' Union No. 1; International Union of Tin, Copper, and Sheet Iron Workers No. 4; and Iron Molders' International Union No. 2. By the end of 1864, the Iron Rollers' Association had formed, and the molders had personally helped the underpaid tailoresses to organize. The assembly met at Troy's new Molders' Hall and, growing steadily, included twenty area unions.[45] Before another year ended, the molders' union claimed 700 members, the stove-mounters 170, the iron rollers 150, and a newly formed puddlers' union 90. In addition, a heaters' union organized. Under the chairmanship of a leading molder, the Troy Trades' Assembly enrolled an entirely different group—100 non-skilled workers—in the new Laborers' Union. This was a development of awesome potential.[46]

"Lazy Ned," the colorful and enthusiastic Troy correspondent to *Fincher's Trade Review*, commented upon these and other accomplishments, proudly noting that the molders now began work at 7:00 A.M. in order to help at home and see their children by daylight. In the context of the Civil War, these seemingly modest gains promised greater ones for Troy's workingmen, so that "Lazy Ned" could exclaim, " 'God bless the movement.' "[47]

ORGANIZING THE WORKER COMMUNITY

The Troy Trades' Assembly did more than knit the unions together. Under its sponsorship, a number of working-class institutions were established. Each union held annual balls and picnics, but the first Trades' Assembly picnic in August, 1864, provided the occasion for display of the unions' combined solidarity and strength. An estimated 2,000 workers met and marched through Troy's streets "to show the capitalist . . . the strength of the working class when combined."[48] Later that day, over 5,000 (roughly 10 percent of Troy's and Cohoes's total populations) frolicked and listened to speeches by Henry Rockefeller, a state labor leader from the Troy molders' union; William Sylvis, president of the Iron Molders' International Union; and a state assemblyman. The day's proceeds went toward establishing the Workingmen's Free Reading Room and Library.[49]

In September, 1864, the Workingmen's Cooperative Association announced that it would maintain a cooperative grocery in Troy for the use of all workers, union and non-union alike. Shares were sold in maximum blocks of ten per person at five dollars a share, with an interest rate of 6 percent payable semi-annually. The store opened around January 1.[50] Two months later, a trio of Troy union men opened the Workingmen's Clothing Store, and before the year ended, Cohoes workingmen had initiated a similar cooperative store in that village.[51] By these ventures Troy and Cohoes workers joined the national movement to establish distributive cooperatives, revealing a consciousness as both consumers and producers.[52]

The Troy Trades' Assembly also served the community in other ways. Seeking to educate its members, the above-mentioned Free Reading Room and Library was opened in July, 1865. The assembly's corresponding secretary boasted that a "minister of the Gospel" attended the inaugural celebration: "Yes, Mr. Editor, a real minister. Just think of it, a minister going among a lot of greasy mechanics."[53] The library had soon collected several hundred books, including thirty-six volumes of William Cobbett's *Weekly Register* which were donated by Thomas B. Carroll, Troy's resident Irish politician, art collector, and friend of labor.[54] Lastly, early in 1866 the Trades' Assembly sponsored a Workingmen's Debating Society, and the first regular issue of a Troy labor paper, the *Saturday Evening Herald*, made its appearance.[55]

Annual union picnics and balls also became institutionalized in the mid-sixties, and ethnic associations such as the Fenians developed. The thousands of participants in Troy Fenian circles suggest the association's working-class base. In addition, by 1865 the working classes of both cities had begun more formal political activities. In October, 1864, the Cohoes Woolen Spinners' Association set up committees to work for the election of an Albany molder as state assemblyman. The local Democratic party committee which officially nominated the man consisted mostly of spinners and Fenians.[56] A year later, Cohoes's textile workers united in a Short-Hour Movement, an attempt to reduce the work week from sixty-six to sixty-four hours. Each of the knitting mills agreed to run either sixty-four or sixty-five hours, but Harmony refused to reduce the hours from sixty-six. The woolen operatives then complained that they had been "sold" by those in cotton and, consequently, voted to dissolve the association between them. The wool hands proceeded to secure their own hourly demands.[57] By 1866, however, the textile workers were again united—and now complained that the increased cost of living had "brought on a credit system . . . with a majority of the working people." Unable to meet their bills, many workers went in debt by purchasing necessities on credit. Three resolutions were drafted by a nine-man committee (no women were mentioned), one from each of the eight knit mills and one from the enormous Harmony Mills. Seeking to ameliorate the credit system, the committee proposed the following: 1) workers should be paid bi-weekly, instead of monthly; 2) only one week's pay should be withheld by the company, instead of two weeks'; 3) all candidates for the state legislature from the district should be asked to support a bill to "give all debts for labor, a precedency over all other debts, in cases of insolvency." Though the manufacturers ignored the resolution on wage payment, both the Democratic and Republican candidates for assemblyman issued public statements agreeing to support the resolution on debts.[58] Thus, by the end of the year, while

Cohoes's cotton workers had not organized a formal union movement or engaged in protracted labor struggles, they had made their
presence felt outside the factory and had protested the conditions of
working-class life.

Troy political life reflected similar developments, only there activities focused around the Workingmen's Eight-Hour League. Organized in February, 1865, this league of city workingmen then
pledged to secure legislation friendly to the eight-hour day.[59] Club
members met later that year and, after the president of the Trades'
Assembly refused nomination, they selected George Thompson,
president of both the league and the molders' union, to represent
Troy in the legislature. Three days later, after Thomas B. Carroll
removed his name from contention, the Democratic city convention
also nominated Thompson.[60] Thompson's candidacy was undercut
by interests in both parties, however. Certain Democrats resented
the "blackmail" represented by the Eight-Hour League's prior
nomination, and the *Times* reminded Republican workingmen that
the Democratic workers had not voted for Simon F. Mann when he
was their (losing) candidate for assemblyman in 1860.[61] Mann was an
ex-president of the molders' union, but his position did not then
appear to have been an issue. Thompson lost the 1865 election by
365 votes, but it was due to the defection of Democrats from the
center-city business wards, rather than from Republican workingmen. In fact, while the Democratic candidate for state secretary
won a 33-vote plurality in Troy, Thompson picked up an additional
125 votes in the south iron wards. In other words, out of the 6,500
votes cast, over 500 men outside the south Troy wards had switched
from the Democratic column when they voted for assemblyman.[62]
The workingmen had lost the election, but they had gained a foothold in the Democratic party that they would not easily lose.

Under the iron molders' leadership, Troy's workingmen had organized social, political, ethnic, and labor institutions which gave
them much influence over urban affairs. As William Sylvis told the
state Trades' Assembly convention early in 1866, "Troy is the banner
city of America upon the trades union sentiment, and everything
concerning the welfare of workingmen," with "excellence . . . in
[the] thoroughness of its organization" and "second to none in
rendering . . . substantial aid."[63] As if to confirm Sylvis's point, a
major threat soon confronted the Iron Molders' International

Union, and the iron molders in Troy's local were asked to join with their Albany counterparts to meet it.

THE 1866 MOLDER LOCKOUT

In mid-March, 1866, the iron founders of Troy and elsewhere met in Albany to consider ways to eliminate the fledgling molders' union and its regulations. Stove manufacturers, for example, considered certain union rules and demands to be unreasonable. During the winter the Troy molders' union had published a list of wages paid by the various area foundries and had insisted that they be equalized, with compensation based on the rates paid at the plant with the highest salaries. In addition, they originally asked (but later withdrew the request) for a 25 percent wage increase. Other issues were more important than wages. The Iron Molders' International Union demanded that, as of January 1, 1867, members be paid by the day rather than at piecework prices; the shop committee required that prospective employees apply to them, not to the foreman, for jobs; and the union sought to maintain a ratio of one apprentice to every ten molders. The founders reacted negatively to these demands: "men working by the piece performed much more work than they would by day work"; shop committees had assumed the authority of the foremen; and the demanded apprentice ratio did not create enough new molders to make up for attrition.[64]

The manufacturers agreed to organize and confront the unions, though William Sylvis suggested that competition between eastern and western founders always marred their efforts.[65] Still, they formed a national trade association, the National Stove Manufacturers' and Iron Founders' Association of the United States; despite the name, they drew support mostly from Troy manufacturers. A Trojan, Charles Eddy, headed the association, and fourteen of its thirty-three members were from Troy, while another nine came from Albany. The members resolved to post notices in the foundries, stating that in the future the owners, and not the union, would regulate the number of apprentices. Furthermore, they would "outlaw shop committees" and "control . . . [their] own workshops."[66] Workers could accept these terms or look for jobs elsewhere. More than the continued existence of the union was now involved; the regulation of the workforce and the source of authority within the industry were also at stake. In asserting the right to regulate the number of apprentices, the manufacturers struck at the heart of the union's power: its ability to regulate the supply of new workers. The further implications of this issue became obvious when Dugald Campbell complained, some years later, that "overproduction in the foundry line is the curse of Troy." The molders, he argued, undercut their own demands by giving the employers more service than their salaries merited, simultaneously providing surplus goods that glutted the market.[67] New workers would mean higher production and lower wages.

On March 17, 1866, the founders' notices appeared and Troy's 745 molders found themselves locked out. In support of the molders, the stove-mounters and pattern-makers promptly quit work. In all, approximately 1,500 men (one out of every nine) in the city were out of jobs. Before it ended two months later, the molder lockout had become Troy's largest and most protracted industrial protest, and the first in the area with explicit national connections.

When the strike began, William Sylvis instructed molders' unions around the country to accept association policies and stay on the job. Troy and Albany would fight the lockout first; the other unions would resist in turn.[68] Simultaneously, he moved to secure funds from the Iron Molders' International Union to start a cooperative stove foundry in Troy.[69] Molders would build their own foundry, in which they could control and regulate production and wages. Cooperatives had been tried in America, England, and on the continent earlier in the century. Now, in the mid-1860s, "cooperation" was again becoming a byword across the country. Led by the molders, Troy's ironworker community translated the cooperative impulse into both a vision of the "worker city" and an impressive instrument of worker power. A month after the lockout began, with the molders ready to break ground for a cooperative foundry, the founders proposed a settlement. The stove manufacturers agreed to guarantee all molders their jobs and not to force helpers upon them if, in return, apprentices could be employed when molders were unavailable.[70] The molders' union debated and then accepted these terms. The notices outlawing the shop committees were removed, and the apprentice ratio officially remained at 1:10. The founders were now able to hire more apprentices, but only when molders could not be found and only if the union approved. Hence the union retained control over the number of apprentices. But the molders remained out upon learning that the founders felt the settlement did not include wage equalization. One by one, over the next month, the foundries also agreed to this proposal, and production was resumed. When the large Clinton Foundry finally capitulated on May 12, the great molder lockout ended.[71] It was a considerable victory for the molders: not only had they defeated an association of Troy's wealthiest and most powerful men, but, in addition to the Trades' Assembly's consumers' cooperatives, Troy's iron molders had established a producers' cooperative—the first of three cooperative foundries.

This most active period in the history of the ironworker community closed with an important victory for labor, but it was only the beginning. In the next decade the manufacturers reorganized to regain and extend their influence over the industry and the city, and the struggle intensified. Even in the flush of victory at the end of 1866, contradictory developments suggested an uncertain future. During the 1866 lockout nearly sixty stove-mounters had withdrawn from their union and returned to work. Before the lockout had ended, the mounters had split into two groups—the Stove Mounters' Union No. 1, which remained firm behind the molders' demands, and a new Stove Mounters' Benevolent Association, which agreed to "pass no law or regulation to conflict with any members' right to dispose of his labor as he may deem proper; or to interfere with the employer's business."[72] In addition, the Trades' Assembly no longer found itself able to sustain the Free Reading Room and Library, and the enterprise was converted to a subscription organization for members only.[73] In contrast, the cooperative foundry was spectacularly successful. Employing fifty molders after six months in operation, it paid higher wages than any other Troy foundry and earned $6,000 in profits.[74]

Troy workers had made a significant start. They had begun to organize trade unions and to create an important network of community organizations. Unionism had taken hold in the iron industry and, in the case of the molders, had led to a cooperative movement. Based on Troy's example, producers' stove cooperatives arose across the country, thereby transforming the molders' union into a cooperative movement as well as a trade union. It was not just a symbolic act when, under Sylvis's leadership, the Iron Molders' International Union changed its name to the Iron Molders' International Cooperative and Protective Union.[75] In Troy, however, it was not only the molders who organized; the entire working class did so. Through a union movement that extended into labor's social and political bases, Troy's working class had laid the foundations for a "worker city." In contrast, Cohoes had become a "company town," and its operatives remained the stepchildren of the union movement. In order to better understand the distinct timing and nature of protest in each city during the two decades after the war, we must first look more closely at changing socioeconomic conditions.

NOTES

1. Charles Tilly, "Collective Violence in European Perspective," in *The History of Violence in America: Historical and Comparative Perspectives*, ed. Hugh Graham and Ted Gurr (New York, 1969), pp. 4–44, calls this earlier pattern of small-scale communal violence "reactionary," and the well-organized later protest "modern."
2. *Cohoes Cataract*, December 26, 1874.
3. Masten, *History of Cohoes*, p. 236.
4. *Public Ledger* (Philadelphia), October 3, 1842. Michael Feldberg kindly furnished this reference.
5. John B. Andrews and William P. Bliss, *History of Women in Trade Unions* (Washington, 1911), p. 67, quoting a letter of October 8, 1849, in the *New York Weekly Tribune* from Lansingburgh.
6. *Cohoes Cataract*, October 10, 1859; Masten, *History of Cohoes*, pp. 146, 182, 242.
7. *Cohoes Cataract*, March 6, 1858.
8. Ibid., January 30, February 6, 13, 1858.
9. Ibid., March 6, 1858. Quoted from a member of the Committee of Ladies who spoke to the company on behalf of the operatives.
10. Ibid., February 13, 1858.
11. Ibid., March 6, 1858.
12. Ibid.
13. Ibid. See also John Wood, treasurer for the strike, to the editor, *Troy Daily Whig*, March 9, 1858.
14. Ibid., March 13, 1858.
15. Ibid.
16. *Cohoes Cataract*, April 8, 15, 23, 1858; *Troy Daily Times*, April 5–28, 1858. Before the Panic, the men received 3 cents per axe. After the Panic, they received 2¼ cents. The strike raised the price to 2¾ cents.
17. *Troy Daily Whig*, July 27, 1858.
18. *Cohoes Cataract*, July 24, 31, 1858. John Cain was arrested for aiding in the rescue, and Thomas Dunn was the striker arrested. Cain posted bail for an appearance at county court; Dunn went to the village "lockup." See also *Troy Daily Times*, July 22–23, 1858; *Troy Daily Whig*, July 26–28, 1858.
19. *Cohoes Cataract*, August 7, 1858. Mention of this strike is limited to this one issue.
20. Ibid., March 6, 1858. This was not unusual, as we shall see in the 1880 and 1882 strikes. Women workers represented themselves in negotiations, but men were looked to

for public leadership and guidance in the union movement. No woman ever spoke at the innumerable labor rallies in Cohoes.

21. "Minutes," Iron Molders' International Union No. 2, of Troy, April 28, 1858.

22. Ibid., April 28, May 1, 6, 1858. Mann became the first president of the Troy Cooperative Stove Foundry in 1866.

23. This is frequently reiterated by the editors of the major labor magazines, *Fincher's Trade Review* (Philadelphia), 1863–66, and *Workingman's Advocate* (Chicago), 1864–72. William H. Sylvis, president of the Iron Molders' International Union during the 1860s, supports this view in *Fincher's*.

24. *Troy Daily Times*, July 7–9, 1858; *Troy Daily Whig*, February 18, July 7, 1858. The Troy ironworks had closed after Christmas, 1858, because the men refused to accept a reduction. The lockout ended six weeks later, when the puddlers accepted a 25 percent wage reduction and other laborers agreed to a 12 percent cut. When the Rensselaer Iron Works and Burden's nail factory resumed production, similar reductions were instituted. Through the spring and summer the foundries operated at only three-quarters time. In July eighteen puddlers and their eighteen helpers at Burden's factory, as well as an indeterminate number of puddlers at the Rensselaer works, struck unsuccessfully for a 15 percent advance and monthly (instead of quarterly) payments.

25. "Minutes," Iron Molders' International Union No. 2, of Troy, March 10, 1859.

26. Ibid., January 20, February 17, 20, March 10, 1859.

27. *Troy Daily Whig*, March 22, 24, 1859.

28. *Troy Daily Times*, March 30, 1859.

29. *Troy Daily Whig*, April 21, May 5, 1859; *Troy Daily Times*, April 2, May 16, 1859.

30. "Minutes," Iron Molders' International Union No. 2, of Troy, June 9, 1859, May 5, 12, 17, June 3, 28, 30, 1860; *Troy Daily Times*, March 15–22, 1860. These advances, however, were not won without some struggle, and, in protest against the uniform-wage decision, the Clinton Foundry foreman resigned from the union.

31. *Troy Daily Times*, April 11, 1861. The union resolved to make all the molders who enlisted honorary members. The Troy papers refer to the 125th Regiment as filled with ex-molders. See also ibid., May 2, 1861.

32. Ibid., April 5, 11, 1861.

33. Ibid., April 5, May 3, 9, 1861.

34. Ibid., July 8, 1861. Smith and Sheldon's Foundry posted the notice.

35. Ibid., July 18, 1861.

36. *Cohoes Cataract*, May 9, 16, 1863. The Clifton Company had refused to accede to the spinners' association's demand that they fire a spinner who had not joined the association. Cotton spinners did not belong to the association.

37. *Cohoes Cataract*, Nov. 21, 28, 1863.

38. *Troy Daily Times*, March 3, 17, 1864; *Cohoes Cataract*, March 12, 1864; "Minutes," Iron Molders' International Union No. 2, of Troy, January 19–March 3, 1864.

39. *Fincher's Trade Review*, May 14, 1864; *Troy Daily Press*, May 2, 1864; *Cohoes Cataract*, March 26–May 7, 1864; *Troy Daily Times*, May 2, 1864.

40. *Cohoes Cataract*, June 4, 1864. Fuller and Safely's Foundry had hired more apprentices than the union allowed.

41. *Troy Daily Times*, February 20, 1864.

42. *Troy Daily Press*, May 19–July 5, 1864.

43. Ibid., May 30–June 28, 1864; *Troy Daily Times*, June 21, 1864.

44. *Troy Daily Press*, June 21, 1864.

45. *Troy Daily Times*, June 22, September 27, 1864; *Fincher's Trade Review*, December 24, 31, 1864.

46. *Troy Daily Times*, November 27, December 11, 1865. Scattered reports in the local papers suggest the Laborers' Union grew rapidly at first. Little, however, is heard of it in subsequent labor conflicts. In 1866 it had 500 members.

47. Ibid., October 15, 1864.

48. *Fincher's Trade Review*, September 10, 1864.

49. *Troy Daily Press*, August 30, 1864; *Troy Daily Times*, August 29–30, 1864; *Fincher's*

Trade Review, September 10, 1864. See also *Cohoes Cataract*, July 30, 1864, for the report on the first woolen spinners' picnic; and *Troy Daily Times*, July 19, 1864, for the report of the massive molders' union picnic.

50. *Troy Daily Times*, September 27–November 15, 1865; *Fincher's Trade Review*, January 7, 1865.

51. *Troy Daily Times*, February 25, 1865; *Troy Daily Press*, February 27, 1865; *Cohoes Cataract*, October 21, 1865.

52. John B. Andrews, "Nationalization (1860–1877)," in *History of Labor in the United States*, ed. John R. Commons (New York, 1918), II, pt. 5, pp. 40–41.

53. *Fincher's Trade Review*, July 29, 1865; *Troy Daily Times*, July 12, 1865; *Troy Daily Press*, July 12, 1865.

54. *Troy Daily Times*, March 15, 1866. Professor Samuel Rezneck pointed out Carroll's role as an art collector to me. Later in life Carroll lent his pictures to Troy's library for their temporary use. Otherwise little is known about him.

55. *Troy Daily Times*, January 10, February 9, 1866. No known copy of the *Saturday Evening Herald* remains.

56. *Cohoes Cataract*, October 8–15, 1864.

57. Ibid., September 16, 1865.

58. Ibid., November 3, 10, 1866.

59. *Troy Daily Times*, February 21, 1865.

60. Ibid., October 24–27, 1865.

61. Ibid., November 4, 1865. Mann lost by 482 votes; 4,926 were cast. He received 15 fewer votes than the Republican gubernatorial candidate in the same election. Mann's working-class credentials were not an issue in this election.

62. Ibid., November 9, 1865.

63. William Sylvis, quoted in the *Troy Daily Press*, February 9, 1866.

64. Ibid., April 12, 1866. The molder's apprenticeship lasted four to seven years; his working career after his apprenticeship was calculated as twenty years. At best, without sickness and occupational mobility, the manufacturers argued that the union would only be training half as many molders as would be needed, according to its suggested ratio.

65. William Sylvis, "Report of the President of the I.M.I.U.," *Iron Molders' International Journal*, January 1867, p. 306.

66. National Stove Manufacturers' and Iron Founders' Association resolutions, quoted in *Troy Daily Times*, March 17, 1866. For a good general history of this lockout, see Andrews, "Nationalisation," pp. 51–54.

67. Dugald Campbell to the editor, *Workingman's Advocate*, May 1, 1869.

68. William Sylvis, "Report," *Iron Molders' International Journal*, January 1867, p. 306.

69. *Troy Daily Whig*, March 19, 1866.

70. *Troy Daily Press*, April 13, 1866; *Troy Daily Whig*, April 16, 1866.

71. *Troy Daily Whig*, April 17–May 12, 1866; *Troy Daily Times*, April 16–May 12, 1866.

72. Stove Mounters' Benevolent Association bylaws, quoted in *Troy Daily Times*, March 19, May 11, 1866.

73. Ibid., October 26, 1866.

74. Ibid., December 8, 1866. The history of the Troy lockout and cooperative foundry is familiar. See Jonathan Grossmann, *William Sylvis, Pioneer of American Labor* (New York, 1945); Foner, *History of the Labor Movement*, I, 417–20; and Andrews, "Nationalisation," pp. 48–56.

75. The change was made at a convention in September, 1868. Andrews, "Nationalisation," p. 53.

CHAPTER 4

Settling In

MORE AND MORE WORKERS of immigrant extraction set-
tled in Troy and Cohoes in the post–Civil War decades. This chapter
discusses some of their experiences and their adaptation as stable,
rooted urban dwellers. First, these immigrants, especially those
who became skilled ironworkers, often found their living standards
improved; by the 1880s, some even became part of an emerging
ethnic middle class. Second, their relative affluence helped them
maintain extensive family and kinship networks that could provide
support in times of crisis. Third, churches were often at the center of
each ethnic neighborhood, and, with ethnic clubs and trade unions,
constituted an important base for worker organization. Finally,
while the general improvement over Old World conditions varied
and was modest, it was real. The occasional example of petit
bourgeois attainment, or the more frequent one of ethnic office-
holding, facilitated the immigrant's adaptation of dominant cultural
attitudes toward success, status, and security. Such a development
helped shape the ultimate direction of urban protest.

The process of settling in, however, is not necessarily opposed to
protest. Factors tending toward accommodation are present, of
course; these insulated people against the continuing pressures
of urbanization, industrialization, and capitalism. But the process of
adaptation was also an important precondition for protest. (One such
precondition, the emergence of an organized associational network,
will be considered more extensively in the next chapter.) Adaptation
emerges unevenly, however, being earlier and more uniform in
Troy than in Cohoes. Low textile wages and the postwar French-
Canadian immigration meant that the expectations of the cotton
workers would be less well formulated and their community less
cohesive than that of Troy's predominantly Irish ironworkers.

THE NEW LIVING STANDARDS

> No English families as rumored plan to leave for
> Europe. The contrast between factory life and
> wages in this country and in Europe is too great.
> —*Troy Daily Times*, as quoted in *Cohoes Daily
> News*, November 2, 1875

During the 1860s immigrant workers entered the iron and cotton mills. Skilled English spinners, weavers, molders, and puddlers arrived first; they were greeted by a shortage of skilled labor and relatively high wages. Next came large numbers of unskilled Irish immigrants, followed in the 1870s by equally unskilled French-Canadian textile workers. These Irish, and to a lesser extent the French Canadians, had probably left their rural homelands under starvation conditions; they quickly found employment in Troy and Cohoes. The Irish gained a substantial number of skilled positions in the iron factories as early as 1860 and dominated all the crafts, including the powerful molder and puddler unions, by 1880. They enjoyed similar success in gaining the more skilled jobs in textiles.

These jobs, however, must be evaluated in the context of the wage and price scales which determined living standards. Cost-of-living estimates based on the relationship between wages and subsistence levels may be calculated. (See Appendix.) The barest subsistence budget, for minimal food, clothing, heat, and shelter only, can be measured by applying B. Rowntree's classic study of poverty in York, England, and by modifying it to account for some variations in the diets of American workers.[1] To this estimate of American eating standards at a subsistence level, the cost of clothing (according to studies of working-class budgets, this amount was approximately one-quarter of food costs), rent, and fuel must be added. But there are, in addition to these estimates of subsistence costs needed for an adult male, the food requirements of the various family members. A woman over sixteen needed 80 percent of the adult male requirement; a girl over fourteen needed 70 percent, and so forth. These figures do not account for periods of pregnancy and lactation, nor were money and food necessarily allocated fairly and equally among all family members. The standard of living of the wife and children might have been lower than the estimates suggest;[2] nonetheless, approximations are possible. (Table 4.1.) The changing subsistence level reflects the rise in wartime food and clothing costs, and their

TABLE 4.1. Subsistence Levels in Troy and Cohoes, 1860–80

	1860	1865	1870	1875	1880
Adult man/week (food & clothing)	$1.06	$1.66	$1.38	$1.34	$1.15
All yearly costs [a]					
1. HW	$201	$280	$258	$244	$228
2. HW C (0–4) C (5–10)	247	362	318	302	272
3. HW C (0–4) C (5–10) C (M 14) C (F 14–16)	384	485	429	410	365
4. W C (0–4) C (5–10) C (F 14–16)	230	328	296	280	255
5. HW, both over 60	169	233	215	200	192

[a] All subsistence costs include food, clothing, housing, and fuel only.
Key: H = Husband
     W = Wife (or widow)
     C = Children (with sex and ages in parentheses)
SOURCE: U.S. Census, 10th Census, 1880, *Reports*, vol. 20, "Statistics on Necessaries of Life." Several Troy and Cohoes groceries and markets submitted records of their prices for basic commodities and necessities almost every year, usually beginning for the 1850s. The variation between cities was small and has been averaged.

decline in the post-1973 depression. These costs must be measured against wages.

Although it is not possible to know the precise number of families below the subsistence line without information on the income of every family member, an estimate is possible. The number of unskilled jobs far exceeded the number of semi-skilled and skilled positions, and even in relatively good times a family headed by an unskilled male laborer or by almost any female worker would find itself below or near the subsistence line. (Some variation would occur with stages of the family life cycle.) Perhaps 20 percent of the iron- and cotton-worker families were below this line. This would be primary poverty, though—the bare minimum for essentials. Secondary poverty—the minimum, plus additional costs for medicine, education, transportation, drink, old debts, etc.—might engulf 40 percent of the ironworker families and, since their wage scale was uniformly lower, two-thirds of the cotton-worker families.[3] A closer look at iron and cotton mill wages suggests the problem of poverty in these workers' lives, and it discloses the higher lifestyle available to the skilled ironworker.

COHOES' HARMONY MILLS

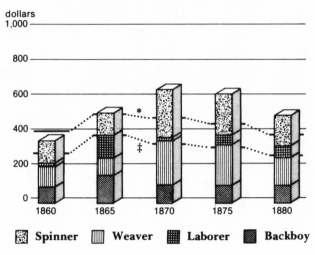

dollars

Spinner   Weaver   Laborer   Backboy

TROY'S IRONWORKERS

dollars

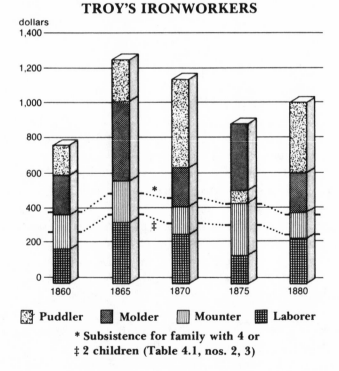

Puddler   Molder   Mounter   Laborer

* Subsistence for family with 4 or
‡ 2 children (Table 4.1, nos. 2, 3)

FIGURE 4.1. Annual Income Earned Relative to Subsistence Levels

Wages for unskilled workers always remained low. A day laborer in the rolling or cotton mills received only about a dollar per day in these years, while children received much less. (See Figure 4.1.) Such a wage did not, by itself, allow a family to subsist; multiple incomes were necessary or the family might, for instance, have to take in boarders or seek charity.

The more ambiguous aspects of ironworker finances and experiences will be discussed in the next chapter. Still, it should be now noted that the unskilled were in an unstable industry that did not employ entire families, so these workers had to devise alternate strategies for survival. In contrast, the low wages of cotton hands must be viewed in the context of family labor and regular textile employment.

The Harmony Mills provided full employment throughout the 1873–77 depression and, despite several wage reductions, *real wages actually increased slightly or held their own*. (For real income, adjusted for annual employment figures, see Figure 5.2.) To be sure, even semi-skilled female weavers paid by piecework only received wages comparable to those of a day laborer. But since there was work for as many family members as might need it, more than one member usually worked. In fact, the first 250 families enumerated in the first ward in the 1880 federal census averaged 2.79 cotton workers each. (See Table 4.4.) Finally, though corporate paternalism could restrict workers, the Harmony Mills built over 800 brick tenements for its hands, and, the meager wages aside, there is ample evidence that the company tried to create a relatively pleasant environment on Harmony Hill. Recent interviews with long-term residents of the Hill generally support the seemingly flowery portrait drawn by the *Cataract* editor in 1864.[4] The mills, he wrote, "have not overlooked in their designs the cultivation of the artistic and beautiful, but have carefully blended utility with refined taste in the arrangement of their factories, grounds, offices, and lecture rooms, so that while they present a scene of busy industry, their surroundings have all the attractions of well kept lawns, luxuriant shade trees, trim walks and ample carriage ways."[5] Unfortunately, low wages and unhealthy living and working conditions contradict this rosy picture.

Low wages meant that most mill families simply got by. However, after the war the families of male skilled mule-spinners earned enough to put them safely over the subsistence level, especially if the small but helpful salaries of children were added. (See Figure 4.1.) The annual income of most mill families was made more secure by regular employment, which also permitted the family's participation in church affairs or in social clubs. Some hands might have even begun to save toward buying their own homes. But a Harmony Mills mule-spinner in 1865 received about $1.65 daily, which hardly compared with the $4–5 a stove molder or puddler might earn, depending on the tonnage he worked.

With the important exception of the stove industry (which, by 1860, had already unionized and won substantial advantages for its workers), *real wages in the iron mills had also kept abreast or ahead of 1860 costs.* Equally important, the high wages of a skilled ironworker meant that with regular employment (ten months a year) he usually earned enough to permit important changes in his family's pattern of consumption and style of life. His wife and children did not have to work; the family did not have to take in lodgers; and there was usually some money available for "extras." If budget information from a later period (New York City around 1900) is any indication, furniture was the first "luxury" purchased by working-class families with incomes above the subsistence level. At the same time, there was increased consumption of food and clothes. Money was available for trade union dues, the church, recreation, and gifts and loans— with all but the last being important to community development (Table 4.2). While the highest percentage increases were recorded in the above categories, the largest dollar growth was actually in "spending money"—an item referring to funds reserved by the husband for his own use. Finally, the two items of greatest expenditure (after "spending money") were drink and medical costs, often a disproportionately high figure for the husband.[6] Clearly, skilled ironworkers and their families were beginning to share many new comforts and luxuries.

This portrait of improved immigrant living standards of course omits much of the degradation associated with rapid urbanization and factory labor. Dangerous working conditions, unsanitary living quarters, and cramped housing characterized postbellum urban society and typified Cohoes mill and community life.[7] Admittedly, an 1882 state legislative committee found that the Harmony Mills management provided conditions "far superior" to those in any

TABLE 4.2. Expenditures on "Sundries" Among New York Worker Families, 1905

Number of families:	40	79
Approximate annual income:	$600	$750
"Sundries" budget:	5–10%	10–20%
recreation	$ 3.63	$ 9.34
union	.30	1.62
gifts/loans	.83	3.39
drink	10.45	18.80
church	1.39	4.49
furniture	2.46	12.86
papers	3.00	5.68
car fare	4.29	8.17
medical	8.09	17.08
"spending money"	11.10	25.62
education	1.60	3.10
domestic service	—	.60
funerals	—	.73
miscellaneous	8.60	13.09
Total	$55.74	$124.57

SOURCE: More, *Wage-Earners' Budgets*, from Table VI, 95.

other factories or mills in the state,[8] but a Cohoes Board of Health investigation in the winter of 1865–66 reported that tenement houses were "overcrowded" and "in a very unhealthy state," with filthy outhouses.[9] As late as 1880, Cohoes and the working-class districts of Troy lacked sewage systems. Stagnant cesspools polluted Troy's alleys and lanes; according to the testimony of doctors, similar conditions in Cohoes affected the health of all residents— dramatically so in 1872, when the town experienced a smallpox epidemic.[10] The Harmony Mills, supposedly offering some of the best-constructed housing and mills at the time, permanently weakened the constitution of the boys and girls whom it employed. Although no details were given, Cohoes doctors reported that mill children were in poorer health and had a higher mortality rate than those outside the industry.[11]

Working-class health related as much to working conditions as to living conditions. Higher wages in Troy's iron mills afforded some real advantages, but they did not improve the fundamentally dangerous, debilitating factory environment. Those employed in the iron and cotton mills worked ten, twelve, or more hours daily. Although mill owners said their factories were adequately ventilated, workers fainted from heat prostration every summer, and operations had to be suspended. In the iron industry, with its open-air furnaces, these suspensions became institutionalized—the so-called heated term, when the works regularly closed.[12] As a contemporary report in the *Medical Press* explained, bronchitis was most pronounced among cotton millhands, and the article's author suggested that operatives use a respirator made of cotton wool over their mouths.[13] Moreover, "deafening noise," especially from the whirling looms in the weaving department, must have been a physical and mental strain.[14] Finally, there was daily physical danger. During the 1870s three boys, aged nine, ten, and fourteen, had their heads crushed in accidents in the Harmony Mills. They were the only ones to die in the mills until the early 1880s,[15] but cotton hands of all ages were regularly maimed. A Cohoes physician estimated that twenty-five to fifty children lost fingers and arms during the period from 1867 to 1882, and weekly items in the *Cohoes Cataract* indicate that this estimate was low.[16] A runaway shuttle could seriously injure a worker in its path; fingers and clothing caught in a machine could easily maim an operative before the mechanism could be stopped; and there were fire hazards, especially in the picking room where cotton was first processed. (For that reason picking rooms were usually separated from the rest of the mill.) Overseers in the Harmony Mills also admitted using physical violence to control the children. Charles Dunn, a spinning-room overseer, explained, "Sometimes we pull their ears and cuff them a little, but not to hurt them; just enough to scare them."[17]

Labor in the cotton mills, however, was less taxing than that in the iron industry. For example, in a glowing tribute to her father's industrial achievement, Henry Burden's daughter eloquently described the fiery hell of the puddling forge:

> In this temple of Vulcan—the puddling forge—the visitor beholds a scene of stirring activity seldom witnessed elsewhere. Scattered in groups or dispersed singly throughout this spacious building are hundreds of brawny men, with faces bedewed by perspiration and begrimed with coal dust, nude to their waists, their feet incased in heavy hobnailed shoes, and their strong hands turning, thrusting,

pulling, and piling the molton of fashioned iron in ways innumerable amid the heat, the smoke and the short-lived splendor of a thousand red-hot metallic sparks. Here are sooty-faced men stirring through open doors of flaming furnaces, glowing incandescent masses of iron that blind one's eyes with their fervent brilliancy. Others again are taking great balls of puddled metal from the furnace in iron buggies and casting them into the devouring jaws of the rotary concentric squeezers, from which, as unpalatable morsels they are ejected in the shape of compact blooms which are immediately . . . thrust between a pair of revolving cylinders—and . . . run forward and backward, until it is shaped into a long bar of crude iron.[18]

This heroic image of the Vulcans notwithstanding, the forge involved hot, hard, and dangerous work. The constant movement of heavy machinery, coupled with molten iron and open furnaces, caused frequent accidents and Troy papers reported almost daily cases of burnings and maimings. But while unhealthy and dangerous working conditions were not unusual working-class problems, the relatively high wages, especially for skilled immigrant ironworkers in the 1860s, were a new development. For previously impoverished laborers, these wages became the measure of their improvement and expectations in the 1870s.

High wages and the demand for skilled labor possibly contributed to an important late nineteenth-century development: the making of an ethnic (in this case, Irish) middle class.[19] The social origins of this growing bourgeoisie remain clouded, although many new Irish shopkeepers probably profited from improved spending power of the ironworkers, while others may have been former ironworkers themselves. As these men grew older, they came to find mill labor too strenuous, as Dugald Campbell had, and, having some savings, opened a small neighborhood shop or a saloon. The latter was a traditional Irish occupational pattern. Less traditionally, a significant number of Irishmen had become traders and dealers. The Irish had not become ironmasters, but by 1880 a higher percentage of employed first-generation Irish immigrants were listed as traders/dealers than among native-born Americans. (See Table 4.3.) While many in this category operated groceries in working-class neighborhoods, most (like mayors Murphy and Fitzgerald, both brewers) represent another dimension of the evolving Irish middle class. In 1889 the importance of this emerging ethnic class was

TABLE 4.3. Troy Shop-Owners and Government Officials by Nativity, 1880

Occupation	U.S.A. N %	Ireland N %
Government officials	106 (0.7)	76 (1.3)
Saloonkeepers	129 (0.8)	114 (1.9)
Traders/Dealers	572 (4.0)	261 (4.4)
Total employed	14,310	5,993

SOURCE: U.S. Census, 10th Census, 1880, "Statistics of the Population," Table XXVI, for Troy, New
York, p. 906.

attested to with the publication of a book chronicling the achievements of Troy's seventy most successful young Irish-American
professionals, businessmen, and politicians. (See Table 7.1.[20])

The development of an Irish middle class had an important effect
on Troy's working class. Most relatively new Irish immigrants
worked in the factories or on the docks, canals, and railroads. Others
already owned saloons or groceries, but they too tended to live,
labor, and associate with the workers. They shared the vicissitudes
of working-class life, remaining men of the worker community,
rather than becoming men of commerce. By the 1880s, however,
the emergence of an Irish middle class meant that the social base of
Irish organizations shifted from an intra-class axis. Since a worker's
ethnic identity was an important extension of his labor identity, this
development had awesome consequences for the direction of
working-class protest and labor's will to persist. Subsequent analysis
of ethnic associations will pursue this hypothesis further, but first we
must look at domestic aspects of working-class life, since these also
tell us how newcomers adjusted to the new urban scene.

FAMILY, KINSHIP, AND NEIGHBORHOOD

The Neighborhood

Ethnicity and class structured the residential patterns of Troy ironworkers and Cohoes cotton hands. Workers in each city tended to
reside in clusters with common ethnic, socioeconomic, and skill
levels. Such clusters usually gave character to a particular section

(often a political ward) of the city.[21] In addition, these residential clusters were likely to be relatively close to the mill in which the workers labored.

Between 1860 and 1880 virtually every unskilled ironworker dwelt in Troy's two or three southernmost "iron" wards, usually on the streets and alleys nearest the river and the mills. Closer to the central business district lived many of the skilled iron hands of the Clinton Foundry and skilled iron labor generally—the puddlers, rollers, roughers, and heaters, and the molders of iron bars. In the northern wards, near their work, resided many of the skilled foundry workers—pattern-makers, stove-mounters, and molders.

The more "independent" skilled ironworkers, like the engineers and machinists, lived in the same wards as the molders. For skilled workers, the ethnic makeup of the area and the location of one's work had greater influence on place of residence than did the nature of one's skill. The Irish gathered around the iron mills in the south wards, although, as could be expected of such a large group, they were well represented throughout all but the center-city wards. Scottish ironworkers lived on Scotch Hill, a small, highly concentrated community in the midst of these southern "Irish" wards. Similar patterns are to be found for other ethnic and/or religious groups. Only the small number of blacks were an exception. They worked as coachmen or maids for families scattered throughout Troy, or they gathered in shanty enclaves in alley dwellings in the city center or near the river. Finally, Troy's manufacturers lived in brownstones near the central business district or in hilltop mansions. Thus, except for the blacks, workers had settled into self-defined, cohesive ethnic neighborhoods, separated from the ironmasters by imposing symbols of money and power.

Harmony Mills, in contrast, relied heavily on female labor and provided accommodations for its workers and their families. Cotton workers of various skill levels all lived within a circumscribed area on Harmony Hill, in neat rows of tenements and boardinghouses built, owned, and leased at slightly reduced costs by the mills. Residence in the company tenements had contradictory implications: company paternalism created conditions of dependence, while it simultaneously structured a common set of experiences upon which workers could draw and organize. For example, the residential community and the network of voluntary associations it spawned offered an important source of stability. The community and associations were also easily translated into social and political power, especially significant after the Civil War, when workers and manufacturers fought to obtain economic self-sufficiency.

The Family

Preliminary evidence argues for family cohesiveness and the importance of strong family ties in aiding members during times of crisis. Such an adaptive family role could be strengthened by both class and ethnic bonds. For instance, studies have shown how female relatives often came to the aid of young girls apprehended as prostitutes in mid-Victorian docktowns, and how families supported textile workers during times of crisis in Lancashire.[22]

Oscar Handlin's classic study of the immigration experience found that the city intimidated and bewildered the immigrant, destroying much of his home and family life: "The street in its strangeness is the evidence of the old home's disintegration . . . . Almost resignedly, the immigrants witnessed in themselves a deterioration. All relationships became less binding, all behavior more dependent on individual whim . . . . The inability to use force was the crowning irony of the immigrants' disorganization. . . ."[23]

Troy and Cohoes immigrants seem to have had a different experience. Troy's Irish workers took active part in the social disorders which characterized these postbellum years; violence, however, can be founded on a coherent and articulated set of shared interests among immigrant workers. As adaptive institutions, household and family structure provide one index to the social base of organization. The key facts are that two-thirds of these iron- and cotton-worker families resided in nuclear households, and that 85 percent of the ironworkers and 75 percent of the cotton workers were part of two-parent families, if they lived with a family at all. Although census data give us a static picture of a family, failing to account for its various life-cycle stages,[24] family cohesion, rather than disintegration, seems evident. (See Tables 4.4 and 4.5.[25])

An important exception to this cohesive family pattern existed within the cotton industry. Cohoes, unlike Troy, had a high percentage of one-parent families. One out of every four cotton-worker families on Harmony Hill was headed by a single parent. Most of them, 80–90 percent, were headed by a "widow"—a woman

BLE 4.4. Household and Family Structure of Ironworkers in Wards 6 and 10, 1880

		Unskilled workers				Skilled workers		
		U.S.A.	English	Irish	Total	U.S.A.	English	Irish	Total
usehold Structure [a]									
clear	N	62	54	215	331	46	26	165	237
amily	%	54.9	45.0	54.0	52.5	67.6	52.0	63.7	62.9
tended	N	8	7	26	41	5	6	17	28
amily	%	7.1	5.8	6.5	6.5	7.4	12.0	6.6	7.4
gmented	N	16	33	46	95	7	7	34	48
amily	%	14.2	27.5	11.6	15.1	10.3	14.0	13.1	12.7
b-family	N	6	3	7	6	1	3	8	12
	%	5.3	2.5	1.8	2.5	1.5	6.0	3.1	3.2
xed adult	N	0	0	6	6	2	2	3	7
roup (MAG)	%	0	0	1.5	1.0	2.9	4.0	1.1	1.9
gle	N	21	23	98	142	7	6	32	45
	%	17.7	19.2	24.6	22.5	10.3	12.0	12.4	11.9
		113	120	398	631	68	50	259	377
nily Structure [b]									
o-parent	N	83	91	250	424	53	40	187	280
	%	90.2	93.8	85.0	87.8	89.8	95.2	83.5	86.2
e-parent	N	9	6	44	59	6	2	37	45
	%	9.8	6.2	15.0	12.2	10.2	4.8	16.5	13.8

[a] Nuclear households are those with parents and children only. The household is extended when other atives are also present, and augmented when non-related persons are present. A sub-family is a nuclear ily living with (augmenting) another family.
[b] MAG and single persons are not included.

whose husband might have left her, but more likely had died.[26] Family structure among the ironworkers suggests that this substantial proportion of one-parent families in Cohoes reflected conditions peculiar to the textile industry. Troy's workers, both skilled and unskilled, lived in one-parent families at about half that rate.[27]

There were differences, however, *between* ethnic groups. *Household* patterns among Irish, English, and American ironworkers were basically similar, but the *Irish family* was noticeably different. The incidence of one-parent households was almost double among Irish families.[28] Statistics compiled by the 1910 U.S. Immigration Commission confirmed as much, recording 12.4 percent of Irish-born immigrant cotton workers as widowed, compared to 5.9 percent of the French Canadians and 7.1 percent of the English.

TABLE 4.5. Household and Family Structure among Harmony Hill Cotton-Worker Families, 1880

		Irish	Canadian	U.S.A.	English	Other	Total
Households							
Nuclear	N	323	125	35	63	18	564
	%	72.7	67.9	60.3	77.8	81.8	71.5
Extended	N	42	20	6	8	2	78
	%	9.5	10.9	10.3	9.9	9.1	9.9
Augmented	N	65	38	15	10	2	130
	%	14.6	20.7	25.9	12.3	9.1	16.5
Mixed adult							
group (MAG)	N	14	1	2	0	0	17
and single[a]	%	3.2	0.5	3.5	0	0	2.2
N		444	185	58	81	22	789
Families[b]							
Two-parent	N	302	157	47	71	17	594
	%	68.0	85.3	81.0	87.7	77.3	75.3
One-parent	N	128	26	9	10	5	178
	%	28.8	14.1	15.5	12.3	22.7	22.6
Percentage of one-parent families headed by a female		89.8	88.5	88.9	80.0	80.0	88.8
Average number of cotton workers per family[c]		2.75	3.63	1.67	2.04	—	2.79

[a] The two boardinghouses are not included.
[b] MAG and single persons are not included.
[c] Based on first 250 families enumerated in first ward.

Significantly, reports suggest that this difference largely disappeared within one generation. For the second-generation immigrant family—the first born in the United States—the percentage of Irish widows more nearly approximated the figure for other ethnic groups.[29]

While some of the distinctive aspects of family structure appear to have diminished with a generation of acclimation, the situation of the first-generation Irish family remains unique. Although many Irishmen first confronted the city with little more than peasant experience, it would be incorrect to ascribe the difference simply to the general anomie of "urban life." Long hours of hot, heavy, and dangerous work in the mills took their toll, but the relatively high percentage of Irish widows could also be attributed to special attitudes toward the family, to the Catholic Church's sanctions against divorce, remarriage, and non-legalized cohabitation, to distinctive immigration or migration habits, or to other features of Irish culture.[30] The fragility of Irish family life reflected aspects of the immigrant experience in industrial America—prejudice, high mortality, and the intense pressures of industrial capitalism. But the higher number of one-parent families also indicates distinct ethnic values. Irish peasant traditions were patriarchal and celebrated community life and kinship. Each father divided his small plot of land among his sons. In towns, where fathers had no land to pass on, paternal control diminished and kinship bonds weakened and changed.[31] Beyond this, though, the willingness to allow young girls to leave home for the factory suggests that the Irish husband subscribed to a set of values distinctly different from those held by Protestant English and native-born males. Finally, Irish peasants brought over unregimented, pre-industrial work rhythms. Adjustment to factory life, with its highly disciplined work patterns, made the industrial experience disruptive and alienating.[32] These hypotheses, then, suggest the importance of ethnic customs, values, and experiences in shaping the working-class experience.

The higher incidence of one-parent families was also characteristic of the cotton industry. These families apparently went to Cohoes because their offspring could then find work in the Harmony Mills. The typical widow was over forty years old, with teenage children. Work in the mills enabled her to stay home with her younger children, or to leave them with kinfolk while she joined those older ones already earning an income. In point of fact, the need for income from adolescent workers prompted parents to send young children only to elementary school, and then for but a few years. Moreover, some youngsters attended night school after their eleven-hour stint in the mills. Except for those few who were able to delay working until the age of sixteen because their fathers had relatively well-paid skilled work, usually in the iron industry, children did not remain in school beyond the age of twelve.[33] Thus the cotton mill also provided employment and financial refuge for the widowed family.

What the census does not make clear, however, is the kinship network among these people. In rural Ireland, before the poor law was enacted in 1838, assistance came from relatives and neighbors.

TABLE 4.6. Kinship in Troy's Sixth Ward, 1880

Families	Part 1	Part 2	Total
Extended	80 (35.1%)	46 (21.1%)	126 (28.2%)
Same surname within three enumerated numbers	23 (10.1%)	17 (7.8%)	40 (8.9%)
Total kin families	103 (45.2%)	63 (28.8%)	166 (37.1%)
N (all families enumerated)	228	219	447

In English cotton towns, like Preston, families provided lodgings to help migrants adapt, and there was a noticeable tendency for kinfolk to congregate near one another.[34] A similar pattern occurred in Troy and Cohoes.

The sixth ward in south Troy reflected the importance and the extraordinary extent of this kinship network, especially in the poorer quarters.[35] The 1880 federal census divided the ward into two sections, placing Irish laborers in the first. This section was clearly Troy's poorest; in order to subsist, more than one-third of these families were of the extended type. (See Table 4.6.) Elsewhere in the ward, where work was probably more regular and wages for skilled labor higher, the percentage of extended families was noticeably lower. In addition, many people had relatives living nearby. Two families will serve as examples of this kinship pattern. First, William Hartnett lived in a nuclear family with his wife and six children, but his home was next to that of widow Margaret Hartnett (perhaps his mother) and her three children. Ed Hartnett, quite likely a brother, lived nearby with his wife and child. Second, Sarah Darby, a widow with three children, lived next door to her brother, Henry Evans; his wife, Sarah's sister Wanda; and her father-in-law, William Darby. Many seemingly nuclear families were, in fact, part of an extended family network.

Further physical evidence emphasized the support that the familial network and neighbors provided in immigrant communities. Harmony Hill was known popularly as "Litrim City" because so many of the residents came from that Irish county.[36] French-Canadian textile workers settled in Cohoes's "Lower Canada," and Scottish immigrants congregated on Scotch Hill in Troy. Immigrants from the same village or county re-created their earlier community in their new environment. This development was widely applicable—whether among north Italians or Polish Jews in Paterson, New Jersey, or Irish or French Canadians in Troy and Cohoes.[37] The gains and losses involved in such transitions are not fully known, but it is apparent that, even though the locale had changed, immigrants were not all total strangers to each other. In addition, first-generation immigrants made extensive efforts to establish functional kinship systems in their new communities.[38]

In time of need, kin and neighbors could share food and housing, provide day care and accommodation, and be emotionally supportive of each other. Troy's poor Irish huddled together during long winters of unemployment in Limerick Alley. An article subtitled "Communism in Poverty" graphically described how neighbors aided each other:

> The destitute are in many cases living together. What one does not happen to have, the other may have. . . . All is thrown into the common stock. In this way many are enabled to live—though not live in any civilized sense. . . . In one instance, three widows, aged thirty-five, seventy-five and eighty years, live together, using all the household goods in common. Yet, so scanty are the comforts, the wonder is how they can contrive to keep death from the door. Indeed, but for the charity of their neighbors, fatal suffering would ensue. A kind family has given the oldest of the trio bread for a year. She receives $2 per month from the overseer of the poor, but this pittance goes for rent. . . . Cases of this kind seem almost numberless.[39]

Kinship ties between generations complemented neighborhood associations and were further strengthened by ethnic bonds.

Figures for ethnic intermarriage suggest how the priorities of immigrant culture helped create communities with kinship bonds. Working-class immigrants, especially French Canadians and Irish Catholics, tended to marry within their own ethnic groups. The two large ethnic groups in 1855—native-born Americans and Irish—rarely intermarried. However, a different pattern appeared among smaller groups of newcomers, who had less choice within their own groups (Table 4.7). By 1880, almost 40 percent of Cohoes's working-class English and native-born Americans married outside their own ethnic groups—unlike French Canadians and Irish, who had only a 7 and 2 percent rate respectively. Similarly, in Troy, with

TABLE 4.7. Intermarriage in the Fourth Election District,
Cohoes (Part) and Watervliet, 1855, Albany County

Husband's Birthplace	U.S.A.	Ireland	Other
Number of couples	194	255	60
Intermarriages	10	14	21
Percentage	5.1	5.5	35.0

SOURCE: New York State, Census Bureau, 1855 *State Census of Population*.

its substantial numbers of Irish, English, and native-born residents,
the Irish intermarried with outsiders at a rate only half that of any
other group.[40] Several factors may account for this low rate of
intermarriage and its persistence among the Irish: nativism and the
bias it implied against the Irish as immigrants and Catholics; the
Catholic injunction against marriage outside the Church on pain of
excommunication; and the exclusiveness of both Canadian and Irish
nationalist cultures. Indeed, the percentage of Irish intermarriages
would most likely be even lower if the Scotch-Irish, the Presbyterian Orange, were not included. Thus working-class marriage patterns suggest how nativist attitudes and ethnic cultural traditions
strengthened connections already existing within the kinship network.

The Accommodating Family

Most social historians agree that the family had a central role as a
stable social institution in the midst of rapid social and economic
change.[41] It provided the working class with a primary organizing
institution for social and economic life. This is not to claim that its
role never altered; the family once might have helped workers develop new institutions (e.g., savings banks, cooperatives, and trade
unions[42]) to perform certain pre-industrial family functions, and at
another time might have helped them organize resistance against
institutional or other encroachments in their social or industrial
lives. Regarding the latter, the family's role would depend on many
factors, including who was involved and the timing and stage of
protest.

Interaction and decision-making within the family remains inadequately understood. We know, of course, that such factors affected behavior. For instance, parents decided which children

would work, and at what age. If jobs were to be defended by strike action, the father's higher-paid labor would likely receive priority. The dependence of most adolescent, and especially female, mill-hands upon the patriarchal family represented a crucial dimension of work experience for these women and helps explain their historic reluctance to organize. Widows and women in female-headed families were free of such patriarchal restraints and took a more active role in protest. The Harmony Mills, however, established only two boardinghouses; most women lived in dependent, patriarchal families.[43]

Of course, general cultural attitudes toward women and their working also affected their ability to organize and protest. In the paternalistic national culture, a "lady" could not publicly protest without risking ridicule or scorn; indeed, public behavior of any sort was discouraged. As a result, women lacked formal involvement and experience in associational life, which itself may have contributed to their difficulty in organizing. Moreover, there was a growing sentiment that the adult female as worker was a contradiction in terms, a sort of sin against nature. This attitude underlay the widely held middle-class belief that for women to work would, as Richard Ely wrote in 1893, mean "the scattering of the members of the family and the breakdown of the home."[44] Carroll D. Wright, writing in 1880, identified the factory as the culprit: "The factory system necessitates the employment of women and children to injurious extent, and consequently its tendency is to destroy family life and ties and domestic habits, and ultimately the home."[45]

Such conventional attitudes towards women's place in the home helped justify lower pay for and displacement of female labor. Ironically, the reverence for the home meant that during protest or when threatened, people turned to the home as an important source of strength. But the home—that is, the role of the family—had varied usage. A series of incidents and anecdotes deriving from local conflicts makes it possible to draw some hypotheses about the role of the family in protest.

Organized family life could provide a necessary but not sufficient pre-condition for protest, but it could be a double-edged sword. The family was able to accommodate, or to organize against adversity; it did both in cities such as Cohoes and Troy. However, the family remained a relatively small private-interest group. It filled the normative role of accommodator, while (as the next chapter will demonstrate) the neighborhood usually remained the arena for collective organization.

Both functions of the family were visible as members entered and left the workforce. Fathers gained jobs for sons and relatives in the iron mills, and whole families were encouraged to work in the cotton mills.[46] On the other hand, family members were also fired as a unit, especially if an overseer felt the discharge would help to defeat a strike. During an 1880 strike John Clark, a tinsmith at the Harmony Mills, was told he would no longer be needed unless his daughter, a union weaver out on strike, returned to work. Clark left the mill immediately. A few weeks later overseers discharged the relatives of all striking spinners.[47]

Family and neighborhood ties helped workers organize, but they could also discourage protest. Timing is important here. With prolonged strikes, economic and social pressures mounted and forced some families to retreat. For example, after a five-month walkout in 1882, one "homesick" cotton worker wrote from Forestdale, Rhode Island: "This is a very pretty place, but not like home."[48] In a less poignant (but probably more pointed) letter, another operative wrote upon returning to Cohoes: "Although he made better wages there [Falls River], he was homesick and longed for the old associations of home, and he was glad to come back and work harder for less money."[49]

The plight of one Cohoes family illustrates the ambiguous role of the family and the centrality of the socioeconomic context in which it existed. Five months into the 1882 strike, a family residing in the Harmony Mills tenements was given an eviction notice by Silas Owen, the superintendent. The wife pleaded with Owen. Her husband and son both worked (the father in town, the son in the mills), she stated, but their income did not leave them enough to pay rent. Owen then made the intent of the eviction notice clear: if the family needed additional money, then she and her daughters should seek employment in the mills. The wife insisted that social pressure from her neighbors—"bulldozing," complained a local editor— would not allow her to come to work. Owen nonetheless persisted, "holding the rent over her head though not mentioning it," and persuaded her to enter the mills.[50] The family and neighborhood had resisted for nearly six months, but the financially pressed family ultimately fell prey to the power of the landlord-manufacturer.

ESTABLISHING A COMMUNITY BASE: THE CHURCH

The kinship network did not constitute the workers' sole supportive institution. Higher wages helped subsidize religious institutions, recreational activities, and voluntary associations which benefited even the poorest. Churches and associational activities, such as picnics or parades, were available to all, and religious and ethnic charities constituted one of the major forms of mid-century urban welfare. The church was the primary non-familiar institution around which immigrant neighborhoods organized. It served a particular ethnic and class constituency, and over the years evolved recreational, educational, medical, and charitable facilities to help its members adapt to life in America.

Of course, the establishment of churches is easier to document than is the influence of religion upon parishioners. Because Cohoes was smaller than Troy and developed later, the history of its churches represents, in simplified form, the general pattern of church growth in both cities. Its churches reflected the immigrant impact. Village life in the 1830s, before large-scale Irish immigration, was dominated by native-born American entrepreneurs, artisans, and "factory girls"; four Protestant denominational churches were established before 1845. These were St. John's Episcopal Church (1833), the (Dutch) Reformed Church (1838), the Baptist Church (n.d.), and the Presbyterian Church (1839). By the mid-1870s merchants, shopkeepers, manufacturers, and professional men seem to have been evenly distributed in these four, or in two small congregations more recently established: the German Baptist Church and the Park Methodists.[51] The combined church membership was about 1,770, approximately 10 percent of Cohoes's total population.

Three more churches were founded before 1890, and their history corresponds to the pattern of immigration. Skilled English textile workers arrived first, and in 1845 the Methodist Episcopal Church was established. Irish immigrants came a few years later, with the famine, and after 1847 they were served by St. Bernard's Catholic

Church. In 1868, when French Canadians began to pour in, the French-speaking St. Joseph's Catholic Church was founded. Like the other Protestant churches, the Park Methodist Church was relatively small, containing 450 members in 1876. In contrast, the Catholic churches claimed an enormous number of communicants by this time, reflecting both the substantial number of Irish and French Canadians and their greater religious devotion. St. Bernard's registered more than 5,000 infant baptisms and nearly 4,000 deaths over thirty years, while St. Joseph's, less than a decade old in 1876, already claimed more than 1,800 communicants, and another 700 were said to be associated with the church.[52] Such associate status suggests that while two out of three French-Canadian Catholics may have attended mass, church activities extended to almost everyone in their community.

Protestants also engaged in church-related activities, and, though fewer in number, they participated with equal vigor. In 1876, the Episcopal Church claimed 500 communicants and the same number of associates. Moreover, the various denominations operated five different Sabbath Schools with about 2,750 members. Significantly, the location and superintendents of the two largest schools suggest that the Harmony Mills intervened in the religious lives of its community. The manager of the tenements, Silas Owen, served as superintendent of the 500-member Methodist Sabbath School, and D. J. Johnston himself was superintendent of the Harmony Hill Union Sunday School with over twice that number. This enormous school also met in the mill buildings and drew children from all of Cohoes's churches.[53]

Troy's churches followed a similar pattern, although, like the city itself, their development was earlier, more complex, and more extensive. By 1890 there were thirteen Presbyterian, five Baptist, seven Episcopal, ten Methodist, and nine Catholic churches (it is not clear if any were French-speaking); in addition, there were three Jewish synagogues and five other churches.[54] The 1890 federal census reported a combined membership of 40,945, or two out of every three city residents. Most impressive, the Catholic churches alone counted 29,000 of them.[55] As in Cohoes, most Catholics arrived after the famine. Their first church dated from 1825, but seven more were built between 1843 and 1872.[56] Troy's ironworkers supported these churches, and the large St. Joseph's Church, "the ironworkers' church," was a proud symbol for the Irish community.[57] Workers filled these churches on Sunday, and their wages undoubtedly helped expand church-associated services to the Irish community.

The city provided some social services, such as poor relief, even before the arrival of the Irish in the mid-1840s. But it was not prepared for the arrival of massive numbers who were hungry and sick, and who needed jobs as well as housing. The beginnings of local Catholic charity may be attributed to this fact, according to a contemporary historian. He concluded that the prevalence of fever among newcomers during the mid-forties compelled the city to treat and quarantine in temporary quarters as many as 700 sick immigrants at a time. Mostly Catholics, they were tended to by the Reverend Peter Havermans, the priest at St. Mary's Church. He then began raising funds for a Catholic hospital to serve his diocese. Completed in 1850, the Troy (Catholic) Hospital was operated by the Sisters of Charity.[58] The Reverend Dr. Havermans, in 1888, summarized the achievements of Troy's Catholic Church during his long tenure, and in so doing he testified to its involvement in the lives of Troy's Irish:

> Now we have here eight Catholic churches with large congregations, a beautiful hospital, two orphan asylums, a grand home for the aged poor, a house for penitent women who wish to change their lives and become useful members of society, a flourishing academy with over 300 pupils under the direction of the Catholic Brothers, a grand theological seminary, numerous well-equipped and elegantly-built schoolhouses, and last of all, a foundling asylum and lying-in hospital for the poor, which I am, at present, trying to establish upon a permanent basis.[59]

Protestant charitable institutions were less extensive, since the older, established Protestant elite operated public institutions which had been created for good works and which were funded by them. Still, the Episcopalians and Presbyterians also operated separate old age homes.

In addition to the church-controlled charities listed by Havermans, Troy's churches sponsored many social activities and organizations for adult parishioners. Irish and French-Canadian males, for instance, joined one of the six St. Vincent de Paul Societies at the Catholic churches they attended. Women organized auxiliary church groups which held annual dances, picnics, and festivals.

Church and church-sponsored institutions and activities permeated the lives of the urban working class. Moreover, these charities, social services, and societies helped the newcomers adapt, but in special ways: they increased worker dependence upon their ethnic identification, at the same time that they absorbed great social problems that otherwise would have burdened or challenged public officials.

It is easier to describe the involvement of Catholic institutions in the lives of iron and cotton operatives than to assess the piety of workers and the impact of church authority on them. Protestant and especially Catholic working-class families evidently attended church in great numbers; women, who had fewer opportunities for public life, probably attended more often and in greater numbers than men. Most Catholics were workers, and most workers Catholics, in these years. Cohoes's merchants and manufacturers, generally Protestants, had to worship with Protestant workers. In Troy, however, separate Catholic and Protestant churches served the parishes in which ironworker families congregated. Most churches there had social class and neighborhood bases, and thus they provided a foundation upon which the parishioners could build other mutual interests.

What message these workers heard in church, and how they responded, is one of the large lacunae in their history. Some sermons, clerical memoirs, and church-related worker behavior, as well as perceptive scholarly suggestions, indicate that some religious values may have encouraged labor protest, while others inhibited it.

Many of the early molders' union leaders appear to have been Protestant English or Scottish laborers with names like Henry Rockefeller, George Thompson, E. S. Douglas, John Glass, and Joseph Hegeman.[60] The last named, a carpenter who was president of the Troy Trades' Assembly as well, was also on the board of managers of the Methodist Sabbath School. Whether or not any of these other men were Methodists is unclear. But the Burden Iron Works housed the Methodist Levings Chapel, which made it likely that many English ironworkers were Methodists.[61] E. P. Thompson has written about the conservative influence of the organized Methodist Church on the English working class—the "Chiliasm of Despair," its work discipline, and its repressive tendencies which bred submissiveness.[62] What, though, of Methodism—and Protestantism generally—in these towns?

Historians of the Gilded Age have noted how conservative Protestant social attitudes reinforced the prevailing business ethic. No connection was made between economic behavior and moral conduct, and traditional Calvinist doctrine equated poverty and failure with sin.[63] These sentiments—famous in the Reverend Russell Conwell's exhortations to parishioners to reap the "acres of diamonds" all around them—found expression among Protestant clergy. The pastor of Troy's First Presbyterian Church for forty years, for instance, asked the indigent at a poor relief meeting, "Is he charitable who gives of his means for the support of idleness, of drunkenness, of every vile practice and vice?" Declaiming "*poverty under the name of imposture,*" he rhetorically continued, "Has any impostor any claim to relief because he is clothed in rags and the den of his family is filthy?"[64] Some ministers disagreed with his sentiment and willingly supported poor relief, but, according to the reminiscences of a Troy Catholic priest, such nativist views struck a popular chord with the "very respectable" Yankees.[65] Still, Protestant sermons generally made little direct mention of social problems.[66] The only known blatantly anti-strike sermon was given by a Methodist minister who subsequently had to defend his position. Workers, he had only meant to say, should "save money" instead of walking out.[67]

Protestantism took many forms, and the traditional authoritarian doctrine bred its antithesis—an evangelical reform strain based on Christian Perfectionism that appealed to discontented workers. Herbert Gutman has observed how pessimistic pre-millennialism translated into a post-millennial Christian justification of trade unionism and even more radical social reform, providing the aggrieved mid-nineteenth-century worker with a "transcendent and sanctioning 'notion of right.' "[68] Labor evangelicals found the new industrial order to be an un-Christian violation of God's will. Two prominent national trade unionists and ironworkers give splendid examples of this union of Protestantism and reform in their speeches. Gutman notes that William Sylvis "found no contradiction between his sympathies for the First International and his belief that the worker's 'task' was 'to found the universal family—to build up the City of God' through trade unionism which . . . [he] called an 'association of souls' formed by 'the sons of God.' "[69] Similarly, John Jarrett, president of the National Amalgamated Association of Iron, Steel and Tin Workers, told a gathering of clergymen that "the climax of the mission of the Savior, beyond a question . . . is that He came here so that the gospel would be preached to the poor."[70]

There is no conclusive evidence to indicate that Troy's ironworkers were converted to Protestant evangelical sects, but Dugald Campbell, an important labor leader, was a Baptist revivalist. Baptist and Methodist revivals occurred in Troy throughout the century, and there is apparently a close connection between youthful religious conversion, temperance, and subsequent labor militancy.[71] The enthusiasm and persistence of Troy's temperance revival movement of the 1870s, highlighted by Campbell's conversion, is linked to the highly charged ideological origins of the Troy and Cohoes trade union movement. The Sons of Temperance were first organized in 1873-74 at the Levings Chapel, a revival took place there in the winter of 1874–75, and Francis Murphy held revivals at the State Street Methodist Church at the end of 1877 and again in 1880.

But temperance organizations could have contradictory effects, sometimes sparking a more general spirit of reform. Troy's temperance revival, with its radical rhetoric, coincided with worker demands for industrial reform; but the temperance movement could also be socially conservative, reflecting well-orchestrated middle-class attempts to alter or adapt pre-factory work habits to the labor discipline demanded by industrial capitalism.[72] Pre-industrial and agrarian work rhythms and rural customs encouraged high rates of absenteeism and labor turnover. The continual search for higher profits and increased production intensified efforts, especially during periods of economic contraction, to create a sober, regular, industrious workforce. From the mid-1870s through the mid-1880s, most churches, both Protestant and Catholic, had active temperance organizations. In Cohoes the D.J.J. Volunteers (the Harmony Hill temperance organization named after the mill superintendent), the St. Bernard's Teetotal Abstinence Benevolent Society, and the Société de Tempérance des Canadiens Français de Cohoes fought the evils of alcohol; in Troy no fewer than ten temperance societies joined the crusade.[73] Finally, several examples demonstrate the clergy's general support for temperance and a conservative social ethic. In 1873 a group of Troy clergymen asked manufacturers to shift the payday from Saturday to Monday to discourage the spending of salaries on rowdy weekend drinking sprees. Rather, we may suppose, they would substitute sober church-going on Sunday.[74] Similarly, at the outbreak of the 1880 Cohoes strike, the Reverend J. F. Lowery of St. Agnes Roman Catholic Church exhorted the operatives against drink while, in the same breath, advising them to place their "respectful submission of grievances" before the mill's director.[75] Lastly, there was William A. Alexander. A temperance lecturer and not a cleric, he crusaded in Troy during the mid-1870s and operated a boardinghouse for scab molders.[76]

The impact of evangelical Protestantism on English workers, as well as the presence of temperance organizations in both Protestant and Catholic churches, have already been noted. But more than half the working class was Catholic, and so the influence of the Church on this labor force must also be considered. The church played an important but ambiguous role in the life of the Catholic worker. Its hierarchy was authoritarian, repressive, and conservative in social and political views. It insisted upon respect for authority and encouraged a repressive deference. French Canadians and Irish attended church in great numbers and relatively often, but their involvement was largely one of custom. The clergy seems to have been particularly influential only in matters of dogma, and not in political affairs. Catholic dogma would, of course, have a conservative influence on social and political consciousness, but on the rare occasions when priests did speak to social issues, they spoke sympathetically of the need for charity. If they were critical, workers wrote letters to the editor, telling them to mind their own business.[77] Only during the 1863 draft riot, when Father Havermans restrained Irish workmen from committing further vandalism, did a priest publicly involve himself in actual protest.[78]

While both Catholic and Protestant workers might have attended church, they used church teachings for their own class purposes. Evangelical Protestantism offered Gilded Age trade unionists what one historian has called a religion "intimately related to the everyday struggles and vicissitudes of an insecure life."[79] Similarly, while the Catholic Church emphasized deference to authority, its social presence seems to have been more important than its direct political influence. Regarding the former, it was especially active in establishing social institutions to serve parishioners in their new urban setting, and it provided an important cultural symbol around which Irish and French Canadians could organize. While workers tended to accept the moral teachings of priests and ministers with regard to self-discipline, self-control, and the like, their notions of political and moral economy flowed partly from their experience as wage earners, partly from inherited traditions about the dignity of labor, and partly from adapting ideas of democracy and individualism from the dominant culture.[80] Consideration must now be given to the formation of these attitudes and values.

THE IMPACT OF AMERICAN CULTURAL VALUES

Whatever attitudes and values the immigrants brought over with them were reshaped by the relatively successful experience of many newcomers, by artisanal traditions about the virtue and rights of labor, and by an entrenched three-part ideology: a "democracy" that denied or obscured the existence of social classes; customary notions of deference (which reinforced traditional peasant attitudes);[81] and a much-celebrated individualism.[82] These ideological strains coalesced into a dominant culture which emphasized opportunity, success, status, and security—values compatible with the needs and experiences respected by workers. Understandably, even if many workers had achieved success by their own lights, they still often sought status and "respectability" from the middle classes.

Troy puddlers served as a model of working-class achievement, and their gains held out the promise of both social mobility and industrial power. Two-fifths of them were Irish in 1860, and four-fifths in 1880. In addition, one contemporary source commented (with rhetoric illustrative of the high value which Protestant society placed on work and thrift) that the puddlers "by frugality and industry acquired for themselves comfortable homes."[83] Finally, while affluence was not part of the average ironworker's experience, a vacation trip to their native Ireland, taken by thirty Rensselaer rolling-mill hands during the summer shutdown, demonstrated to all that (for some, at least) the dream of mobility could come true. Workers living on meager subsistence had reason to believe the

Times when its editor exclaimed, "A trip to Europe is no longer a luxury for the wealthy alone."[84]

More modest potential for success and status existed in Cohoes during the 1870s. The average cotton-mill family struggled to survive, and its plight cannot be minimized; nevertheless, the expectations accompanying factory labor are central to these workers' perception of themselves and their response to social conditions. Irish and French-Canadian families found many employment opportunities in the cotton mills. Increasingly, sons and daughters also found more skilled work available. Most families remained in debt, but some managed to save money—enough, in a few cases, to support a family during a strike and to encourage union militancy. In 1868, for example, the Cohoes Savings Bank reported $112,000 on deposit—much of which, according to the local paper, belonged to factory operatives: "The girls know how to take care of their hard earnings and are interested in having the value of them maintained."[85] The personal values of hard work and thrift (read labor and capital) brought modest success and enabled some workers to struggle against management.

In sum, life in Troy and Cohoes could meet labor's expectations. Individual workers had a measure of success; so did the working-class community as a political and social whole. The higher wages of skilled iron or textile workers, and the differentials existing even between trades, gave a financial emphasis to status occupations. But many of these workers did not feel that they received the merited social recognition for their achievements, at least not from elite circles in the city. The perception of workers is elusive, since they did not leave diaries or customarily report their attitudes to newspapers. Moreover, important differences existed among workers. Some led, others followed; some took radical social positions, while others held conservative ones. Still, they shared many experiences in the factories and in the community, and these experiences provided a shared set of attitudes. Two local workers—one a Cohoes factory girl and the other a striking Troy molder—sent series of letters to their local newspapers which reiterated a common refrain: workers who succeeded in terms celebrated by the dominant culture were denied the respect due them according to the democratic ethos. Neither of the two was necessarily a typical worker, but each testified to the persistence of traditional beliefs about the openness and "democratic" character of American society, and each responded to negative public reaction to the economic rights and social status of workers. Their letters suggested something of workers' concerns for social status and security, as well as indicating their involvement with the new industrial ethic of work and the cult of progress.

A series of anonymous letters from "A Striking Molder" in 1859 illustrate the continuance of pre-factory traditions about the rights and dignity of labor. Artisans were raised in the popular Revolutionary tradition of resistance to authority and defense of the liberty tree; these traditions persisted through the antebellum period in the celebration of republicanism and what Alan Dawley calls the "philosophy and practice of Equal Rights" for labor.[86] Molders— unmechanized factory workers whose high wages and skill made them a distinctive factory subculture[87]—were logical carriers of such traditions, though as workers in a relatively new industrial trade they might carry them in somewhat muted form. Letters from "A Striking Molder" suggest as much, also reflecting the search for social recognition and illustrating how hegemonic cultural attitudes about work, morality, and the "democratic" experience had been proudly incorporated into the worldview of some workers. This molder's views express those of the two worlds he bridged: the radical pre-factory workshop, and the new urban industrial marketplace.

In the spring of 1859 the molders struck to regain the wage levels which had existed before the 1857 depression. During this walkout the *Times*, which had recently editorialized that all strikes were "foolish . . . at any time,"[88] published an article which stated that labor-saving machinery had transferred labor power from the worker's hands to his head. One anonymous molder, obviously provoked, found such sentiment symptomatic of a general bias that minimized the intelligence and, consequently, the status of the skilled worker. Signing his letters "A Striking Molder," he responded defensively, asserting both the intelligence and "rights" of the working class: "We claim, sir, that we can think. We pretend to understand what are the true relations of capital and labor. In the bright light of this nineteenth century, with its freedom, its inventive progress, its cheap and diffuse information, we assume to belong to the order of men who know their rights, and knowing, dare maintain them."[89]

"Striking Molder" knew "his rights"; significantly, his view of them was informed by an ironic vision of his nineteenth-century world. Not poverty and deprivation, but "freedom," opportunity, openness, and "progress" stimulated workers. All workers demanded was a fair share of profits, now that the worst of the 1857 depression had passed. The *Times*, however, felt that unionization—the secret and unfair combination of men—was a separate problem. "Striking Molder" consequently felt compelled to defend the position of the union and the honor of the working class.

The molder, asserting traditional values of radical American workers, borrowed much from the language of classical political economy. His arguments also reflected a belief in Jeffersonian equations of work with virtue, and hostility to the "artificial" labor represented by capitalism. According to him, the union was merely the great equalizer. Without such collective self-protection, the capitalists held all the power. Manufacturers organized "to serve and force markets for their wares"; so, too, labor would combine. The molders wished only the same rights as their employers: not equal wealth, but equal bargaining power and self-protection. After all, said the molder, this was America, where there were no social distinctions, as opposed to some monarchy ruled by a privileged elite. In the United States, hard work was the measure of virtue, and no one worked harder than the millhand. "Striking Molder," then, did not claim his right to a higher wage so much as the right to organize. Equality of virtue would lead the industrious to those rewards merited by talent. The molder's thinking revealed a general confusion between the worker's economic status and his status as a citizen:

> In this republican land, is it anarchical for the laborer to do what it is an ordinary and everyday matter for his employer to do without subjecting himself to odious comments . . . [for] the idea that workmen degrade themselves by combining for such purposes is preposterous and absurd. Such talk will do very well for monarchial countries, where the oligarchist of capital stands but one removed from the crown. . . . But it will not go down smoothly in communities where distinctions of caste are fictitious rather than arbitrary, and where an intelligent workman is by virtue of his talents held

in more honorable repute, and more valued by his fellowmen, than a
clownish millionaire.[90]

"Striking Molder" applauded America's progress and defended
the honor of the iron molders' union and its strike. But "A Stricken
Mounter," another working-class writer, viewed the walkout differently. He reminded the readers that the striking Clinton Foundry
molders had adversely affected all the mill's employees, including
mounters like himself, as well as pattern-fitters and carpenters (with
a combined total almost equal to the number of molders). "Many,"
he said of the non-strikers, "have families, and all . . . I believe
have stomachs." Nor was this undeniable hardship the only cause for
complaint. Suggesting that the molders were a labor aristocracy, he
observed that they earned over $20 a week, while mechanics like
himself averaged $1.50 a day.[91] In addition, mounters who traveled
up and down the Hudson River valley, unsuccessfully searching for
work, heard manufacturers uncharitably note that "their depressed
condition was in some measure attributable to the exorbitant prices
heretofore paid to molders."[92]

"Striking Molder," in response, angrily attacked capital and urged
working-class solidarity. Labor and capital, he stated, were not
equal: "Capital is a shadow and a myth—labor is a fact and a realiza-
tion." Extending the yeoman farmer's notion of work and virtue to
the factory, the molder vigorously defended his position: "What
is money, save for what it brings? . . . Labor is real
wealth. . . . Money does not grown grain, . . . money does not
carry on the machinery of government. . . . When laborers unite
to guard against the aggression of the power they themselves origi-
nate, how can you pronounce it anarchy, tyranny?"[93] Labor combinations maintained a balance for workers against the forces of capital. Rather than jeopardizing the national equilibrium, trade unions
and the labor movement helped preserve the uniqueness, the "cho-
senness," of the American experience. For proof, the writer asked
the reader to compare the servile working classes of England and
France with "the comparative strength, intelligence, and good social position of the mechanic working classes in America generally."[94] But what of the mounter and his gnawing hunger? The
molder reminded him that the molders' union had made strike
provisions available for all the workers. The mounter's complaints,
therefore, were not simply unjustified; they were those of a man-

ufacturer in disguise or a class traitor. If the mounter was, in fact, an ironworker, his critic urged him to sympathize with the working class: "If his hands are blackened, it is from attrition with pens used in making out bills of sale and writing pithy letters to business correspondents—not from contact with dirty iron. . . . If I am mistaken, and your correspondent is really a 'stricken mounter,' permit me to say, he is a disgrace to his class."[95]

Almost two years before the letters from Troy's "Striking Molder" appeared, a series of letters in the *Cohoes Cataract* from "A Factory Girl" provoked a comparable debate. Textile work had broken with its artisanal past: work was now almost completely mechanized, and immigrants had displaced the native-born. "A Factory Girl" suggests the textile workers' involvement with the new industrial ethic of work and status, and she describes one working woman's attempt to challenge elite attitudes toward cotton hands. Her first letter, in March, 1857, complained of the elite's social snobbery and asked the editor to explain the reasons for it:

> Assuming that you would be an Apollo to me, I would first ask you some questions in relation to "social distinctions" in Cohoes. This subject has been particularly impressed upon my mind by a remark which I overheard at one of the lectures here last winter. Said one of the "Upper Tendom," (for such a circle there is in Cohoes . . .) "who are those ladies in front of us?" "Oh, I don't know; factory girls I should think," was the reply, in accents of contempt, "they must have come here to see, and be seen, for I don't suppose they will understand one sentence of the lecture." Again, said another lady (?), "When I go from home I am ashamed to say I live in Cohoes, lest people should think I am a *factory girl*."[96]

Subsequent correspondence, and the responses it evoked, generated reader interest in this unknown and articulate operative and her plea for respect.

"Factory Girl" complained that Cohoes's social elite was generally contemptuous toward the women millhands. Neither their alleged outlandish dress nor foul odor, she thought, explained the contempt toward these workers. She observed: "Those who passed the greater part of their early lives as factory operatives, [were] . . . most given to making contemptuous remarks about factory girls." Furthermore, not only were "the most extensive circumferences" in Cohoes "*not* worn by factory girls," but the disdain toward the female operatives was due less to the factory air than to "the potent aid of money."[97] To "Factory Girl," the arguments of the "upper tendom"—the elite—only masked the actual reasons for their prejudice: in ridiculing female operatives, the elite tried to obliterate its own adolescence, and to elevate and distinguish itself by dressing with certain cultural accoutrements which customarily adorned those of higher financial status.

Many women workers, "Factory Girl" informed one of her critics, were well educated and were the daughters of respected and intelligent members of the community. In fact, ignorant and ill-bred people could be found both within and outside the factory. For the elite, certain behavior constituted a privilege; for the average factory girl, it was considered boorish. Gum-chewing was a case in point. Different standards existed: "A lady (?) sits in church, with her jaws in constant motion—her eyes very seldom resting upon the speaker—and she has a certain position in society, and *should* know better, it passes for eccentricity in her (no fancy sketch). A factory girl does the same and how shockingly vulgar."[98]

One anonymous letter from "A Teacher" accepted this description of social distinctions as largely correct: Cohoes did divide into an upper and a lower class, and the latter included nine-tenths of the factory girls. Moreover, although the distinctions related to the kind of labor one did, women millhands were despised, she argued, *not* because of their labor per se, but because of their class characteristics—what she called their "ignorance" and "unladylike demeanor." Amplifying her idea, she exposed her real complaint against these workers: they had not embraced the cultural values and moral postures which she cherished. Her prescription was blunt. Factory girls should frequent libraries, dress with neatness and simplicity, and go to church on Sundays instead of *"going over to Green Island to swing."* They should read art, history, music, philosophy, and "the Art of Good Behavior," instead of "yellow covered literature," and should reject the company of factory boys who spend all their money on liquor, and should visit the Troy Adelphi three times a week.[99]

In reply, "Factory Girl" accused "Teacher" of constructing a moral utopia that did not exist anywhere—even in the supposed paradise of Lowell. Social behavior varied, she agreed, but the distinctions that "Teacher" suggested were artificially maintained.

Ignorance and folly were not exclusive to any one class. Because she was literate, people called her exceptional, "Factory Girl" said; yet no one knew or suspected that she was the author. To them, she was just another millhand. She was "contending," she explained, "not [for social] position, but [for] justice," not to be other than she was, but to be respected for what she was. In her own words, she was merely "a quiet, tolerably sensible factory girl."[100]

In these letters, Cohoes's "Factory Girl" and Troy's "Striking Molder" articulated values and sentiments that sounded much like those which might have been expressed by Lowell mill girls or Lynn shoemakers twenty-five years earlier.[101] Troy and Cohoes workers at mid-century were similarly anxious to demonstrate loyalty to their new land and its culture. They celebrated a mythic America, the glorious vision of national destiny and uniqueness that excited the nineteenth-century American imagination. In the traditional republican view, expressed for instance by "Striking Molder," England and France were "monarchical countries" dominated by "oligarchists of capital." In America, however, "distinctions of caste are fictitious," for each "intelligent workman" would reap the "virtue of his talents."[102] Such workers were "free-born" and, unlike the Chartists, did not have to struggle for their enfranchisement.[103] For workers like "Factory Gril" and "Striking Molder," America remained the land of opportunity, unbridled by a titled aristocracy. In the litany, success was attainable and was directly related to labor, virtue, and intelligence.

What these workers sought was recognition of their status and achievements. The *Cohoes Daily News* editor made explicit the sentiments which had only been implied by working-class correspondents: labor was concerned with status and personal esteem. The mills could fulfill these needs. Women operatives perceived their positions as preferred to those of domestic workers. Understandably, then, the *News* complained,

> It is next to impossibility to get competent, reliable girls who are willing to do housework at any price. . . . Cohoes' women have the feeling that as operatives in the mills they take a higher place in the social scale than is accorded them when they do housework. The fact is, they don't like the idea of being servants, or being treated as such, and unless compelled by lack of the employment of their choice, they avoid it with scorn.[104]

For Cohoes and Troy workers, then, some measure of the status and security that the dominant culture celebrated could be found in the mills and in the community.

Notwithstanding the above, the matter of social identity was not easily resolved. Iron and cotton workers did strike, and at times even engaged in collective violence. Evangelical Protestantism, native-born artisanal traditions, and Irish traditions of association and resistance all informed such behavior. But although workers acted collectively (a radical enough tactic) in the age of *laissez-faire*, their attitudes and perspectives continued to be dominated by this personal vision of a society in which each person would reap the rewards of status and security through industry and frugality. Demonstrations of loyalty toward the corporation and deference toward management may have reflected a pre-industrial tradition, but they continued to exist in American industrial relations.[105] For example, it was not uncommon for workers, even strikers, to pledge their loyalty to management. In the course of an appeal for a wage increase for molders, "Striking Molder" conceded that "the employers have the best interest of the employees at heart."[106] According to the conventional wisdom, if success was personal, so was failure. For most of the working class, personal hardship could be attributed to laziness or bad luck, or to the miserliness or cruelty of a wicked employer. Vacillating between these alternatives, workers might strike at one time and give their boss a testimonial gift at another.[107] This paradoxical behavior had its parallel in labor's equivocal view of the relationship between political and economic action. The economic system was free and unfettered, said the myth, and there was the risk of imposing controls if political and economic issues were mixed. Such fears prompted newspaper appeals, during the 1880 strike in Cohoes, that workers not allow legitimate economic grievances to bias them in the town election. Such a plea was unnecessary. Despite their grievances, the striking cotton workers helped re-elect Mayor William E. Thorn, the Harmony Mills treasurer. As one of the strike leaders stated (in French as well as English) on Thorn's behalf: "It is not a political question, but a cause of yours and your children; you want an hour for dinner, and an advance in your pay. . . ."[108] Yet, two years later, after the bitter 1882 lockout, textile hands elected their leader, an evicted tenant, to the state legislature. They had potential political power, but whether and how they chose to use it were distinct, if related, questions.

Industrial workers settled into Troy and Cohoes, establishing elaborate kinship groups in ethnic working-class neighborhoods. The church and other institutions facilitated the development of a supportive associational network. These institutions helped the workers adapt in the industrial city and were important preconditions for protest. While such associations did not stimulate protest, they provided essential organizational connections and support. As workers adapted, they also developed a political and social consciousness that would shape their protest—based partly on values from the aforementioned associations, partly on inherited traditions, and partly on values from the dominant national culture. Values were not uniformly shared; subgroups of workers divided by skill or ethnicity shared certain traditions and attitudes. Molders, for instance, enjoyed high living standards and status, as well as unmechanized work traditions which could be significant resources for their protest. The ethnic experience was also important. Some workers (especially the native-born and English) inherited traditions of the dignity of labor and carried the reform spirit of evangelical Protestantism. Others (like the Irish) carried traditions of association and resistance which will be discussed shortly. But for the increasingly immigrant Irish workforce, their traditions, the immigrant experience, and the hegemonic national culture, rather than the native-born artisanal inheritance, shaped attitudes and values.

These immigrant workers lived with greater security than ever before, as well as with some small measure of success. They continued to seek more, but some important ambiguities involving living standards threatened their achievements. The nightmare was over their shoulder, the dream before them; they stood in limbo. These polar visions were influenced by the negative pre-immigrant experience, the immigrant's aspirations, and the impact of the success myth. By the 1880s among iron and cotton workers, minimal but real achievements, as well as the emergence of an Irish middle class, took on great importance, facilitating the integration of Irish labor into American society. Such integration included political co-option by ethnic leaders into national political parties which were committed to a classless "democracy," as well as acceptance of traditional attitudes toward work, opportunity, and moral equality, and it could have an ambiguous effect on protest. Integration of this sort could leave workers content or docile, but it could also raise new expectations and provide impetus for labor organizations which would realize them. The belief that American society was "open"— that opportunity and status mobility were possible—could stifle or shape protest, and could encourage wage and trade union consciousness. The outcome depended on many different factors, including whether the need for protest appeared urgent. Once protest erupted, the dominant cultural values and attitudes tended toward a narrow trade union perspective, rather than toward the cooperative vision of the 1860s. Before surveying the order and disorder of these cities, the specific bases for protest should be described.

NOTES

1. The English diet was heavy with bread and potatoes. The weekly diet included 118 oz. bread, 21½ oz. cheese, 45 oz. oatmeal, 34 oz. potatoes, 4½ pints skimmed milk, 9 oz. bacon, and minute amounts of coffee, tea, sugar, and margarine. Comparable studies of American working-class diets early in the twentieth century and an 1899 nutrition study by the U.S. Department of Agriculture suggest small modifications for a subsistence diet based on American eating standards that would also be nutritious. Louis Bolard More, *Wage-Earners' Budgets: A Study of Standards and Costs of Living in New York City* (New York, 1907).

2. Peter N. Stearns, "Working Women in Great Britain," in *Suffer and Be Still*, ed. Martha Vicinus (Bloomington, Ind., 1971).

3. Similar poverty levels are estimated for English manufacturing districts in the nineteenth century. See Foster, *Class Struggle and the Industrial Revolution*, and Benjamin S. Rowntree, *Poverty: A Study of Town Life* (London, 1901).

4. In a walking tour of Harmony Mills tenements connected with a seminar on industrial archaeology sponsored by Rensselaer Polytechnic Institute, June 26, 1974, several elderly residents commented on how pleasant it was with the manicured lawns, shade trees, and garbage collection by the company.

5. *Cohoes Cataract*, December 10, 1864.

6. More, *Wage-Earners' Budgets*, p. 95.

7. See, e.g., Oscar Handlin, *The Uprooted* (New York, 1951).

8. New York, Bureau of Statistics of Labor, Legislative Assembly Document no. 26 (1882), p. 341.

9. *Cohoes Cataract*, December 2, 1865.

10. Tenth Census, 1880, Vol. 18, *Social Statistics of Cities*, pp. 509–13, and *Cohoes Cataract*, June 8, 1872.

11. New York Legislative Assembly Document no. 26 (1882), "Sanitary," interview with Drs. J. D. Featherstonhaugh and J. W. Moore, pp. 183–88.

12. *Cohoes Cataract*, June 18, 1868; August 24, 1872; *Troy Daily Times*, August 16, 1857, June 28, 1873, July 1, 1874. The expression "heated term" first appeared in 1874 and referred to the mill closing for the month of July. Reduced orders during depressions most likely facilitated this shutdown; in any case, the hot weather was not confined to one month.

13. "Diseases of Factory Hands," *Medical Press*, reprinted in *Cohoes Cataract*, April 15, 1871.

14. *Cohoes Cataract*, October 26, 1872.

15. Ibid., February 19, 1870; May 20, 1876; April 21, 1877.

16. New York Legislative Assembly Document no. 26 (1882), p. 184.

17. Ibid., p. 78.

18. Proudfit, *Henry Burden*, quoted in Rezneck, "Office Building," pp. 88–89.

19. In a doctoral dissertation on the federal census occupational structure, Margo Conk confirms the development of a substantial *petite bourgeoisie* in New York City by 1880. See Margo Conk, "The U.S. Census and the New Jersey Urban Occupational Structure, 1870–1940" (Ph.D. dissertation, Rutgers University, 1977).

20. Edward H. Lisk, *Representative Young Irish-Americans of Troy* (Troy, 1889).

21. Ethnic residential clusters are evident from the 1880 federal census, where ethnicity and street addresses appear. Local newspaper accounts confirm this pattern. See *Troy Daily Times* and *Cohoes Cataract*.

22. Judith R. Walkowitz and Daniel J. Walkowitz, " 'We Are Not Beasts of the Field': Prostitution and the Poor in Plymouth and Southampton under the Contagious Diseases Acts," *Feminist Studies* 1, no. 3 (Winter 1973/74):73–106; Anderson, *Family Structure*; and Foster, *Class Struggle*, pp. 125–31. Mayhew also finds families playing an important supportive role among London needlewomen. See *The Unknown Mayhew*, ed. Eileen Yeo and Edward P. Thompson (New York, 1972).

23. Handlin, *The Uprooted*, pp. 155, 163.

24. See Anderson, *Family Structure*, p. 202. At different points in a family's history it might have been nuclear, extended, or augmented, according to the needs of kin, financial pressures, etc.

25. Based solely on structural evidence, these conclusions are put forth tentatively, though I think the limited evidence available confirms them. For a fuller discussion of my data on family and household structure, see my "Working-Class Women in the Gilded Age" and "Statistics and the Writing of Working-Class Culture."

26. Almost every "widow" was over forty years old; this fact suggests that most husbands had died, rather than deserting their wives.

27. The percentages of one-parent families among skilled and unskilled ironworkers were 13.8 and 12.2 percent respectively.

28. For example, in Cohoes, 28.8 percent of the Irish families were single-parent, compared to only about 14 percent of the families of other ethnic groups. Combining skilled and unskilled Troy ironworkers, approximately 15 percent of the Irish, 6 percent of the English, and 10 percent of the native-born Americans lived in one-parent homes.

29. U.S. Immigration Commission, *Reports of the Immigration Commission to Congress*, 1910, Vol. 10, part 3, *Immigrants in Industries*, pp. 154–55. The percentages for the American-born Irish, English, and French Canadians were 5.9, 4.8, and 3.8 percent, respectively.

30. This is a terribly complex matter. The strength of Irish culture, particularly the influence of the Catholic Church, has been seen in the low intermarriage rate among the Irish. Similarly, the Church provided strong sanctions against divorce. The small number of divorced individuals enumerated in the census, however, suggests that the expense of divorce and the Church opposition to it made separation the practical alternative for members of the working class. In addition, during this period of rapid industrial growth, with frequent strikes and lockouts, men were continually forced to seek new employment. Lateral occupational mobility could only increase the considerable geographic mobility which Thernstrom (*Poverty and Progress*) and others have found in urban America at this time. This, in turn, would increase the number of men likely to be out of town in search of work until one of two situations arose: either the Troy strike was settled, or a new position was secure enough to send for the family. Lastly, Trojan "widows" may have lost their husbands to the workingman's perennial enemy—unemployment, under-employment, and poverty, and the resulting psychology of failure that turned men to drink, dissipation, and/or flight. Irish family structure may have been simply the product of the trauma involved in the nineteenth-century industrial crunch.

31. Anderson, *Family Structure*, p. 96.

32. Edward P. Thompson, *The Making of the English Working Class* (New York, 1963), pp. 436–44.

33. Manuscript federal censuses for 1860 and 1880; monthly and annual reports in the *Troy Daily Times* and *Cohoes Cataract*; and New York Legislative Assembly Document no. 26 (1882), "Child Labor," pp. 60–83, 270–81. John Modell has told me that preliminary data for Philadelphia at about the same time indicate that nearly half of the children there were still attending school at age twelve.

34. Anderson, *Family Structure*, pp. 46, 58, 97.

35. Were it possible to check matrilinear relations, the frequency would undoubtedly be even higher.

36. Clark, *History of Manufactures*, p. 57.

37. The Paterson dyers were Italian immigrants, while the weavers were Polish Jews, with each group hailing from particular villages in their homeland. An interview with a group of long-time Paterson labor activists first brought this to my attention. Interview with Isadore Geller et al., Highland Park, N.J., April 1974.

38. Anderson, *Family Structure*, p. 153.

39. *Troy Daily Times*, December 18, 1874.

40. Only 13.7 percent of the Irish married someone outside their ethnic group, while the rate rose for those of native-born and English background to 23.2 and 32.4 percent respectively. My data on intermarriage in these cities appear in my dissertation, "Working-Class Culture in the Gilded Age," and in my article on "Statistics and the Writing of Working-Class Culture."

41. Anderson, *Family Structure*; Richard Sennett, *Families against the City* (Cambridge, Mass., 1970); Neil Smelser, *Social Change in the Industrial Revolution* (London, 1959).

42. Smelser, *Social Change*.

43. Thomas Dublin, "Women, Work, and the Family: Female Operatives in the Lowell Mills, 1830–1860," *Feminist Studies* 3, nos. 1/2 (Fall 1975), argues that first-generation factory operatives in Lowell boardinghouses had a camaraderie and personal independence that aided their organization and protest. Later immigrants had family responsibilities that restricted independent action.

44. Richard Ely, "Introduction," in Helen S. Campbell, *Women Wage-Earners* (Boston, 1893). Ivy Pinchbeck, *Women Workers and the Industrial Revolution, 1750–1850* (London, 1969 [1930]), pp. 196–98, recounts similar arguments against women's labor in England.

45. Carroll D. Wright, quoted in Campbell, *Women Wage-Earners*, p. 90.

46. Dugald Campbell to the editor, *Iron Molders' International Journal*, December 1866; *Cohoes Daily News*, August 14, 1882.

47. *Cohoes Daily News*, April 1, 19, 1880. See also issue of June 5, 1882.

48. Ibid., August 11, 1882.

49. Ibid., August 12, 1882.

50. Ibid., August 16, 1882.

51. Masten, *History of Cohoes*, pp. 252–53.

52. Ibid., pp. 253–55.

53. *Cohoes Cataract*, December 28, 1872; Masten, *History of Cohoes*, pp. 252–55.

54. Weise, *Troy's One Hundred Years*, pp. 348–54.

55. Eleventh Census, 1890, *Report on Statistics of Churches in the United States*, "Denominations by Cities," p. 112.

56. Weise, *Troy's One Hundred Years*, p. 353.

57. The dean of the School of Humanities and Social Sciences at Rensselaer Polytechnic Institute, the Reverend Thomas Phelan, whose family are long-time residents of Troy, provided this common designation for St. Patrick's Church.

58. Weise, *Troy's One Hundred Years*, p. 216.

59. Ibid., pp. 295–96. The full text of Havermans's speech was printed in the *Troy Daily Times* sometime in 1888.

60. "Minutes," Iron Molders' International Union No. 2, of Troy, 1858–66.

61. Joseph Hillman, *The History of Methodism in Troy, N.Y.* (Troy, 1888), lists the more prominent figures in each of Troy's Methodist churches, but does not include the names of

any prominent ironworkers. The Levings Chapel no longer exists, and attempts to uncover its records have thus far proven unfruitful.

62. Thompson, *The Making of the English Working Class*, ch. 11, "The Transforming Power of the Cross."

63. Conservative Protestant social attitudes are summarized by Herbert G. Gutman in "Protestantism and the American Labor Movement: The Christian Spirit in the Gilded Age," *American Historical Review* 72, no. 1 (October 1966):74–101.

64. The Reverend Nathan S. S. Beman, paraphrased by the Reverend Augustus J. Thebaud, in *Forty Years in the United States of America* (New York, 1904), p. 114.

65. Ibid., pp. 112–20.

66. See, e.g., George Colfax Baldwin, *Notes of a Forty-one Years' Pastorate* (Philadelphia, 1888); Thaddeus A. Snively, *A Half-Century of Parish Life* (Troy, 1881); Peter Havermans, *Golden Memories* (Troy, 1880); Hillman, *History of Methodism in Troy*, and Weise, *Troy's One Hundred Years*, pp. 290–97.

67. *Troy Daily Times*, March 17, 25, 26, 1873.

68. Gutman, "Protestantism," p. 87. See also Timothy L. Smith, *Revivalism and Social Reform in Mid-Nineteenth-Century America* (New York, 1957); Thompson, *English Working Class*, ch. 11; and Eric J. Hobsbawm, *Primitive Rebels* (Manchester, 1959), pp. 134–40.

69. Gutman, "Protestantism," quotes William Sylvis in James Sylvis, *Life, Speeches, Labors and Essays of William H. Sylvis* (Philadelphia, 1872), pp. 96–117, 443–45.

70. Gutman, "Protestantism," quotes John Jarrett from his *Labor: Its Rights and Wrongs* (Washington, 1886), pp. 252–61.

71. Hobsbawm, *Primitive Rebels*, p. 139.

72. Edward P. Thompson, "Time, Work-Discipline, and Industrial Capitalism," *Past and Present*, no. 38 (December 1967):56–97; David Montgomery, "The Shuttle and the Cross; Weavers and Artisans in the Kensington Riots of 1844," *Journal of Social History* 5, no. 4 (Summer 1972):411–46; and Gutman, "Work, Culture, and Society."

73. Weise, *City of Troy*, p. 134; and *Troy Directory, also Cohoes*, 1880, p. 239.

74. *Troy Daily Times*, July 30, 31, 1873.

75. *Cohoes Daily News*, March 2, 1880.

76. *Troy Daily Times*, May 8, 1876.

77. Augustus J. Thebaud, in *Forty Years*, wrote movingly of working-class poverty among his Catholic parishioners and urged charity, never labor reform. Anti-labor comments were rebuffed by workers. See *Troy Daily Times*, July 30, 31, August 1, 2, 1873. Even the Reverend Hiram Sexton waffled on the meaning of his anti-strike sermon; *Troy Daily Times*, March 25, 26, 1873.

78. Weise, *City of Troy*, pp. 246–49.

79. Liston Pope, *Millhands and Preachers* (New Haven, 1942), p. 86. Gutman, "Protestantism," suggests this reference.

80. The last half of this chapter has benefited from a series of insightful suggestions by Milton Cantor, for which I am especially grateful.

81. See, e.g., Carl Bridenbaugh, *Myths and Realities; Societies of the Colonial South* (New York, 1963); and, for the North, Kenneth A. Lockridge, *A New England Town: The First Hundred Years—Dedham, Massachusetts, 1636–1736* (New York, 1970).

82. Three classic statements are appropriate here: Frederick Jackson Turner, *The Significance of the Frontier in American History* (New York, 1963 [1893]); Alexis de Tocqueville, *Democracy in America*, trans. Henry Reeve (New York, 1945); and Philip E. Slater, *The Pursuit of Loneliness; American Culture at the Breaking Point* (Boston, 1970).

83. *Troy Daily Times*, January 27, 1875.

84. Ibid., July 19, 1881.

85. *Cohoes Cataract*, November 7, 1868. Additional evidence of these savings appears ibid., February 7, 1857; and *Cohoes Daily News*, April 25, August 5, 1882.

86. Alan Dawley, *Class and Community: The Industrial Revolution in Lynn* (Cambridge, Mass., 1976), p. 227.

87. This molder subculture is discussed more fully in ch. 5.

88. *Troy Daily Times*, March 17, 18, 19, 31, 1859. The editor wrote on March 19, "There are no more intelligent, upright and honorable workmen in our city than the molders."

89. Striking Molder to the editor, March 22, 1859, ibid.

90. "Combinations," Striking Molder to the editor, March 23, 1857, ibid.

91. See Eric J. Hobsbawm, "The Labour Aristocracy in Nineteenth-Century Britain," in his *Labouring Men* (New York, 1964), pp. 321–70.

92. Stricken Mounter to the editor, March 24, 1859, *Troy Daily Times*.

93. Striking Molder to the editor, March 25, 1859, ibid.

94. Ibid.

95. Ibid.

96. Factory Girl to the editor, March 21, 1857, *Cohoes Cataract*. In the first sentence, the writer asked for the editor to be her "Apollo"—like the British journal *Apollo* (1708) that answered moral, social, scientific, and religious questions.

97. Factory Girl to the editor, March 28, 1857, *Cohoes Cataract*.

98. Factory Girl to the editor, April 11, 1857, ibid.

99. The Adelphi was an entertainment center in Troy that had a reputation for gambling. It was a center for lower-class life, and it conjured up visions of unmentionable "sin" in the minds of the "respectable."

100. Factory Girl to the editor, April 25, 1857, *Cohoes Cataract*.

101. Lucy Larcom, *A New England Girlhood* (New York, 1889); Abbott, *Women in Industry*, and Alan Dawley and Paul Faler, "Working-Class Culture and Politics in the Industrial Revolution: Sources of Loyalism and Rebellion," *Journal of Social History* 9, no. 4 (Summer 1976).

102. Striking Molder to the editor, *Troy Daily Times*, March 23, 1859. In this rhetoric and ideology, notions of Manifest Destiny neatly overlap with the assumptions and language of social Darwinism and the gospel of wealth that would appear full-blown later in the century.

103. Dawley and Faler, "Working-Class Culture and Politics."

104. *Cohoes Daily News*, May 4, 1881.

105. Deferential colonial attitudes in both north and south are seen in Bridenbaugh, *Myths and Realities*, and Lockridge, *New England Town*.

106. *Troy Daily Times*, March 18, 1855.

107. Such happened to Thomas Norton, the renegade Democrat who opposed Mayor Murphy in 1877. While foreman of the Clinton Foundry's molding department in 1864, the union actively opposed Norton's decision to fire a man he considered an inferior workman. When he moved from Troy to St. Louis in 1880, the men presented him with a "valuable gold watch and chain," "a pair of goldmounted spectacles," and "other substantial testimonials." See *Troy Daily Times*, March 18, 1864, December 18, 1880. For other testimonials, see ibid., January 26, July 14, 1857, May 14, 1858; *Cohoes Cataract*, February 3, 1872, December 29, 1877.

108. *Cohoes Daily News*, February 28, 1880. The speech was by Arthur E. Valois.

CHAPTER 5

Groundwork for Protest

MANY IMMIGRANT WORKERS in Troy and Cohoes enjoyed an improved standard of living, but contradictory features of their experience made their positions tenuous. Although most obtained jobs and a few saved money, they still found survival a day-to-day affair dependent on multiple family incomes and regular employment. Strikes, layoffs, and technological redundancy all threatened to impoverish workers, but neither poverty nor conditions of dependence entirely explain labor protest. Those who struck—the molders, puddlers, mule-spinners, and weavers— were skilled and semi-skilled workers whose higher wages put them in a decidedly stronger economic and political position. Their position, however, also carried certain risks: they had more to lose. The molders and puddlers who engaged in the violent protest of the 1870s and 1880s were well paid and skilled, with established work traditions and status. But they were predominantly Irishmen as well, and working in trades which experienced vast wage and income fluctuations during the depression. Such fluctuations exposed the marginality of their achievements, threatened their gains, and could evoke protest. Some previous Irish associational traditions, a leadership core, and a support network could be necessary to help direct and sustain such protest. While examining the more tenuous aspects of labor's living conditions, it would be wrong to try to isolate the relative impact of any factor. Work experiences and work traditions intersected with ethnic traditions of resistance and struggle, providing the moral and political bases for protest; the conjunction of a disruptive event and the capacity to organize resistance influenced its timing.

Developments specific to each city also affected the timing and shape of protest. Such factors include the character of the textile and iron industries, the later immigration of French Canadians to Cohoes, and the differing social and economic structures of each city. The major industries were affected differently by technology and by the 1873–77 depression. New textile machinery was continually introduced that increased production, modified skills, and imposed new working conditions. Though the entire rolling mill was threatened by the conversion to open-hearth steel furnaces, jobs in the iron mills and foundries remained relatively unchanged throughout this period. Moreover, the iron industry was much more sensitive to changing market conditions than the cotton industry, in two respects. The Harmony Mills, as noted above, ran full-time through the 1873–77 depression (partly because speed-ups increased production without raising costs), whereas the iron mills frequently shut down. Perhaps more important, railroad expansion, which sharply affected subsequent iron production, initiated this depression. Thus the iron industry provided a more tumultuous industrial setting than the cotton industry.

By way of contrast, the cotton-worker community experienced greater ethnic diversity and change during the depression. English and Irish workers had migrated from similar regions to both cities at around the same time, adapting and settling into each city by the 1870s. But French Canadians immigrated later and mostly to textile centers. Their later adaptation, then—their development of a leadership core, an associational network, and an ethnic neighborhood—influenced the timing of protest. Cohoes had a well-established Irish community, but if problems arose, the presence of many French-Canadian newcomers would complicate the consolidation of ethnic interests into a cohesive working-class response.

Finally, the differing morphology of the two cities was also an important factor in the history of order and disorder. Harmony Mills' paternalism controlled the daily experiences of cotton workers; Troy's ironmasters could not control their workforce likewise. Troy manufacturers, therefore, had to use alternative methods to discipline their labor force or to break its power, as the next chapter will demonstrate.

INCOME FLUCTUATIONS AND TECHNOLOGICAL IMPOSITIONS

Poverty

Most acute in depression years, poverty was a chronic problem for the working classes. Cohoes's more affluent residents established a soup house and gave out hundreds of bread tickets during the 1857–58 panic. Troy's overseer to the city poor also reported a dramatic increase in applications to his office, "a great proportion of which," as the *Times* matter-of-factly reported, were "turned down."[1] During the 1873 Christmas week, the Troy Relief Association distributed 479 quarts of soup and substantial quantities of bread, pork, and flour.[2] And during the spring of 1877, 300 unemployed workmen, claiming to represent 4,000, marched to City Hall under the banner "Work or Bread."[3] Such were the more dramatic expressions against actual or imminent destitution.

Poverty was always feared, for it was always present or nearby. One year might be relatively good, with labor in demand; the next could find the working-class family mired in poverty. For example, in Oldham, an English textile town, John Foster estimated that only 15 percent of the families had incomes below the subsistence level in the relatively good year of 1847; during the depression year of 1848, however, the figure climbed to 41 percent. In two neighboring towns, Northampton and South Shields, approximately one-fourth of the families lived in poverty in 1848.[4] Furthermore, as discussed earlier, there was a secondary level that defined poverty; those who were poor owing to costs of medicine, transportation, drink, etc., constituted a larger category.[5] Poverty also varied according to the family's stage in the life cycle: its incidence increased when young children had to be supported, and in old age, when earnings declined.[6] Many families climbed out of poverty only by adopting alternative practices: boarders were taken in, mothers and children went out to work, or relatives combined households.[7]

From 1850 to 1880, Troy and Cohoes underwent a stage of industrialization comparable to these Lancashire towns. We have already estimated that similar levels of impoverishment existed among American families dependent on unskilled ironworker wages or on most textile labor; skilled work in America paid exceptionally well. Most important was the marginal character of family existence when wages—of the skilled as well as the unskilled—depended on work in the iron or cotton mills. Available data enable us to assess the changing stress of such work in these years and disclose the frequent need for and sources of additional income—from boarders, child labor, the wife's homework or work in the factory, and so forth.[8] The figures are not always accurate; for example, they fail to measure adequately the high level of under-employment, especially in the iron mills and foundries during the depression years. Even if the mills did not close, they often operated with reduced workforces. Extremely variable market conditions and seasonal layoffs, as well as lengthy strikes, marked living standards and frequently left iron-workers unemployed.

After 1873, the wage and income structure in the iron industry underwent tumultuous changes. Molders' wages crashed after the union's defeat in 1877, and lengthy lockouts and depressed conditions halted production for long periods. High wages therefore do not tell the full story: ironworker income rose and fell precipitously. Consequently, while puddlers and molders earned well above the day wages of unskilled iron workers, their incomes fluctuated violently, reflecting their work situation, the vicissitudes of their trade, and the fortunes of their militant unions.

Each puddler worked with a gang of helpers. This group was small relative to the larger mill workforce and, with the heaters and rollers, comprised a powerful elite. The molders made up about half of a foundry's workforce, and the income of mounters and pattern-makers was very much tied to them. Owing to dull trade conditions, wages declined after the Civil War. Then, led by the molders' union, income rose rapidly until 1876, when the union was defeated. Between 1876 and 1877 daily molder wages fell from a high of $3.67 to $2.75. Annual income figures more accurately suggest how close to poverty their families might have been. (See Figure 4.1.) The puddlers also struck for six months in 1875–76, so their total income for the year fell well below that of the molders, to a level where they might have to send their wives and children to work. In sum, marked wage and income fluctuations, not high wages, were the central feature of Troy's skilled ironworkers' existence after 1875. This instability threatened to neutralize their recent gains, crush their expectations, and enforce modes of accommodation associated with the families of un-

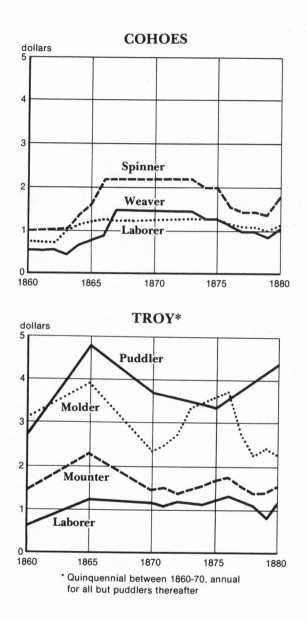

FIGURE 5.1. Wage Fluctuation: Day Wages for Selected Occupations in Cohoes's Harmony Mills and Troy's Iron Industry

SOURCE: Tenth Census, 1880, *Statistics on Wages*, Harmony Mills (annual listing), Albany and Rensselaer Iron and Steel Company (quinquennial listing), Perry and Co. (stove works), Albany (annual listing, 1870–80); "Minutes," Iron Molders' International Union No. 2, of Troy; and *Troy Daily Times, passim.*

COHOES

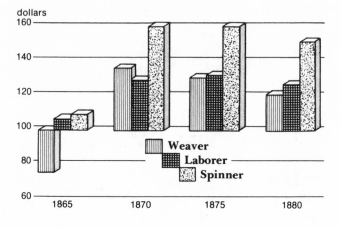

TROY

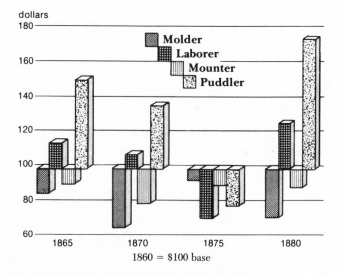

1860 = $100 base

FIGURE 5.2. Income Fluctuation: Adjusted Real Income for Selected Occupations in Cohoes's Harmony Mills and Troy's Iron Industry

skilled workers. (See Figures 5.1 and 5.2.) During years of full employment they could be expected to assist the poorer among them, but without work their own subsistence became more marginal.

Several examples show the dimensions of poverty in Troy during the 1873–77 depression. Many striking puddlers went on relief during their 1873 strike, the *Times* reported, and the 1874 strike resulted in widespread poverty. These strikes affected the entire industry. One *Times* article blamed Troy's poverty upon the huge strike-incurred debts, as well as upon dull trade and high unemployment.[9] Moreover, everyone was affected when the mills operated only eight and a half to nine months a year (excluding slowdowns and frequent, occasionally lengthy, strikes),[10] but seasonal unemployment was most severely felt by the large number of unskilled. According to one reporter's account in the winter of 1874–75, "The suffering among the families of the unemployed workmen in South Troy almost exceed the credit of the senses."[11] Noting that, even with steady employment, laborers could "do little more than support their families in an indifferent manner," he graphically described the extent to which suffering pervaded the ironworker community, especially during the bitterly cold Troy winter:

> During the summer and fall a precarious living might suffice, but with the advent of winter extreme suffering has ensued. . . . . If one wished, columns could be filled with detailed descriptions of misery which have resulted from the suspension of work during the past year. *Families that once could help destitute neighbors cannot help themselves now.* The struggle for bread and fuel has become desperate with a larger class than was ever before known in our city. Fifteen hundred or two thousand men are out of employment, and are likely to be the remainder of the winter, on account of suspension of work at Corning's and Burden's mills. Not one, it is safe to say, can afford this idleness. *Most of them can scarcely keep above suffering in their most prosperous days.*[12]

Such reports tend to confirm what wage and income data suggest: any family dependent on the wages of an unskilled ironworker had a marginal existence in the best of times, but during the 1873–77 depression, when the rolling mills and foundries were frequently closed, even the annual incomes of skilled workers plunged precipitously. Consequently, the *Times*'s estimate that

one out of every three families was suffering in Troy's southernmost iron wards (near the Albany and Rensselaer iron and
steel works and Burden's nail factory) hardly seems exaggerated.[13]

In contrast, the Cohoes cotton industry provided stability. The
community may have been uniformly poorer, but it was better
housed and more regularly employed. Harmony Mills provided
full and steady employment virtually throughout the 1860s and
1870s. Constantly changing technology made textile hands more
dependent on the company than their Troy counterparts were,
but company paternalism met their needs and stifled their protest. Finally, wages paid to female and adolescent textile labor,
semi-skilled or unskilled, were comparable to those of the
unskilled iron hands, but the Harmony Mills engaged family
labor, with resulting multiple incomes. Even so, poverty would
threaten these operatives and their families if the industry closed
down, or if the family did not send its children into the mills.
Even the higher-paid male mule-spinner occasionally depended
on supplementary income from his children, his wife, and other
relatives or boarders. When the state legislative committee investigating child labor in 1882 conducted random interviews about
life in the mill town, the economically fragile character of
cotton-worker family life became obvious.[14] One typical exchange
between an investigator and the wife of an unskilled millhand
went as follows:

> Q. How many children have you in the mills?
> A. Four now—three girls and the old man [her husband]. . . .
> Q. Could you support your family without the help of the children?
> A. No, it would be too hard to support all of them.
> Q. How many have you?
> A. Just eleven. . . .
> Q. Are you able to save any of the earnings?
> A. No sir, not and keep clothes on them.
> Q. Are you in debt?
> A. No sir, I do not get in debt at all; I try to keep out of debt and
> pay as I go.[15]

Such testimony was not unusual. Thirteen Cohoes families testified that their children worked in the mills, and only one felt it
could survive without child labor.[16] Thus, at a time when well-
situated ironworkers were increasingly seeking to emulate "re-

spectable" middle-class working and living conditions, child labor allowed cotton-worker families a modicum of security. Such dependence on low-paid work made their position marginal, and it remains an important factor in accounting for the lack of protest in Cohoes in the 1870s. Regular employment is not a sufficient explanation.

Low wages, under-employment, and unemployment left most unskilled iron- and cotton-worker families impoverished or marginally sufficient. Many survived and, perhaps by their own account, did reasonably well: seven of the Harmony Hill families interviewed claimed to be out of debt, the minimum measure of success available to workers.[17] For most, especially during particular stages of the family life-cycle, solvency could be accomplished only with supplementary incomes. But iron industry fluctuations—often traumatic changes—created special circumstances for even the skilled workers, and a distinctive mentality, as well as periodic misery. Skilled male operatives in textiles, also likely to remain out of poverty, would be similarly influenced by their industry's relative stability.

Dependence and Technology

Various forms of dependence and technological innovations also threatened to engulf iron and cotton workers. Although corporate paternalism provided desirable facilities and services, it also restricted the options of the beneficiaries—often intentionally, to shape behavior and attitudes in accordance with entrepreneurial needs. Such paternalism celebrated the status quo, subservience, and respect for the rights and privileges of wealth. It did little to encourage protest.

Dependent conditions extended beyond those created by the inculcation of the elite's values and morality. There was the dependence on full employment and adequate wages; then, too, there were the market's chronic fluctuations, intensified in Cohoes by dependence on the corporation for housing and even for food. Profiteering frequently resulted—and was attacked. "Let this order business and company storekeeping be denounced, as it should be," one workingman wrote, "until it is abandoned. Let the laborer receive his pay regularly in cash. Let less credit be required and less given." Rent, coal, and medical costs were high, he continued, due to the "large profits charged [by nonproducers] on the articles after being produced by the hands of labor."[18] This store credit system was only one of the several ways by which wages were controlled. To discourage strikes, the Harmony Mills withheld earnings for the first two weeks; in addition, any over-seer could deduct pay for work deemed unsatisfactory.[19] Various ironmasters tried to regulate work and prices in other ways; they paid the workers every three months, introduced the "check sys-tem" (time cards), and supported and operated the contract sys-tem of prison labor.[20] Seasonal labor limited workers to sporadic wages and increased their dependency on the mill. Moreover, both Troy and Cohoes manufacturers restricted union activity by compelling workers to sign "yellow dog" contracts—though opera-tives knew that, without the union, any "disreputable" action, political or social, could be the basis of dismissal. When workers found employment in other cities, manufacturers often attempted to force them to sign contracts that restricted their behavior and associations inside *and outside* the mill. Workers, then, could not join unions and could only engage in "socially respectable" activi-ties. When they were troublesome, mill owners used blacklists to isolate and screen them out. By such means employers extended their control over aspects of working-class life, from gambling and drinking to union organizing. If they felt any particular activity was detrimental to efficiency, high production, and effective dis-cipline, they reserved the right to dismiss the offending employee.[21] Whether the restrictions were intimated or im-plemented, they had an intimidating effect, producing fear of re-prisals among those dependent upon mill employment.

Technological innovations posed perhaps the most serious threat to workers. Machines served to de-skill and intensify labor. In both the cotton and iron mills, skilled work afforded some in-dependence and identity, and was the basis for material and oc-cupational improvement. With the tradition of artisan's rights, it represented status and achievement for the craft practitioner. It also represented industrial power: as long as the manufacturer had to rely on him for production, the skilled worker could bar-gain from strength. But if standards were reduced, if excess ap-prentices were trained, or if the skill was made obsolete through new technology, the craftsman lost a measure of independence. It is within this framework that unions fought to regulate the number and training of apprentices. Technological innovations steadily exacerbated problems, however, especially for textile workers. The introduction of newer, faster, and more complex textile machinery in these decades eroded whatever protective status these workers had gained, further crippled union power, and pressed new, seemingly insurmountable obstacles to control over the conditions of working-class life. In the Harmony Mills, for example, slashers—machines that prepared the thread— replaced skilled dressers in the 1870s; by the end of the decade, double slashers had reduced "the number of slash-tenders necessary by one-half."[22] Similarly, the speeding up of other machines increased production. During one week in 1847, one girl wove thirty-two cuts of cloth averaging thirty-three yards per cut on six looms, and this was considered quite a feat. During one week in 1870, one girl wove thirty-seven cuts averaging forty-five yards per cut on six looms while on a workday two or three hours shorter. Production had increased almost 65 percent, while the weaver worked an almost 20 percent shorter day. Through mechanization, the work pace had increased dramatically in a little more than two decades.[23] A worker who had earlier tended one or two looms soon was expected to tend as many as eight.

In 1880 the Harmony Mills reported on the impact of their modernization:

> The improvements introduced within the past 25 years have enabled the same number of employees to produce 30 percent more work than formerly, the quality of which is also better. In 1866 it took 12 dressing frames, at a cost of $6.40, to what in 1880, with 3 slashers, cost $1.75.
> In 1866 a cut cost for labor 84.5 cents.
> In 1880 a cut cost for labor 52 cents.
> In 1872 labor was 12 cents per pound of cotton used.
> In 1880 labor was 8½ cents per pound of cotton used.[24]

This report seems typical for this time. Speed-ups allowed manufacturers to reduce the number of employees, or to expand and increase production. On the whole, they chose to expand, and the Harmony Mills was no exception. For workers, an adverse effect upon wages was the more important fact of the speed-up. Production increased the market supply and caused prices of goods to fall. The selling price of printed Harmony Mills cloths, 64 inches square, fell steadily from 7⅛ cents in 1870 to 3⅞ cents in 1880. Fortunately for the industry, mass production of cotton cloth was partially met by rising consumption of ready-made apparel. The speed-up often augured wage reductions, cotton hands argued, since wage rates were tied to piecework, and since the piece rate was often lowered more than the rate of the machine was increased.[25] Faster machinery might enable a weaver to produce 15 percent more cloth under "usual" conditions, and the piece rate would be lowered proportionately. But conditions were frequently *un*usual: spinners might not be able to supply enough thread, the thread might break more often, or a weaver might not be able to maintain the faster pace. Then perhaps only 10 percent more cloth was produced, but the piece rate remained 15 percent lower. Equally important, the speed-up did not necessarily mean easier labor. To the contrary, it meant greater drudgery, insecurity, and dependency, a more frenetic pace, and more intense clamor. Consequently, Joseph Delehanty, the leader of the 1882 textile strike, asserted that a wage increase was called for, rather than the decrease that actually occurred. Dependency was at issue for workers. Delehanty said he "would rather have his right arm paralyzed and his tongue struck dumb than accept the slavery of the mill reduction."[26]

The Molder and Puddler Subculture

Without a constant stream of innovations similar to those which had occurred in textiles, work in the iron mills in 1880 remained much as it had been twenty years earlier. The horseshoe machine had been developed by Henry Burden before the Civil War, and work in the puddling forges and stove foundries was not easily mechanized. In their response to the 1880 federal census inquiry, Troy ironmasters and foundrymen could agree with the terse statement by the Albany and Rensselaer Iron and Steel Company: "There has been no change in the efficiency of labor."[27] The Schenectady Stove Company's report simply added, "and no labor-saving machinery of any consequence has been introduced."[28] For the molder and puddler, the aristocrats of the iron industry, work had retained its artisanal character. Their craft and world of work distinguished them throughout the workplace: they were respected for their long apprenticeship, skill, and strength; their higher wages afforded them a better lifestyle; and their work routine still had a distinctive, privileged pre-factory pattern. Puddlers worked in "heats"—intense stints of heavy labor with the molten ore—followed by regular rest periods. During these intervals they went to the local tavern to fortify themselves for the next stint. "Ramming" and "pouring" were similarly regulated by molders, though the latter usually remained in the foundry during their breaks. Such patterns allowed both groups to regulate their own work rates, a privilege denied most factory hands by the relentless cycle of the machine. In addition, their world of work provided for an *esprit de corps* and camaraderie—a chance to share joys and problems. Molder and puddler work routines and experiences constituted a unique and vital ironworker subculture, and were an important social context for their union organizing.[29]

While no major changes occurred within any particular craft, the entire iron industry was undergoing a fundamental shift to steel production. The Bessemer process made its American debut in Troy as early as 1866, but steel production did not "take off" until production costs were lowered in the mid-1880s. The bituminous coal reserves and the new open-hearth furnaces of the West challenged eastern producers and threatened to render their furnaces and puddlers obsolete.[30] Hence, while cotton hands faced more technological changes than ironworkers did in these years, the specter of technological obsolescence hung over all workers. As early as 1866 the *Troy Daily Times* forecast a "complete revolution in the process of iron molding." A new machine then in experimental operation claimed to do the "most essential and most laborious in the whole process of manufacturing stoves," presently done by the skilled molders.[31] Three years later, a new spinning machine was introduced at Cohoes's Eric Knitting Mills. It was safer, easier to operate, and more efficient than its predecessor, and the local paper warned: "Were 'ye local' a spinner I should be looking for some other business very soon. The manufacturers will control the spinning operations in spite of the spinners."[32] The message could not have been lost on the working class, whether they were spinners, molders, or other ambitious, hard-working laborers.

Labor's position was at best tenuous. The factory provided an important avenue to fulfillment and social mobility for immigrant Irish and French-Canadian workers, but enforced dependence inside and outside the mills and technological innovations threatened whatever gains they had made. Poverty also loomed as near as the next depression or price decline. Living and working conditions exacerbated poverty and led to a high mortality rate—even for Cohoes cotton workers, who had relatively good living conditions. Income fluctuations meant that even skilled ironworkers were often "marginal men." Much like children in the cotton industry, those in the iron mills (boys, in this instance) worked in increasing numbers between 1860 and 1880. In addition, most young men delayed marriage until their late twenties or early thirties. This practice may have reflected financial considerations, since only by then had they gained sufficient occupational and financial independence. But most important, in contrast to Cohoes cotton workers, skilled Troy ironworkers with strong artisanal traditions—molders and puddlers in particular—felt the brunt of inflation-depression wage cycles.

These fluctuations did not occur in a social vacuum. In Troy, they coincided with and augmented political and industrial assaults on the ironworkers and their militant unions after 1873. Meanwhile, textile employment remained much more stable, although cotton workers constantly confronted speed-ups, long hours, and other conditions of dependence, and endured periodic wage reductions. The basis for protest existed in their lives, too, yet they did not strike until 1880, after their fourth wage reduction since 1873. Harmony Hill workers may not have had *sufficient* cause or political and social resources for protest until 1880. Timing of protest depended on many interrelated factors, including leadership, broad-based support, and a capacity to resist, and we must next examine when and if such a groundwork for protest developed in each city.

THE ASSOCIATIONAL NETWORK

Three previously discussed aspects of working-class life suggest how working-class community structure helped to sustain workers. First, laborers usually settled near where they worked, on Harmony Hill or in the "iron wards" of south Troy. Neighborhoods with distinct ethnic characteristics existed within these worker communities. Second, these ethnic neighborhoods had strong family interconnections. Nuclear families with extended kinship networks had been maintained, and these family units served as a cohesive base for the web of urban social and political institutions. Third, ethnic ties also extended from the family and kinship circles to the labor movement, the church, and club life, thus cementing the several worker neighborhoods into a cohesive working-class community. This associational network represents the fullest extent to which the working-class community had established itself within the city.

Club Life

During the immediate postwar years, workers had organized a trade union movement with a plethora of associated social and benevolent organizations. The molders' union had provided the organizational impetus. The Troy Trades' Assembly, with twenty-one area unions, had been formed. Cooperative stores had been opened in both cities, and the first producers' cooperative had been built—the Cooperative Stove Foundry. Finally, the Trades' Assembly had organized a Workingmen's Free Reading Room and Library, a Workingmen's Debating Society, and a Workingmen's Eight-Hour League. More than 2,600 union members and their families enjoyed the benefits of union membership and the round of annual balls, picnics, festivals, and excursions which each union sponsored.[33]

During the next twenty years, these trade union social activities were dwarfed by the rapid growth of non-union social and benevolent clubs (Table 5.1). Many of these proliferating organizations—the Masonic orders, charities, professional associations, and most of the leisure-time clubs—served predominantly middle-class constituencies; others, like the ethnic, benevolent, and political clubs, had sizable working-class bases. Since so many Irish initially were workers, special attention must be paid to their ethnic associational life. Their non-labor social activities began to compete with union-sponsored affairs and tended to be under inter-class, rather than intra-class, sponsorship.

Both the number of voluntary associations and degree of middle-class involvement in them mushroomed after the Civil

TABLE 5.1. Troy Associational Life

	1864–66	1884
Labor		
Unions	21	14
Benefit	0	3
Cooperatives	2	0
Social and Benevolent		
Educational	3	11
Masonic	18	67
Military	forming	9
Ethnic	4	18
Leisure	5	25
Reform		
Temperance	8	8
Charity	5	10
Political (Irish)	3	5
Religious	3	12
Professional, Business	4	8

SOURCES: *Troy City Directory*, 1864–66, 1884. Data on labor organizations in 1864–66 and Irish politics (Fenians, Land and Labor Leagues, Clan na Gael) are from the *Troy Daily Times*, November 28, 1865, March 4, 1881.

War.[34] The reasons for such growth remain unclear, though it coincides with the growth of an urban middle class. Organizations such as Apollo Lodge No. 49 had been established by Troy's Masons as early as 1796, but the fraternal clubs of antebellum years were composed of the city's "upper crust." After the war, in addition to the new charities, there were gun or bicycle clubs, choral or dramatic societies, and veterans' organizations. By the 1850s and 1860s workers in various mills challenged one another to Saturday afternoon cricket matches and, later, to baseball games; by the 1880s they could watch the Harmony Hill Blue Stocking Baseball Club play neighboring towns, or the professional Troy Haymakers challenge such teams as the Cincinnati Red Stockings.[35] Admission was now charged, as entrepreneurs turned leisure into business, and social class participation into general spectator sport.

The flowering of middle-class associational life was illustrated most dramatically by the growing number of Masonic clubs which were open to an expanding managerial elite. Between 1866 and 1884 the number increased nearly fourfold, from eighteen to sixty-seven. These included Odd Fellow associations, Orangemen clubs, lodges of Rangers, chapters of Foresters, Knights of Pythias lodges, and numerous "symbolic," "capitalar," "cryptic," "chivalric," or "ancient" orders and lodges. These were united in eleven "grand," "Supreme," or "Imperial" councils.[36] No membership lists for these clubs have been found, and city directories only list the officers. These officers were almost exclusively manufacturers, well-established merchants, clerks, or professional people.[37] Significantly, three foremen in different stove foundries appear in the 1866 list of officers of the Apollo Lodge No. 49 of the Masons.[38] Men from the same managerial strata presumably recognized their common social position and joined the same chapter. Most Masons usually held slightly lower social positions in the community than their officers did, though.[39] The Masonic stress on a rigid hierarchy, with its highly ritualistic titles and behavior, encouraged deference, as is demonstrated by the tendency to name benevolent orders after prominent manufacturers: the Erastus Corning Lodge, Ancient Order of United Workmen; Camp Henry Burden, International Order of Rangers; Erastus Corning Lodge No. 47, Ancient Order of Foresters.[40]

Membership in Masonic clubs extended to artisans and occasionally to a well-paid skilled worker. Initiation fees, regular contributions to charitable efforts, and dues totaling perhaps five dollars a year restricted working-class membership.[41] Equally important, membership was limited to Protestants; Roman Catholics, including the Irish working class, were excluded. While some particularly skilled workers joined these predominantly middle-class social and benevolent societies, they participated in such organizations much less often than tradesmen. Nonetheless, the very existence of these lodges probably had an impact on working-class life: the desire to enter a secret order or to engage in the new leisure activities may have prompted workers to demand shorter hours and higher wages.[42] This relationship between social class and leisure activities may have been dialectical: the "middling" classes created clubs to fill time and to mark themselves off from labor; in turn, these clubs may have created new expectations for leisure among workers. Thus Masonic lodges could have an important indirect effect on labor's attitudes. Meanwhile, however, a group of other voluntary associations developed—Irish and French-Canadian ethnic and nationalist clubs—which had substantial working-class involvement.

Ethnic Republican Roots

After the war, in addition to labor unions, the largest and most important organizations of male workers were the ethnic clubs such as the Sons of Scotia, the Hibernians, the German Mutual Aid Society, and the St. Jean Baptiste National and Benevolent Society. Fraternal associations of this kind provided leisure activities for their numbers. The French-Canadian Atheneum, for instance, contained both a debating society and a dramatic society.[43]

The Irish, as the largest working-class ethnic group, had extensive and supportive social and political associations. The Troy draft riot of 1863, for example, underscored their political and religious connections. During the riot, several thousand workmen marched from the nail factory and attacked the pro-Republican *Times* while the Catholic priest urged them to stop.[44] Irish nationalists and their international political associations—the Fenians, Clan na Gael, and Land and Labor League—were also active and powerful in both cities. When the iron molders' union rented its hall, each society paid three dollars a night, except the Fenian Brotherhood, which paid only two.[45] Given the close relationship between Fenians and molders, it is instructive to note the Fenian organization and militancy. The 1866 Fenian national convention met in Troy, and Thomas B. Carroll, molders' supporter and future mayor, donated $100 to the group. Later, as fundraiser and organizer, Carroll informed the Fenians when their boats and arms were ready for an attack upon Canada. A brigade of approximately 200 Troy Fenians participated in this attack in June, 1866, while the Irish community gathered around the telegraph to follow their daily exploits.[46] In the spring of 1870, in another raid, one of twenty-five Cohoes Fenians was captured.[47] Then there was the secret revolutionary brotherhood, the Clan na Gael; it supposedly claimed Mayor Murphy, as well as the Troy police chief and controller, as members. Indeed, according to

Thomas N. Brown, Troy "had the distinction of being the home of the largest and perhaps the most influential city organization."[48] Finally, within a year of its formation, Troy's Land and Labor League claimed over 600 members, organized into three branches; nearly 400 additional Irish workers belonged to the Cohoes chapter.[49]

In Cohoes, the French-Canadian community, with its own ethnic clubs and nationalist concerns, nearly equaled the Irish community in size by 1880. Although mass strike rallies were addressed in both French and English in order to unite the two groups around their common needs, separate ethnic associations and institutions existed. There were Irish and French Catholic churches; the Irish organized the Fenians and the Land and Labor League, and the French formed the St. Jean Baptiste Society; a French newspaper, *La Patrie Nouvelle*, was begun in 1876. Each ethnic group established benevolent societies, and, while Cohoes Irishmen usually voted Democratic, it was not uncommon for Republican French-Canadian groups to form before the fall elections.[50]

While the two ethnic groups had ample bases for competition, there were also certain similar experiences. Both groups were Catholic; both had the nationalist fervor of a colonized people under the thumb of nineteenth-century imperial England; both emigrated in search of economic advancement. Moreover, social conditions involved them in similar experiences. Harmony Mills paternalism pervaded all their lives. Usually several members of each family, and occasionally whole families, worked in the mills. They labored side by side, were neighbors on the Hill, and struggled against the manufacturers to preserve their jobs and control their work conditions.

Community Organization

Irish and French-Canadian organizations only begin to describe the variety and scope of working-class community life. These activities did not all weigh equally; the baseball team, for example, had less political impact than the union or the church. But this network of associations had important social functions and illustrates the supportive and reciprocal role of clubs and recreational activities.

Mill labor was indeed taxing, but social existence in the Harmony Hill "ghetto" and the south Troy iron ward helped workers develop close relationships, and community organization helped sustain their families. When workers walked out, the whole city was affected. Community pressure helped to maintain the strike: some businessmen offered discounts and contributions to strikers; reluctant strikers were threatened and intimidated by their more militant neighbors; and money raised through social events sustained the struggle. Furthermore, working girls and women, especially important in Cohoes, joined the women's and children's auxiliaries of the Land and Labor League. There they performed supportive tasks, running picnics, strawberry festivals, and so forth, to augment general fund-raising efforts.

This community network also contained political organizations which often overlapped with other ethnic and social activities. On April 18, 1865, between six and eight thousand workingmen held a mass meeting in Troy to protest the Hastings Bill, a repressive state labor measure. The procession was headed by an ex-molder who had been wounded in the war; George Thompson, president of the molders' union, chaired the meeting, and Henry Rockefeller was the main local speaker. The keynote speaker, from New York City's coopers' union, angrily attacked lawyer-politicians, celebrated the work ethic and American freedom, and appealed to the ethnic pride of his Irish audience:

> The workingmen made the Monitor, and when the 'little cheesebox' met the enemy no lawyer crawled in there. It was built and manned and fought by the sons of toil. Keep lawyers out of the Senate and Assembly—they know too much. We may soon be called to lend a helping hand to friends across the Atlantic—many know what I mean (allusion to the Fenian brotherhood—cheers and sensation)—organize and determine to keep America a free and happy land. (cheers).[51]

Fincher's Trade Review, reporting the event, simply noted that the workingmen of Troy "partake of the same spirit of determination which marked the other great demonstrations in the state, only a little more so."[52]

Led by the Irish, these Troy and Cohoes workers created a diverse and extensive community life with social and political interconnections. Each community maintained the full spectrum of institutions: military corps, fire brigades, police, ward political clubs, church groups, bands, and fraternal groups. Every organization, whether political or social, held annual picnics, balls, soirees, excursions, and strawberry festivals. Each nationality had its own fraternal organization; if women could not join, they established an auxiliary.[53] Different trades also formed their own baseball teams (or cricket teams, in the 1850s), and an internal rivalry developed within the Harmony Mills.[54] Finally, political rallies occurred regularly—and not only at election time. At one rally held in Troy in January, 1880, the Irish patriot Charles Stewart Parnell spoke for the Irish Land League; three separate Land Leagues, each with a women's auxiliary, formed over the next few years. Then, on April 11, 1883, Troy's Knights of Labor sponsored Henry George, and free copies of *Progress and Poverty* were distributed to his audience.[55]

Cultural activities were also an integral part of the working-class community's social network. These included a wide range of events, such as cock fights, temperance revival meetings, concerts at the nail factory, debates and lectures at the Workingmen's Free Reading Room and Library, and theatrical performances, or evenings with an entertainer like Wild Bill Hickok and his Indian troupe. When the Irish moral drama "Arrah na Pogue" was performed in Troy on December 2, 1865, extra trains had to be dispatched to Cohoes to transport all those who wished to see it.[56] Then there was the saloon, traditionally condemned for its debilitating effect on the working class, especially on the Irish. In reality, the neighborhood bar, like the neighborhood church, played a more ambiguous part in these communities. The pub had a traditional place in British society, especially for males and for the poor. As a predominantly male institution, it extended the male subculture from sex-segregated work (for instance, in the iron mills) to sex-segregated leisure outside the home.[57] It also provided shelter and warmth in what was usually the town's only public building besides the church. Finally, clean water was often not available, and drink was a thirst-quenching alternative that could fortify against the cold as well as relieve social tensions.[58] This pub tradition, with the social and physical sustenance it offered, was readily adapted by British immigrants to America, especially when they were faced with the pressures and hardships of industrialization and cold upstate New York winters.

In America, one measure of the saloon's importance is the frequency with which newspaper accounts placed both labor-related brawls and meetings in various bars. Here working-class men (and, to a lesser extent, women) enjoyed themselves, shared the problems of working-class life and drowned them in ale. Clubs and saloons, and the events occurring there, provided pleasures that punctuated—if only for a few hours—the otherwise tenuous and difficult life of labor in post–Civil War America. The saloon provided a relatively inexpensive and convenient center for camaraderie, gaming, gossip, and local news. Like the church, it nurtured other institutions, such as the music hall and trade union, and we have noted its central role in molder and puddler work traditions. The saloon helped bind men together and facilitated community organization. It was the ward's communication center, and working-class tensions throbbed through it.[59]

The saloon also offered an avenue to middle-class entrepreneurship—a road taken, for example, by both Dugald Campbell, Troy's prominent labor organizer, and Mayor Murphy, the ex-brewer who would be the city's first and only U.S. senator. Such entrepreneurial and political developments, part of the emergence of an ethnic (in particular, Irish) middle class, would reshape class allegiances within ethnic associational life.

Clubs such as the French-Canadian Political Club, the Fenians, and the Land and Labor League had a strong working-class component, as well as an ethnically homogeneous bond. But we might tentatively suggest that the rise of the new ethnic middle class within these organizations began to shift the members' loyalties from social class to ethnicity. (See Table 5.2.)

Although no comparable information is available for the 1860s, by the 1880s almost half of the leaders of these groups were from the middle or manufacturing classes, while many others were engaged in non-factory artisanal production. Efforts by the Irish-American associations to free Ireland would have channeled worker energy away from industrial struggle to the attack on English colonialism. Furthermore, anti-colonialism attracted an inter-class constituency. For example, though the 1882 Cohoes

TABLE 5.2. Leadership in Troy-Cohoes
Land and Labor Leagues and the French-
Canadian Political Club, 1880–82

Manufacturers	3
Middle class*	16
Skilled/Artisan	14
Unskilled/Semiskilled	6
Total	39

* Includes shopkeepers, tradesmen, clerks,
bookkeepers, professionals, managers

strike was in its fifth month, the mills' superintendent, D. J.
Johnston, chaired the Irish Relief Committee meeting.[60] In this
manner, iron and textile workers who had contributed so much to
the region's labor movement found themselves increasingly
cooperating with middle-class leaders in nationalist political
movements.

While the community's social network helped organize and sustain worker protest, contradictory developments occurred within
it. The growth of the Masonic lodges and other benevolent
societies also reflected the emergence and establishment of
middle-class culture. Finally, the Irish immigrant, as noted, had
developed a substantial petite bourgeoisie by 1880. While many
worker associations had been created immediately after the war,
twenty years later they had to share center stage with thriving,
increasingly inter-class ethnic groups and city-wide social clubs
led by middle-class tradesmen and manufacturers. The labor
movement was ultimately weakened by the fluid class dynamic, as
there emerged an ethnic middle class with roots in the immigrant
community.

Despite these developments, the supportive role of the ethnic
neighborhood and working-class community remained prominent.
The community continued to be united by bonds of family, kinship, ethnicity and neighborhood, and it continued to be defended in both labor and political contests. Police "inefficiency,"
"mobs" who freed neighbors arrested while on strike, regular attacks on non-union labor, local-shop discounts to striking workers,

and local fund-raising fairs and picnics—all these testify to the ongoing support network. As a final case in point, the *Cohoes Daily News* declared the lengthy 1882 walkout at an end when weavers and spinners "from neighborhoods which have heretofor kept a bold and unbroken front" resumed work. Eighteen spinners, all belonging to three housing clusters, had returned to work. The strike committee tried to apply community pressure on these "Rat Spinners" by posting their names in public places around Cohoes, but the community's spirit of resistance had been broken, and the six-month strike ended within days.[61]

Traditions of Association

Many workers had Old World associational experiences that shaped their attitudes and informed their present behavior. Unfortunately, however, evidence of workers consciously drawing upon such experiences remains fragmentary, and the discussion that follows must remain tentative.

The English had come first. Many, of course, were artisans and skilled workers who arrived with some prior trade union experience.[62] They would become molders, puddlers, and mulespinners, and eventually the early labor leaders. The post-famine Irish came mainly from southern and western Ireland. The social history of Troy and Cohoes was influenced by their origins, and by their rural and religious identities. Most were Roman Catholics and had been landless rural laborers. Their church was a community center and charitable organization as well as a cultural symbol, and it promoted deferential, socially conservative attitudes. In their other identity, however, the Irish had joined labor combinations at home, and carried with them traditions of organized agrarian and anti-colonial resistance.[63]

Bands of Irish rebels organized into clans had resisted English colonialism since the seventeenth century.[64] Specifically, they opposed tenant evictions and Anglican tithes. This tradition of peasant resistance continued and grew with the increasing population of landless rural laborers in the nineteenth century. Insurrection spread throughout southern and western Ireland, owing to high rents and low farm prices, and drove many of the rebellious to the New World.[65] Cohoes, we may recall, was called "Litrim City" after the Irish Limerick who congregated there, while Troy had its "Limerick Alley." After a particularly fierce period of rebellion, Limerick County had been placed under the Insurrection Act in 1814.[66]

English colonialism continued, with its increased taxes and growing anti-Catholicism, and it produced mounting landlessness. Irish anti-colonialism also deepened, but a Republican tradition which paralleled agrarian resistance began to redirect it toward new political goals.

The associations and social protest of Troy and Cohoes immigrants from southern Ireland reflected this background. Robert Emmet led an 1803 uprising of the United Irish against English rule; Troy's Irish residents founded the Robert Emmet Benevolent Association. Similarly, the many Land and Labor Leagues testified to the continuing appeal of Republicanism and agrarian land reform; so did the Fenian groups in both cities. Perhaps most important, the 1866 Fenian raiding parties that attacked Canada, and the Irish mobs that terrorized non-union labor in Troy during the 1870s and 1880s, suggest the viability of these old traditions of association and resistance.

Prior to the Civil War, fire companies staffed by Irish adolescents and young men were active centers of working-class life. Firehouses provided informal meeting places, and the gangs may have been linked with pre-immigrant associational patterns, as well as providing preconditions for later industrial protest. The centralization and professionalization of the fire department in 1861 apparently curtailed the social role of adolescent gangs,[67] but they continued to exist and made their presence felt during labor disputes. To middle-class observers, their behavior was hooliganism, but the camaraderie and clubbing tradition strengthened associational ties. Conversely, the absence of such a tradition hindered women's ability to organize.

Cohoes Irish were not especially violent, but once protest erupted, these traditions may have legitimized certain familiar modes of behavior. The tactics of terror and insurgency used by some protesting Irish peasants—the Thrashers—in 1806 is illuminating:

> The mode taken . . . has been by assembling themselves at night
> in disguise, sometimes with arms, going to the houses of such per-
> sons as refuse to associate themselves in their body, and if neces-

sary for their purpose, breaking open the houses of those persons, and robbing them of their property; inflicting torture upon those who become objects of their enmity; and, if necessary for the final completion of their designs, if any person be honest or bold enough to give information against them, the business which began in lawless combinations is consummated by *murder*.[68]

Compare this description with the April 25, 1876, assault by fifty to one hundred men on the boardinghouse of non-union molders from Filley's Foundry. This attack also occurred at night, the men were masked and armed with bludgeons and revolvers; the leader, in an act reminiscent of the eighteenth-century "whiteboys," had covered his face with a white piece of knit goods.[69] Before the battle had ended, nearly a hundred shots had been fired, one "special" policeman guarding the boardinghouse had been wounded, two non-union molders were beaten, and a third was wounded four times. The attack leader had also been shot, but all the men escaped.[70]

The *Troy Daily Press*, recognizing a familiar pattern, headlined its article "The Molly Maguires." Though shrouded in legend, the origins of the Molly Maguires could be traced to Irish secret societies of the 1830s and 1840s which violently defended tenant rights.[71] Irish-American secret organizations within the Fenians, Clan na Gael, and Hibernians continued this tradition of lawlessness and violence.[72] For example, the Hibernian orders out of which the Mollies emerged in Pennsylvania, John R. Commons has noted, existed in the United States as early as 1852 and also carried forward this heritage:

[The] Ancient Order of Hibernians was organized in Ireland as a means of opposing the encroachments of the landlords, but in the United States [in Pennsylvania] it was maintained in an effort to control the relations between the miners and mine owners. The Irish organization was composed of men who in their own country, had lived through a period of storm and stress that had made them lawless and tenacious of their rights.[73]

Irish traditions of resistance seem to have similarly informed the struggles between Troy's ironmasters and ironworkers. For molders and puddlers, such traditions were linked with artisanal notions of labor's dignity and provided their work subculture with a powerful combination: traditions of equal rights (carried forward

by the earlier native-born and English unionists), and violent resistance in defense of those rights. Indeed, militant Irish unionists
and their supporters could join a range of well-organized,
politicized, and often secret Irish-American nationalist associations, including the Clan na Gael, the Irish Land and Labor
League, and many Fenian as well as Hibernian orders. More to
the point, though, the pattern of violence in the "reign of terror"
of the 1870s further suggests Molly Maguirism and the legacy of
resistance. The 1876 attack on Filley's boardinghouse was particularly dramatic, but incendiary fires, shootings, beatings, and general efforts to intimidate non-union labor occurred almost nightly
throughout the mid-1870s. Moreover, some of these militant
workers consciously saw themselves acting much like the Mollies.
For example, James Morrissey, a strike-breaking apprentice at
the Clinton Foundry, was among those non-union molders assaulted. On April 4, 1877, he had been told to quit work, and his
mother had been stoned by a gang "aged 17–20." Two days later,
a small boy gave his father the following note: "If you [the son]
want to lose your two hands and get your house burned down,
work to-morrow. Signed, M.M." The *Troy Daily Times* railed
editorially against these would-be Mollies, and Morrissey—either
determined, stubborn, or hungry—continued to work. On April
26 the Morrissey house was set afire.[74]

Much like skilled English workers with their trade union background, the Irish seem to have brought traditions of resistance
with them. Further, this resistance had a strong Catholic cultural
identity and was directed increasingly in behalf of Republican
nationalist interests. Such traditions could feed labor militancy,
but, as suggested earlier, they could also drain working-class solidarity into exclusively inter-class ethnic concerns in later years.

In contrast to the Irish, Cohoes's French Canadians lacked a
legacy of agrarian resistance. In English-controlled Canada, they
had been engaged in a struggle to preserve their distinct French
and Catholic identities. Hence they would share with the Irish a
common enmity toward English Protestant manufacturers, but
their celebration of French-Canadian culture and the defeat of
Great Britain in the American Revolution translated into a fervent
nationalist separatism and a highly individualistic republicanism.

Moreover, and most significant for us, neither attitude encouraged unionization. In contrast to the dual traditions of English trade unionism and Irish resistance, French Canadians lacked the associational experience of the Irish and English. According to a leading historian of the French Canadians, they brought a "profound individualism" to America, and were "willing to pay the price of being distinctly French and Catholic in an industrial system dominated by the Anglo-American Protestant world."[75] Though their culture might not stimulate industrial protest, the French-Canadian community could provide impressive coherence and solidarity once such protest was underway.

In sum, an extensive associational network existed in both these cities, though later in Cohoes. But when the basis for mass industrial protest was laid, it was laid earlier and more firmly in Troy.

WORKING-CLASS LEADERSHIP

Since Cohoes's French Canadians migrated after the Irish did, the town's worker community fully organized later. Not surprisingly, a labor leadership cadre also emerged first in Troy. During the 1860s the core of this working-class leadership in both cities came from the iron industry, especially the molders. Unfortunately, biographical data do not exist for most leaders, and we can only speculate as to what induced some to seek leadership positions. But information about them, drawn from census reports, city directories, and newspaper accounts of their activities, enables us to construct their general social profiles. Two groups can be distinguished: those who served as officers in labor-related institutions (Working Men's parties or city-wide labor federations and their spin-offs, such as cooperatives and libraries), and those— "organizers"—who spoke at labor rallies. (See Table 5.3.) Since cotton workers had not organized extensively in the 1860s, the only prominent figure at the time was an officer of the Woolen Spinners' Association who also served as vice-president of the Troy Trades' Assembly. In this early period, Cohoes workers who did organize—molders, puddlers, or woolen spinners, for example—joined Troy area locals or, as with the woolen spinners, belonged to the Troy Trades' Assembly. Troy's molder leaders in the 1860s (as Table 5.1 notes) played the major role.[76] Their

TABLE 5.3. Occupations of Working-Class Leaders

	Troy (1860s)				Troy (1873–84)					Cohoes (1877–82)				
	Organizers	Trades' Assembly	Other†	Total	Organizers	Industrial Council ('75)	Workingmen's Assembly ('82)	Labor politics	Total	Organizers	Strike executives	Labor politics	Organizing committees	Total
Molder	6	5	5	10	4	6	5	6	14					
Puddler		1		1	1	3		2	5					
Roller		3	1	4										
Stove-mounter		3	1	4			2		2					
Machinist			1	1										
Pattern-maker						1		1	1					
Spinner		1		1^b						3	3	3	1	6
Carder										1			1	1
Operative											1	2	3^c	6
"Widows"^a													3	3
Carpenter	1	1	1	2		1			1	1				1
Printer			4	4		3	2	1	4					
Painter	1	1	1	1	1	2		1	2					
Mason						3			3					
Tailor						3			3					
Shoemaker					1	1			1					
Cigarmaker						1			1					
Collar cutter			1	1										
Sash & Blind			1	1										
Coachmaker			1	1										
Laborer						1			1					
Porter							1		1					
Music teacher^a													1	1
Shopkeeper					3	2		1	3	1	1	1	1	1
Clerk/ bookkeeper			1	1								1		3
Reporter										1				1
Editor										1				1
Lawyer										1		1		2
				32					42					26

* Not including leaders of local and international unions.
† Including the Cooperative Store, Free Reading Room and Library, Debating Society, Eight-Hour Movement and an Unemployment Committee.
a Females with relatives working in the cotton mills.
b A wool-spinner from Cohoes.
c Two are women.

union included nearly 800 members, perhaps four times as many
as any other in the city. It follows, then, that a relatively large
number of molders went on to hold important positions within
their locals and the International, and were also influential in
urban affairs generally.

The biographical sketch of Dugald Campbell in the introduction to this volume illustrates molder prominence and the labor
leadership network which such involvement created. Further
examples existed. Simon F. Mann, the first molder president, was
the unsuccessful Republican mayoral candidate in Troy's 1860
election. He later became superintendent of the molder cooperative, as well as president of the Charles Eddy Steamer. Henry
Rockefeller, another molder president, also was president of the
state convention of trades' assemblies and a trustee of the Workingmen's Cooperative Association. James Hegeman, the union
carpenter who served as president of the Troy Trades' Assembly,
as mentioned previously, was also on the board of managers of the
Methodist Episcopal Sabbath School, while Thomas Norton, an
early molder organizer, was the ninth ward alderman throughout
the 1860s, as well as an Irish nationalist leader. One final example
from Cohoes suggests the leadership ties that were beginning
there, too. The Woolen Spinners' Association endorsed a rump
Democratic mechanic for state assemblyman in 1864. The secretary of the nominating meeting was an officer of the spinners,
while the three-member nominations committee consisted entirely of Fenians.[77]

The leadership base shifted somewhat by the mid-1870s. Many
union activities were now assumed by inter-class organizations
often run by the middle class. During a bitter 1877 strike, the
molders' union was broken and forced to suspend activities. Similarly, the worker-supported social clubs closed down—to be replaced by very different associations after 1880. Management of
the non-union Clinton Foundry founded a benevolent association
for its molders in 1881 as an alternative to the union.[78] Other
ironmasters followed suit, establishing benevolent associations in
each of the ironworks.[79] Likewise, the workingmen's clubs were
replaced by ethnic or religious-sponsored societies such as the
Young Men's Catholic Literary Association or the Hibernian Rifle
Corps, or by middle-class institutions such as the Free Reading

Room Association and the Young Men's Association Debating Society. Working-class leaders received early experience in public speaking by participating in such debate societies, but they could also be coopted by their newfound "friends."[80]

Limited data keep any conclusions tentative, but Troy labor leaders during the 1870s and 1880s now seem to have been drawn from the different craft unions, especially from those outside the iron mills and foundries. Labor leadership, for example, came from among the printers, tailors, painters, masons, and shopkeepers. (See Table 5.3.) In Cohoes, meanwhile, the 1880 and 1882 strikes had the support of middle-class radicals. Their appearance helps explain the character of protest. In Troy, the mounting power of craft unions coincided with growing violence and the increased emphasis on political solutions usually associated with craft unionism in America. But the development of a radical middle-class cadre in Cohoes occurred after the settlement of the French-Canadian and Irish communities. By 1880 this leadership cadre had grown to the point where a critical mass of leaders existed to help galvanize protest, in an organized social environment that could translate that protest into action.

Several other characteristics of working-class leaders relate to the impact of family and ethnic traditions upon protest. In contrast to the predominantly young, unmarried Irishmen arrested in militant protest during Troy's "reign of terror" between 1874 and 1884 (see Table 6.1), most activist leaders in both cities at the time were generally older (over thirty) and married.[81] If the militants arrested were relatively free from family obligations, the leaders were immersed in such concerns. As their relative age suggests, most were in the later stages of the family life cycle, with spouses, children, and relatives dependent on them. Of thirty-two Troy leaders who could be traced, twenty-nine had dependent children living with them. In fifteen of those twenty-nine families, the offspring were all under twelve years old, and the father provided the family's sole reported support. The mother may have earned income from unreported part-time work at home, but without the availability of child labor, the family economy was vulnerable to any fiscal setback, whether a wage cut or a layoff. Thus, leadership came from those likely to feel and understand familial pressures. They could perceive the need to defend material gains and family obligations vigorously, yet cautiously.

Cohoes's few women leaders shared one important social characteristic: four of six who served on a negotiating committee during the 1880 strike were widows. Only one of the four still worked in the mills, though undoubtedly they all had at some time. The other two were older single women from large families who still lived with their parents. All had children, siblings, or other relatives employed in the mills at the time of their own involvement with the labor movement. Not only did the cottonworker community look to them for leadership but, equally important, these women accepted their roles as agents of social change. Like Lowell's mill girls of the 1830s, these Cohoes widows were without male authority figures in their families, and such independence may have facilitated their involvement and leadership in the labor movement.[82] But unlike Troy's Kate Mullaney, the president of the Collar Laundresses' Union who became a vice-president of the National Labor Union, they remained subordinate to male organizers. After conferring with the mills' superintendent, they retired to the background and let the male leaders tell a mass strike meeting what had transpired at their conference.[83]

Finally, Englishmen like Joseph Egolf, George Thompson, Henry Rockefeller, John Glass, and Mark Smith had joined Scotsmen like Dugald Campbell in guiding the molders' and puddlers' unions in the halcyon days of the 1860s. By 1880 most labor leaders were Irish, though an important minority, especially in textiles, were still English or Scottish workers likely to have had some prior trade union experience.[84] Equally important, under the new leaders the Working Men's party was absorbed into the Democratic party—now an Irish-dominated machine with a working-class bias. Biographical sketches of Troy's James P. Hooley and Cohoes's Joseph Delehanty are representative of the new young Irish leadership in the 1880s, and of their political, labor, and ethnic connections.

Hooley, a second-generation Irish-American, attended St. Paul's School, and at age seventeen became an apprentice molder. Eleven years later, in 1882, he helped organize the Workingmen's Trades' Assembly. He was nominated for state assemblyman the next year as Working Men's party candidate. The Democratic party endorsed his nomination, and he won handily. Hooley at this time was the third vice-president of the Iron Molders' International Union, and during the first of his two terms in office the state legislature, under his leadership, finally abolished the contract prison labor system in New York. He later became a factory inspector, remaining active in the International. An accomplished musician, he was well known throughout south Troy as a member of Doring's Band.[85]

Joseph Delehanty's career was equally impressive. Born of Irish parents in Stonebridge, England, in 1845, he may have shared with other English-born cotton workers some early familiarity with the trade union movement. Little is known about his first years or his migration to America, though he apparently learned the trade of a cotton-spinner at an early age and worked for many years in the Harmony Mills. In 1874, as the Democratic candidate, he was elected to represent the Harmony Hill ward on the Cohoes city commission. After failing in an attempt to lead the reform Democrats, Delehanty worked for the Greenback-Labor party in Cohoes. By early 1882 he had assumed positions of leadership across the spectrum of Irish working-class institutions. He was elected first vice-president of both the Albany Trades' Assembly and Cohoes Irish National Land and Labor League. He drafted a resolution on behalf of the League as well as the Cohoes Irish-American societies, urging the federal government to protect all Irish-American citizens (Fenians) still "incarcerated in British dungeons." In March, 1882, he was elected school commissioner from Cohoes's first ward. Perhaps most important, he led the 1882 Harmony Mills strike, and with labor support was afterward elected to the New York legislature.[86]

Working-class leaders, then, seem to have been older married men, or widows with family responsibilities. Irish leaders may have helped catalyze local labor activities, while those of English origins provided practical trade union experience. Moreover, the leadership occupational base broadened between the 1860s and 1880s, gaining support from non-factory craft unionists, and established itself within the Democratic party. Finally, as we have seen, Troy molders organized that city's unions in the mid-1860s,

TABLE 5.4. Bases of Protest in Troy and Cohoes, 1860–85

	Troy	Cohoes
Ambiguities of living standards	high wages *fluctuations* poverty	marginal family income 4th wage reduction, 1880
Associational network	1864–	late 1870s (French-Canadian immigrants) (inter-class later?)
Leadership	1857–	late 1870s (trade union consciousness later?)
Experience	trade union (English) resistance (Irish)	trade union (English) resistance (Irish) (less for women and children) NOT for French-Canadians
Technology	artisanal work traditions	fully mechanized

while Cohoes's radical leadership nucleus emerged only in the late 1870s. (On this matter of timing, see Table 5.4.)

Ambiguities within the standard of living existed within both worker communities, though fluctuations within the iron industry, beginning in the mid-1870s, especially challenged a worker's hard-won gains. In contrast, a Cohoes cotton worker's family economy remained stable though marginal, and the effects of wage reductions were less immediate than cumulative. As important, the workforce of each city developed the capacity to initiate and sustain active protest at different times. For instance, the French Canadians arrived in Cohoes in the 1870s, lacking the previous trade union experience of the English, or the Irish traditions of resistance. Molder and puddler work subcultures combined with these Irish and English traditions, encouraging labor organization and militance. Finally, a supportive associational network and leadership core developed later in Cohoes than in Troy.

When violence and strikes did erupt in each city, they took different shapes, reflecting the specific urban context. Our discussion has, however, largely omitted one central factor: efforts of manufacturing interests to instruct, regulate, discipline, or, in their own terms, improve the lives of their workers. These efforts in each city depended on the needs, attitudes, and power of the manufacturers, as well as on the opposition they encountered. Such efforts were the immediate cause of protest, or helped to define the socio-political context in which such protest took place. They, too, are a part of the social history of worker protest, and to that aspect we now turn.

NOTES

1. *Cohoes Cataract*, February 13, 1858; *Troy Daily Times*, November 4, 10, 16, 18, December 8, 1857.
2. *Troy Daily Times*, December 29, 1873.
3. Ibid., April 28, 1877.
4. Foster, *Class Struggle and the Industrial Revolution*, p. 96. A precise figure for Troy or Cohoes cannot be given without compiling additional data on the actual families in these cities, but in chapter 4 I suggest that the Troy-Cohoes situation is roughly comparable.
5. Rowntree, *Poverty*, p. 117. Rowntree estimates the incidence of secondary poverty in York, even much later in the century, as twice that of primary poverty.
6. Foster, *Class Struggle and the Industrial Revolution*, pp. 98–99. The figure was 89 percent in the first case and 4 percent in the second.
7. Ibid., p. 96.
8. Manufacturers provided most of the available wage data to the Census Bureau. In the accompanying figures, annual income has been adjusted according to the number of months the mills were supposedly open in a given year.
9. *Troy Daily Times*, February 20, 1875, February 5, 1876.
10. Tenth Census, 1880, *Statistics of Wages*, p. 216.
11. *Troy Daily Times*, December 18, 1874.
12. Ibid. Emphasis added.
13. *Troy Daily Times*, February 1876.
14. The interviewer wrote, "In gathering this evidence great care was used to take it in such a manner as to preclude any possible charge of prejudice or unfairness. The houses visited were taken just as they came, and therefore, the testimony adduced can be said to represent the average conditions of these people." New York, Bureau of Statistics of Labor, Legislative Assembly Document no. 26 (1882), "Establishing the Fact of the Existence of Child Labor in the State," p. 112.
15. Ibid., pp. 115–16.
16. Ibid., pp. 111–20. Compiled by the author.
17. Ibid., pp. 115–16.
18. "A Workingman" to the editor, March 30, 1875, *Troy Daily Times*.
19. *Cohoes Cataract*, February 28, 1880.
20. *Troy Daily Times*, May 5, November 10, 1873, December 20, 1876.
21. For a brief but good summary with evidence of such forms of dependence, see Herbert G. Gutman, "Labor's Response to Modern Industrialism," in *Main Problems in American History*, ed. Howard H. Quint, Dean Albertson, and Milton Cantor (Homewood, Ill., 1968), II, 83–105; and Leon Litwack, *The American Labor Movement* (Englewood Cliffs, N.J., 1962).
22. Baker, *Technology and Woman's Work*, p. 17; *Cohoes Cataract*, June 15, 1878.
23. *Cohoes Cataract*, February 26, 1870.

24. Tenth Census, 1880, *Statistics of Wages*, p. 363.

25. *Cohoes Daily News*, August 7, 1882.

26. Ibid.

27. Tenth Census, 1880, *Statistics of Wages*, p. 216.

28. Ibid.

29. Ed Hamilton, a member of the American Foundryman's Society, in a letter to Barbara Abrash, March 10, 1977, discusses the molder's work routine. I wish to thank Ms. Abrash for sharing his letter and her research on foundry work. See also Thompson, "Time, Work-Discipline, and Industrial Capitalism," *Past and Present*, no. 38 (December 1967):56–97. Milton Cantor impressed the importance of molder and puddler work routines on me, for which I thank him.

30. Temin, *Iron and Steel*, pp. 138–40.

31. *Troy Daily Times*, May 1, 1866.

32. *Cohoes Cataract*, June 19, 1869.

33. *Troy Daily Times*, November 28, December 11, 1865, March 30, April 3, 1866, and *passim*.

34. Weise, *City of Troy*, pp. 198–99.

35. *Cohoes Cataract*, 1856–60, *passim*; *Cohoes Daily News*, January 17, 1880; *Troy Daily Times*, 1880–84, *passim*. The cricket and baseball games seem to have been played on Saturday even before the Civil War, though it is not clear when the half-Saturday holiday began.

36. *Troy Directory*, 1884.

37. Ibid.

38. Ibid., 1866.

39. Brian Harrison, *Drink and the Victorians* (London, 1971), and Peter H. J. H. Gosden, *The Friendly Societies in England, 1815–1875* (Manchester, 1961).

40. *Troy Directory*, 1884; *Troy Daily Times*, January and February 1882.

41. No good evidence on actual dues was available, but the molders' union, for example, apparently maintained an initiation fee of $1.50, asked almost weekly for contributions of 25–50 cents for indigent relief or for striking molders, and charged perhaps 50 cents per month in dues. "Minutes," Iron Molders' International Union No. 2, of Troy, November 4, 1858, August 11, 25, 1859.

42. General studies of protest suggest that, in more mature industrial societies, workers' wage demands increase with increased leisure time. See Stearns, *European Society in Upheaval*, pp. 246–49.

43. *Cohoes Daily News*, August 12, 1881.

44. Weise, *Troy's One Hundred Years*, pp. 198–200.

45. "Minutes," Iron Molders' International Union No. 2, of Troy, June 23, 1864.

46. *Troy Daily Times*, September 5, 1865, March 5, June 1–8, 1866; William D'Arcy, *The Fenian Movement in the United States: 1858–1886* (Washington, 1947).

47. *Cohoes Cataract*, May 28, June 4, 1870.

48. Brown, *Irish-American Nationalism*, p. 66.

49. *Troy Daily Times*, January 2, March 4, 1881; *Cohoes Daily News*, July 1, 1882.

50. Carl Wittke, *We Who Built America* (Cleveland, 1964), pp. 315–28.

51. Mr. Roberts, quoted in *Troy Daily Whig*, April 19, 1864. See other accounts in *Troy Daily Press* and *Troy Daily Times* of that date.

52. *Fincher's Trade Review*, April 30, 1864.

53. Weise, *City of Troy*, pp. 337–57; and *Troy Directory*, also *Cohoes*, 1880, pp. 237–89. There were, of course, clubs that served the native-American and English population. For example, Troy had chapters of the American Protestant Association and the American Club, as well as four boat and row clubs, four medical societies, and a Young Men's Christian Association. These organizations, however, were mostly supported by middle-class and manufacturing interests.

54. *Cohoes Cataract*, 1855–79.

55. *Troy Daily Times*, January 30, 1880, April 12, 1883.

56. Ibid., December 3, 1865.

57. I am most grateful to Judith Walkowitz for pointing out the connection between sex-segregated work and leisure.

58. Harrison, *Drink and the Victorians*, pp. 37–63, 165–70, 298–99.

59. Ibid., p. 54.

60. *Cohoes Daily News*, July 1, 1882; *Troy Daily Times*, December 19, 1881.

61. *Troy City Directory, Including Cohoes*, 1882. The sixteen "rat spinners" were listed, with addresses, in *Cohoes Daily News*, August 21, 1882.

62. Charlotte Erickson, *Invisible Immigrants: The Adaptation of English and Scottish Immigrants in Nineteenth-Century America* (Coral Gables, Fla., 1972).

63. Bernard Reavey documents early nineteenth-century Irish trade union activities in his forthcoming doctoral dissertation on rural Irish protest between 1800 and 1850 (University of London). My discussion of the Irish political culture of resistance has benefited considerably from Andor Skotnes, "Irish Peasant Political Culture in the Pre-famine Era," unpublished MS, Rutgers University, March 1974.

64. George Cornwall Lewis, *On Local Disturbances in Ireland* (n.p., 1836), pp. 4–13.

65. Minutes of Evidence, House of Lords, 1824, p. 36, testimony by Richard Griffith, a civil engineer employed by the government; quoted in Lewis, *On Local Disturbances*, p. 70.

66. Ibid.

67. Weise, *City of Troy*, pp. 127–38, relates the boisterousness of Troy fire companies prior to 1861. Weekly accounts of fire companies' social activities—their competitions and entertainment of one another—are related in the *Cohoes Cataract*, 1855–60. Accounts of Irish gangs in fire companies prior to the Civil War appear, for New York City, in Skotnes, "Irish Peasant Political Culture," esp. pp. 190–93; and, for Philadelphia, in Bruce Laurie, "Fire Companies and Gangs in Southwark: The 1840s," in *The Peoples of Philadelphia*, ed. Allen F. Davis and Mark H. Haller (Philadelphia, 1973), pp. 71–88.

68. W. Ridgeway, "Report of Proceedings under a Special Commission in the Counties of Sligo, Mayo, Litrim, Longford, and Cavan, in December 1806," in Lewis, *On Local Disturbances*, p. 41.

69. The "whiteboys" were groups of eighteenth-century peasant insurgents who protested land enclosure; they wore white shirts as a bond of brotherhood.

70. *Troy Daily Press* and *Troy Daily Times*, both April 25, 1876.

71. Wayne G. Broehl, Jr., *The Molly Maguires* (Cambridge, Mass., 1964), pp. 27–29.

72. Ibid.; Brian Arthur Jenkins, *Fenians and Anglo-American Relations during Reconstruction* (Ithaca, N.Y., 1969); Leon O'Broin, *Fenian Fever, an Anglo-American Dilemma* (London, 1971); Commons, *History of Labor*, II, 181–82; England, Irish Office, "Secret Societies in Ireland and America," Balfour Papers (April 9, 1889).

73. Commons, *History of Labor*, II, 181–82.

74. *Troy Daily Times*, April 5–27, 1877.

75. Wade, *The French Canadians, 1760–1967*, I, 337–43.

76. Since the data focus on city-wide organizations, those workers whose activities were confined to a local or international union have been omitted.

77. *Cohoes Cataract*, October 8, 15, 1864.

78. *Troy Daily Times*, September 10, 1880.

79. Ibid., January 19, 1881. E.g., the Bessemer Steel Works Mutual Benefit Association was formed.

80. See, e.g., the biographical sketch by George H. Dyer, "Edmund Jones," *National League Journal* (London), October 1, 1877, pp. 3–5. In Troy, Dugald Campbell and several pro-labor cohorts were featured at the debating society in February and March, 1880, against a team of manufacturers and professional men. They dealt with two questions: Resolved, "that strikes are opposed to interests of both capital and labor"; and "are inventions detrimental to the laboring classes?" The pro-laborites won one of the debates and do not seem to have returned for a third tryst, but their presence indicates a certain interclass involvement in the club. See *Troy Daily Times*, February 9, March 22, 1880.

81. In Troy, 85.7 percent (42 of 49) of the leaders were between the ages of 30 and 49,

and an equal percentage were married. In Cohoes, 61.5 percent (24 of 39) of the leaders were between the ages of 30 and 49, while 74.4 percent were married or widowed.

82. Dublin, "Women, Work and the Family."

83. *Cohoes Daily News*, February 28, 1880. Troy's Kate Mullaney was also single (she later joined a religious order in the midwest). Her more public leadership may be attributed to the fact that the laundresses had an almost exclusively female union in an almost exclusively female industry. The molders always remained their protectors, however: molders organized them, and Dugald Campbell helped establish and became superintendent of the laundry cooperative.

84. In Troy 73 percent of the leaders in the 1870s and 1880s were Irish; 16.2 percent were English or Scottish. In Cohoes during the same period, the percentages were 60 and 22.

85. Lisk, *Representative Young Irish-Americans*, pp. 193–94; *Troy Daily Times*, September 28, November 7, 1883, September 11, November 5, 1884; *Troy Press*, April 13, 1882; and Samuel Rezneck, *Profiles out of the Past of Troy, New York, since 1789* (Troy, 1970), p. 208.

86. *Cohoes Daily News*, July 21, December 13–17, 1880, March 8, 10, 1882. For a biographical sketch of Joseph Delehanty, see *New York World*, quoted in *Cohoes Daily News*, December 28, 1882.

PART III

Protest

"BURGLARIES!"

Dear Times—I wish to state to you,
that times down here look wond'rous blue,
Or b'ack, I rather ought to say,
Since all our puddlers are at play.
Their wages are reduced, 'tis true,
and so their circumstances too.
And times are really very hard,
Especially here in this Sixth Ward.

Burglaries now are very rife,
amid these scenes of want and strife.
Last night, a house was slyly enter'd,
and in a gang of burglars ventur'd,
with dry goods, groceries—all were arm'd.
Truly the inmates were alarm'd,
When lo! Instead of stealing from them,
the burglars heap'd these goods upon them.
Success attend these burglars bold,
who deeds of kindness thus unfold.
May they continue to steal,
and not a pang of conscience feel.

P.S.   Since writing the above I've learn'd,
their *avaricious* mind return'd,
and not content upon the whole,
to-day sent half a ton of coal.
The burglars who create *these panics*,
are *gentlemen* although *mechanics*.

—J. H. N., Nail Factory,
Troy, February 13, 1858

CHAPTER ⑥

Manufacturers' Counter-Attack
and Workers' Response, the 1870s

THE SOCIAL HISTORY of Troy and Cohoes during the 1870s presents a study in contrasts. Tough company efforts to crush the iron unions sparked recurrent violence and lengthy disorders, while cotton workers remained quiescent, only slowly beginning to organize politically and industrially toward the end of the decade.

After the Civil War, industrial capitalists in both cities sought ways to lower costs. Their quest was simple initially, since the immediate postbellum years were relatively prosperous. The textile and iron industries expanded, wages rose, and industrial harmony reigned. To be sure, there was an occasional strike, like the 1867 lockout in the iron mills; but the puddlers and ironmasters agreed to a sliding wage scale for puddling based on the price of iron, settling a major souce of mill conflict. By the 1870s, however, the need to economize had become more urgent. Competition from western iron entrepreneurs who had lower labor costs and better distributing facilities for the new western markets increasingly forced Troy mill owners to cut costs. The onset of the 1873 depression intensified the economic squeeze on manufacturers. Rails had been overproduced, the demand for nails and stoves fell, and the price of cotton cloth plummeted. Both iron and cotton manufacturers had to improve ways to maintain profits and minimize losses. There were various options: they could try to lower wages, further mechanize work, intensify labor, dilute well-paid skills, increase hours, or assert discipline on the labor process. The options chosen depended on their existing power over the workforce and the resistance that they might meet.

That Cohoes was a "company town" greatly facilitated management control over the labor process. Harmony Mills remained
firmly in charge and periodically enforced wage reductions and
speed-ups. Moreover, mill workers accepted the perquisites of
company paternalism which rendered them dependent and which
were supported by particular historic conditions. The predominantly unskilled female and adolescent workforce was
supplemented by the large influx of French Canadians; given cultural and linguistic barriers, it took time for the established hands
and the newcomers to work out a common *modus operandi*.
Moreover, the relative stability in textiles contrasted with conditions in the iron manufacture. The iron mills and foundries operated only about eight and one-half months a year during the
1870s, and often with only half a complement of men. The Harmony Mills, however, kept running almost without interruption.
Harmony operatives were painfully aware of the under-employed
or unemployed status of their neighbors in Cohoes's wool mills,
and in the iron and shirt-and-collar industries of Troy.

By way of contrast, Troy's molders' union had succeeded in establishing closed shops, gaining substantial wage increases, and,
perhaps most important, controlling apprenticeship regulations in
the foundries. The last gave them the ability to protect their craft
from efforts to dilute the skill or to produce a surplus of skilled
hands who could replace them during a strike. Furthermore, the
Troy working class, led by the molders, had built a community
network of social and industrial organizations, established a political base, and helped to elect a sympathetic Irish Democrat
mayor, Thomas B. Carroll. In the mid-1870s, under the leadership of four-time mayor Edward Murphy, Jr., they cemented
their hold on the mayor's office. Finally, the police and molders
shared common ethnic and neighborhood bonds, strengthened by
the fact that many policemen had once been molders themselves.
The ironworkers were in an unprecedented position; a national
association of wealthy and powerful manufacturers recognized as
much when they unsuccessfully fought against those workers in
1866. When the lockout ended, the ironworkers' cooperative vision had become a reality—in the form of a cooperative store and
the first of three cooperative stove foundries. Troy had become a
"worker city."

By 1873, with the depression, Troy's cooperative movement lost its luster and was replaced by a resurgent trade unionism. Although one of the three stove foundry cooperatives continued to operate, the movement lost its special attraction for Troy workers by 1873, as the stockholders' demand for profits increasingly forced abandonment of cooperative principles.[1] On a national scale, as one labor historian has written, "the return to prosperity in 1869, the disappearance of employers' organizations and last but not least the failure of cooperation as a panacea turned the Molders' Union again into the groove of trade unionism."[2] But, with the Sons of Vulcan (the puddlers), the molders remained in the vanguard of the Troy labor movement. The Irish overwhelmingly dominated both trades by the 1870s and, by their lights, had improved their status. Not wealthy men, they were still the "aristocrats" of the ironworkers, with a distinctive lifestyle and work tradition. Less skilled labor (laborers and helpers, or the hookers, and catchers in the rail mills) were paid lower wages. Usually having no union to lend them support, they claimed it was "unfair for the puddlers and heaters to ask them to stand out."[3] The higher-paid skilled workers, then, could sustain a strike, had a greater stake to defend, and retained some measure of industrial control. Consequently, ironmasters had to use more than economic controls and dependence to enforce discipline, and the battle they fought with workers extended from the factory to law enforcement. Throughout these years, in their efforts to reassert control over Troy, the masters had to take aggressive action to break the union's power and seek an alternative to the more pervasive paternalism and technological control exercised in the Harmony Mills. They found their alternative in the police and the courts.

COHOES AND PATERNALISM

Management at Harmony Mills had three distinct advantages unavailable to their counterparts in Troy's iron industry: a sizable, cheap, reserve army of labor composed of women and children; textile technology which permitted continual increases in production over a shorter period of time and with less skilled workers; and pervasive company paternalism which inculcated work discipline and worker deference while at the same time creating worker dependence on the corporation.

First, while only men labored in the iron mills and foundries, two out of every three cotton workers were females. Moreover, in 1880 only 7.6 percent of the molders and 17.4 percent of the unskilled ironworkers were under twenty years of age. By comparison, 58 percent of all Harmony Mills operatives were under twenty years old; perhaps more significant, only 16.6 percent were males *over* twenty years old. There was an extra advantage to the use of female workers: women were not expected to engage in social or economic protest or to participate in public affairs. Rather, the national culture celebrated the American woman as mother, the protector of the family hearth. Most working-class wives did not continue in the mills, although women occasionally did participate in social action. The activities of Troy's collarmakers and tailoresses, as well as of the Cohoes cotton workers, testified to their acute sense of oppressive conditions and the extent to which the myth concerning women's roles did not entirely define their social reality. Nonetheless, women cotton workers as a rule organized later and less successfully than men in the iron industry.

Second, as the previous chapter has demonstrated, technological changes were diluting skills, displacing workers, and intensifying mill labor. Such changes made it crucial to have a pool of inexpensive female and child labor. And so, for example, in the 1880s female ring-spinners increasingly replaced male mule-spinners, at a third of the latter's wage.[4]

Third, and perhaps most important, was the pervasive company paternalism. We have previously described its more beneficial aspects, e.g., the brick tenements and reduced rents. But these material amenities combined with corporate power, much like the carrot and the stick, as handmaidens for effective social control. They served to reduce absenteeism and turnovers, encourage company loyalty, discipline the workforce, and inhibit unionization and protest. The company was not primarily motivated by benevolence; its ultimate objectives remained increased production and higher profits. As the "cow sociologists" of a century later would formalize it: "contented workers give more milk."[5]

Harmony Mills paternalism was distinguished by its thoroughness, pervading almost every aspect of working-class life. The company operated over 800 tenements, comprising a model village that effectively controlled its working-class residents. This Hill community was self-contained, isolated from the rest of Cohoes by a sheer cliff and accessible only through the mill. The tenements themselves were built along angled but parallel streets running off an artery (Vliet Street) that bisected the development. They sat on an incline that sloped gracefully down to the factory gate and to the two boardinghouses and company store. Long View, David J. Johnston's mansion built in 1874, overlooked the entire complex. The Harmony Hill community was an organic, structured piece of industrial social engineering.

Company paternalism reached into the home itself. Company housing, for example, was only available to company workers; while rentals were modest, they were not automatically reduced with every wage decrease. A company store opened in 1857, also exclusively for the operatives.[6] Rent, and possibly store bills, were simply deducted from the family's paycheck. Since tenure in company housing existed only as long as someone in the family worked for the mills, it was thus at the pleasure of the company, and strike action could result in eviction. That no one was evicted until the 1882 strike speaks as much for the way in which paternalism intimidated protest as it does for company benevolence.

House and factory, however, were not the entire life of an operative; accordingly, the company did what it could to shape the whole person. Workers engaged in recreational and associational activities which sustained them in important ways. But corporation culture must be seen as the alternative to working-class culture, as a bourgeois vision of the well-educated, well-behaved worker. Management built a reading and lecture room with a "well-selected" library for its operatives. To inculcate them in the virtues of obedience and charity, the walls of the room were engraved with scriptural scenes that blended in with the "tastefully frescoed ceiling."[7] Methodist religious services were held there on Wednesday evenings, and hundreds of working-class children packed the Harmony Hill Sunday Sabbath School, under David J. Johnston's direction. By 1864 the school claimed 360 pupils, making it Cohoes's largest.[8] Omnipresent company paternalism followed the working-class family from factory to home to leisure activities and moral education. Within this semi-controlled environment, the manufacturer sought to instruct his workforce in that "moral" discipline which would reinforce factory work discipline. As one editor innocently observed, with all these marvelous institutions this "model factory" would be able to achieve "perfect discipline."[9]

Company paternalism in Troy was the same as that of Cohoes only when religious and leisure activities were involved. Harmony Mills management was more extensive, invading almost every part of the cotton workers' lives. Its tenements and company store tied the workers' wages to their living conditions and encouraged dependence on the company. Its superintendent directed the Sabbath School and lent his name to temperance drives, such as the D. J. Johnston Volunteers, the Harmony Hill temperance association. The company, by becoming involved in the lives of its labor force, sought to make them more productive workers and better citizens. It could not have been displeased when the lessons of dependence were translated into political deference and its workers helped elect mill managers to public office. But paternalism did not, by itself, improve profit levels, though it did shape reactions to wage decreases, such as the one of 1873. The relatively passive acceptance of this management decision was a product of paternalism, of that mixture of worker faith in and dependence on the company.

By 1873, wages had not been reduced for nearly a decade, but trouble was brewing. The Harmony Mills had made its owners millionaires, but in October management reported that it had to borrow money to meet the payroll. A few weeks later, the mills closed.[10] The *New York Herald* correspondent described the effect of the closing and tried to dramatize the depression's impact upon Cohoes. The company had 4,500 employees, three-quarters of whom were women and children; when it shut down, the entire city suffered. The article melodramatically concluded by saying that Cohoes storekeepers, who were owed $100,000 by the unemployed workers, vowed to supply their customers; consequently, "no suffering may be felt for two or three weeks yet."[11]

A month after the shutdown, two seemingly contradictory items appeared in the *Cataract*. The company announced that, to aid the large number of unemployed, it would resume full production with an average wage reduction of 12½ percent. Probably in response to worker complaints, management noted that this salary cut did not correspond to the decline in print goods prices and "will hardly save the company from loss." Nonetheless, the employees, it declared, could now expect to work through the winter. Rents on company tenements would be halved. Another column in the same issue, without a hint of irony, quoted a description of the mayor's new house as a "mansion in the sky." The mayor was David J. Johnston, the mill superintendent.[12]

As management promised, the Harmony Mills did not close during the 1873–74 winter, or, for that matter, the next year. Although the woolen mills periodically suspended operations, the cotton mills did not. No record of accounts for the period exists, but the drop in cloth prices must have cut into profits. Still, in the winter and spring 1875, the company found the money to add French roofs with decorative towers to the Ogden Mill, thereby maintaining an elegant uniformity with the other mills.[13] Then, late in October, two years after the first reduction, the company announced another 12 percent decrease, owing to the glutted cotton market.[14] The workers' protest amounted to one letter in the local paper which questioned how full production would solve the problem of a glutted market and suggested curtailing the work day.[15] Rumors filtered through the community that some dissatisfied English families planned to return home. Denying these stories, the *Troy Daily Times* showed an understanding of one aspect of the workers' perspective when it concluded that "the contrast between [the better] factory life and wages in this country and in Europe is too great."[16]

As some workers had feared, the market remained glutted. Management announced a third reduction in wages—10 percent on those earning more than four dollars per week, and 6 percent on those receiving less. This time, however, the cotton workers decided some discussion was necessary. They sent two operatives from each room in the mill to ask the general manager, Robert Johnston, to operate at three-quarters time with the present wages, rather than at full time with reduced wages. Johnston refused, stating that a reduction in the work day would not lower inventories because competing mills would only increase their production so as to obtain a larger share of the market for their owners.[17] In contrast, the Knit Goods Manufacturers Association then meeting in Cohoes unanimously resolved to recommend a work stoppage.[18]

Although Cohoes's cotton workers were hardly in a position to regulate national production, they believed someone had to start cutting back production somewhere, and hence found Johnston's answer unsatisfactory. A week later a majority of the No. 2 Mill weavers assembled in order to organize a protest against the wage reduction. When the women could not agree on tactics—whether to fight for reduced hours or for an hour break for lunch—they all returned to work. That same afternoon, the No. 3 Mill weavers left their looms and debated their position in the factory yard; then they stopped work a few hours early and demanded "short time" and no wage reduction. The next morning, only sixty to one hundred weavers stayed out, and the following day, after a mass rally, the mill hands agreed to the salary cuts and returned to work. The weavers' protest had failed.[19]

Working-class protest in Cohoes remained low keyed throughout the rest of the decade. In September, 1876, a committee of cotton operatives met with general manager Robert Johnston to find out if their old wage level would be restored. Some months earlier, a delegation of mule spinners had asked superintendent David Johnston for a wage increase. At both meetings the workers received assurances that management would do what it could for them, but they gained no tangible commitments.[20]

The working-class community itself was no more successful. Cohoes's workingmen's cooperative closed its doors in early April, 1867, after a year and a half of operation. In addition, some cotton workers tried to elect pro-labor candidates on the Democratic ticket or as part of a third-party movement, but they received no strong support from the community. Although it held the balance of power at election time, the Working Men's party had collapsed, mustering only 175 votes in the 1867 town elections.[21] Labor had some political success in 1874 when a spinner, Joseph Delehanty, was elected to the City Commission from the Harmony Hill ward. He led the labor wing of the local Democrats until, in 1877, he joined the newly formed Greenback-Labor party, a national organization appealing for workers' votes. Cotton-worker voting patterns revealed several attitudes: a limited sense of the connection between politics and labor issues, no little naivete and a remarkable faith in the intentions of management, and, perhaps most important, deference to management and fear of company reprisals. During these years Harmony Hill's first ward, composed almost entirely of cotton workers, voted consistently Democratic by an almost two-to-one majority, except when David J. Johnston or William E. Thorn, the company treasurer, ran for mayor, or when Silas Owen, the tenement superintendent, ran for commissioner. Then the ward voted Republican.[22]

Only near the end of the decade did the political consciousness of Cohoes workers change in significant ways. In its first campaign in 1877, the local Greenback-Labor party nominated Joseph Le Boeuf, a French Canadian who had organized the French Catholic Church in Cohoes. He received only twenty-one votes and shortly thereafter moved to Holyoke, Massachusetts.[23] In the November, 1878, election the Greenback-Labor party received 25 percent of the Cohoes vote, having converted enough Democratic voters to enable the Republicans to come into office. Local Democrats now knew they could no longer take labor's vote for granted. Then, early in the new year, the Harmony Mills announced it would cut back operations, owing to overproduction in the industry. But local action could not overcome a national problem; entrepreneurs elsewhere simply filled the vacuum. After two months on a half-time schedule, the company ended its experiment and resumed full production. Simultaneously, wages were slashed 10 percent, the fourth decrease since 1873. Real wages had not declined over the next six years, but the four wage reductions (with some increases) had reduced the millhand's average salary about 30 percent, or to its 1863–64 level.[24] Worker response was moderate but significant. In the local election which followed, a company official, Silas Owen, lost his bid to represent Harmony Hill on the city council. He was defeated by three votes, with the Greenback-Labor candidate receiving eighty-six votes.[25]

Cohoes's cotton-worker community had remained largely quiet throughout the 1870s, until French Canadians settled into the community and, with their Irish and English neighbors, began to establish a network of associations. For these workers, reduced employment, while preferable to unemployment, was not preferable to the reduced wages suffered by workers in many other industries. Though hard-pressed, they absorbed successive wage reductions with comparatively little protest and only slowly began to develop the first stirrings of political consciousness. In Troy, however, iron manufacturers faced a different set of conditions and had to find different solutions.

TROY

The Manufacturers' Search for Power

Power took varying forms for manufacturers and for workers, with circumstances structuring their alternatives. Technology had not penetrated the iron industry as it had textiles; molding and puddling remaining unmechanized trades. Moreover, paternalism was decidedly less pervasive in Troy than in Cohoes, and on a smaller scale. Troy's ironmasters provided similar services, with company stores, and some tenement housing available at reduced rents. The iron industry involved itself comparably in worker religious and leisure activities. The Albany Iron Works contained a public hall, a library and reading room, and held weekly Episcopal services; the Rensselaer works ran a store for its employees; and the Burden mill supported a Methodist chapel and Sabbath School in that part of the city called "The Nail Factory."[26] Paternalism extended to other activities, including company-sponsored railroad or boat excursions and picnics for employees and their families. Each company held an annual garden reception for the Sabbath School picnickers from the south Troy Methodist Chapel. Accompanied by a band and more than a thousand friends, the students marched to the mansions of three or four different ironmasters, where they were greeted with refreshments. They received a brief tour of the grounds, recited their lessons, and were given a contribution for the school.[27]

Such paternalism taught workers deference but did not provide Troy ironmasters with adequate industrial control. Consequently, the masters sought other ways to enforce their authority in the industry. The most powerful authority—the police and the courts—constituted one arena in which a power struggle ensued. This contest reflected attempts at social regulation and gives another dimension to the pattern of protest. Law-and-order advocates tried to oust local police who had ties to the Irish ironworker community, replacing them with a more impartial Rensselaer County force. That this conflict centered in Troy testifies to the need of the city's entrepreneurs for a system which would provide legal stability comparable to the social stability provided by paternalism.

Four related developments shaped this contest: the growing immigrant labor force; fluctuating market conditions in the iron industry, with their attendant social dislocations; employers' demands for a disciplined workforce; and the bourgeois cult of success which insisted that poverty was the result of personal weakness, rather than social injustice. The immigrant influx made for rapid urbanization, usually accompanied by increased problems of sanitation, housing, and infant mortality. To long-term city dwellers, the unfamiliar customs and strange languages or dialects of the newcomers were coterminous with urban decay. Second, the protracted economic crises after 1873 stimulated efforts to return to what was believed to have been a simpler, older order and set of values. Third, industrialization reinforced the celebrated Protestant work ethic. It required a sober and orderly workforce, the need for which was strengthened by increasing competition. Drunkenness, violence, and vagrancy violated this work ethic. The fourth and final factor involved the social Darwinist Gospel of Wealth, which equated industry with virtue and which insisted that habits of hard work and thrift could prevent impoverishment. According to classical economics, depressions were an inevitable part of the trade cycle, and one had to save for such "rainy days." These four themes combined to create a negative image of the urban working class. They associated the deteriorating physical environment of working-class neighborhoods with the social and moral decay of those living there.[28] As such, middle-class fears of contagion, originally a real response to declining health standards, became confused by a growing intolerance toward traditional working-class habits and consequently involved anxiety over working-class unrest, rather than sympathy toward the poor. Problems of crime, labor unrest, and control of the police took place within this complex of social developments and attitudes.

Labor protest and violence markedly increased in Troy after

1873, coincident with the onset of the depression and with efforts to professionalize and reorganize Troy's law enforcement. But police were often recruited from working-class ranks, and, during periods of social or economic stress, discrepancies between the demands of the law, inequities in the social order, and the interests of their working-class and ethnic community tested police allegiances and provoked middle-class charges of police-worker collusion. Manufacturers and workers fought industrial battles that often spilled over into street brawls involving union and non-union ironworkers. The police were called upon to maintain order, and manufacturers found them wanting: "inefficient." In a series of Twelfth Night reversals, events in 1874 turned the Troy social world upside down. Criminals roamed free; police locked themselves into their station houses, rather than turn over authority to a rival county force supported by the business community; workers cheered from the sidelines. The clash originated, however, in the history and nature of the police force itself.

The development of an urban police force is a familiar story, and Troy and Cohoes provide no exception.[29] Briefly, a night watch existed in Troy as early as 1786. Formalized in 1838, it was updated in 1851 into a night police force with forty-eight members. The first jail, built in 1793, was replaced by a newer facility in 1826, while the first Cohoes "lock up" dated from 1857.

By mid-century Troy and Cohoes each had a small regular police force supplemented by a larger number of night police, since most problems then occurred after dark. With the increasing population and rapid industrialization, criminal activity continued to rise, and attention focused on the most efficient way to police the entire area. This concern led to the replacement of both police forces by a centralized force, the Capital Police District, in 1865. It encompassed Rensselaer, Albany, and Schenectady counties; Troy and Cohoes were both placed under the eighty-nine-man Troy division. The division was then subdivided into six precincts: three city precincts with sixty policemen, and one precinct each for West Troy, Cohoes, and Lansingburgh (North Troy). Cohoes had six policemen.[30] The reasons for this reorganization are not fully clear. The local press editorialized on how it would enable the new force to be free of politics, since the governor appointed the five commissioners.[31] In addition, it

COUNTER-ATTACK AND RESPONSE   195

would provide twenty-four-hour service. And, perhaps as important, it would mean that this new, largely Irish force would
be less influenced by the increasingly "partisan"—that is,
ethnic Irish—local government. Possibly the reorganization
was an elite response to the shifting membership of Troy's
twenty-member board of aldermen. The board had been dominated by manufacturers in 1857 and included only two, or possibly three, ironworkers; but by 1865 there were six workers on the
board, with another three being skilled artisans. In addition, a
number of Irish brewers—including Edward Murphy, Jr., the
prominent political boss who would become mayor for eight years
in 1874—lent a decidedly Gaelic tone to the board. In contrast,
the new commissioners of the Capital Police District were all respectable members of the business community. The Troy commissioners included an attorney and a lumber merchant who was
also treasurer of the First National Bank; the only identifiable Albany commissioner was a real estate broker.[32]

Confirming the political character of this supposedly non-
political force, the police were again placed under local control on
April 29, 1870, during the tenure of Thomas B. Carroll, the first
Irish mayor.[33] The new arrangement—a board of three police
commissioners selected by the mayor—meant that the force
would now reflect the mayor's political interest in the Irish and
working-class Democratic strongholds.

Troy police traditionally had strong ethnic and class ties to the
Irish working-class community. In 1880 they were mostly Irish,
resided among the iron workers, and were well integrated into
the worker community. They very likely worshipped together and
intermarried, and many had once been ironworkers themselves.
When the Capital Police District was formed in 1865, a long-time
south Troy grocer, James McMulkin, was chosen high constable.
In the iron wards, constable William Connors (sixth ward) most
recently worked as a laborer; constable John Conway, Jr. (seventh
ward), lived with his father, still a south Troy laborer; constable
Dennis McCarthy (eighth ward) had been a furnaceman; and constable John Shelly (ninth ward) resided near his relatives, all
laborers in the iron mills.[34]

As mentioned above, former molders held an important place
in the Troy police hierarchy by the 1880s. The superintendent

and the chief of detectives had been molders; one of the two detectives had been a mounter for twenty-two years. Of the four
captains, one had been employed at the Burden works and
another had molded stoves in the Clinton Foundry. Furthermore,
eight of the fifteen sergeants had earlier worked in the iron
industry—two as molders, three in the stoveworks, and one each
as mounter, pattern-maker, and rolling mill hand.[35] This social
and geographic proximity to the iron industry inevitably aroused
suspicion among "respectable" members of society about the ability of the police to maintain a professional distance from the Irish
poor.[36] There was no problem while criminal activity consisted
largely of indirect political acts like stealing, or anti-social acts
such as drunkenness and disorderly conduct. The police would
then be "responsible." But during periods of extreme economic
stress and direct political protest, the ties binding police to the
demands of law and order became more fragile. As their communities became mobilized against the dominant social and economic order, the claims of their class and ethnic identity would
press more heavily on the police. Such was the case in Troy during the mid-1870s and in the early 1880s.

In the midst of the 1873 puddler strike, an imbroglio erupted
between county and city police which would threaten the
working-class community for years to come. Its relationship to
labor protest remained indirect, for the moment, but these simultaneous conflicts prefigured a time when the two fronts would
become one. Each conflict involved two management goals: to
discipline the predominantly Irish ironworkers and their allies,
and to maintain law and order so as to protect entrepreneurial
interests and priorities.

A series of small strikes began it all. In January, 1873, sixty
men at the Bessemer Steel Works walked out after rejecting company efforts to change their wages from the customary "day system" to the "ton system." According to the former system, the
men received $2.25 per day and worked about ten heats; accord-
ing to the latter, they would be expected to work eleven heats.[37]
When Chester Griswold, their employer, reversed his policy,
they returned to work. Four months later, he implemented a
"ticket system" (time cards) for the laborers. The machinists and
blacksmiths claimed this was "a species of servitude that they will

not submit to," and promptly gave two weeks' strike notice. Again Griswold retreated and agreed to postpone implementation of the system.[38] Thus failed efforts, early in the depression, to increase productivity and maintain worker discipline. The lesson was not lost upon management: once again the need for greater authority and more decisive action had been demonstrated.

It was apparent, too, on June 10, when the puddlers at Burden's nail factory—members of the Empire Forge of the Sons of Vulcan—struck against an arbitrary foreman. The foreman had refused to allow a puddler to return to a rebuilt furnace which he had earlier operated. When workers complained, claiming that he was being vindictive, the foreman threatened to move or discharge anyone he pleased. He was thus challenging not an individual, but overall job security and the union itself; in response, the puddlers walked out. James Burden, a managing partner, supported his foreman and offered back pay to the strikers in exchange for their permanent departure. They refused, he closed the plant, and the strike became a lockout.

Complicating the issue was a subsequent clash between the two rival police forces. Both manufacturers and Republicans wanted to have the Rensselaer County police replace Troy's police, a largely Irish force with family and community ties to the Irish working class. On August 7, 1873, the city police refused to hand over their authority, barricading themselves into the three stationhouses for about a month. In November the courts ruled that the act establishing the county force was illegal, and 5,000 Troy workingmen celebrated the victory with bonfires and a triumphant march through the city.[39] Although this victory parade was the only evidence of worker sympathy for and involvement in the cause of the local police, incidents growing out of strikes and violence over the next few years confirmed the existence of their bond.

Meanwhile, the puddler lockout continued, seemingly unaffected by the police issue. A national arbitration committee was sent by the annual convention of the Sons of Vulcan, then meeting in Troy, to confer with the Burdens; the committee advised the city's puddlers to return to work and concentrate upon matters more substantial than a single obnoxious foreman.[40] This report was followed by a stormy debate, and the convention dele-

gates resolved instead to "sustain the Troy brothers in their present struggle against the tyrannical actions of Langley, their boss,
in removing union brothers in order to make room for inferior
workmen, or in other words, woodchoppers, whom he expects to
use for his tools in case of emergency."[41] The *Vulcan Record*'s
account further clarified the issue: Troy's iron manufacturers had
collusively established a de facto blacklist. When released without
a discharge paper, a puddler could not find similar work
elsewhere in Troy. This paper, management said, was a "a kind of
passport conveying a secret understanding between the iron
manufacturers of that section that the bearer of such document
can be employed."[42] Discovering a secret conspiracy of ironmasters arrayed against them, the Vulcans united behind Troy's
puddlers.

Union membership quickly soared, and money poured in to
sustain the puddlers and their families. Seventy-eight puddlers
joined the two Troy forges in August. The National Forge sent
$1,375 to sustain the Empire Forge, and an additional $583 was
received in donations from puddler locals across the country
and from the Troy stonemasons' and tailors' unions. For the seventeen weeks that the National Forge supported the walkout,
each of seventy-three strikers received an average of $34.[43]

Again the manufacturers took the offensive. On October 3,
James Burden arranged to have Erastus Corning discharge all of
those puddlers' helpers who had worked for Burden before the
dispute. It was done, the *Times* reported, "to throw the strikers
entirely on their own resources, and to more speedily bring them
to terms."[44] When all of Troy's iron and steel mills closed down
the next day, ostensibly because of the depression, 3,100 men
discovered themselves out of work. Notices appeared two weeks
later announcing a 15 percent wage decrease (10 percent less than
the usual winter wage), and the stoppage became a strike. By
mid-November, a month after they had walked out, the workers
at the Rensselaer and Albany works resumed work, only to find
that the reduction had been revised upward to 20 percent. On
December 5, when negotiations between the Burdens and their
striking puddlers suddenly broke off, Corning and Company announced a plant shutdown.

Simultaneously, rumors spread through the worker community that the nation's leading iron mill proprietors had decided "to steal the working men's thunder" and move against them. The closing of Corning's works was supposedly a part of that plan.[45] Two days later, on December 8, the puddlers at Burden's mill reached a settlement with the manufacturers. The agreement granted much to the strikers: the foreman was retained, but his authority was undercut; no employee could be discharged by him. The Burdens agreed to oversee the forge department personally, and promised to abolish the "infamous discharge or passport system . . . from the works."[46] That winter, the Sons of Vulcan reported, Troy's puddler forges had doubled in number—from two to four.[47] On December 10, Corning's works also resumed, though the terms of settlement are unclear. Thus, six months after it began, the longest labor conflict in Troy's iron industry ended. Originally just a strike among Burden's puddlers, it eventually overlapped with a struggle to control the police as well as millhands in Troy's three large ironworks. The "obnoxious" foreman remained, but more important, the discharge system had been eliminated and the union had grown stronger. Little did the puddlers suspect that an even more extended and bitter test awaited them. Having failed to break the union with a prolonged lockout and crippling wage reduction, and having failed to replace the local police with a more sympathetic force, Troy's ironmasters would next try to replace union with non-union labor and would defend these scabs with their own special police force.

The "Reign of Terror" Begins

For workers, Troy's labor history during the mid-1870s was less a Gilded Age than an Age of Resistance. The collective strengths of ironworkers and their employers continued to be tested into the 1870s, but the tone of such encounters changed sharply, especially after the 1873–74 puddler strike, when management decided to import non-union labor. Lengthy strikes and recurrent violence marked these depression years, with bitterness and violence continuing through 1885. Although the protest corresponded to dramatic fluctuations in the income of skilled ironworkers, at issue were more than purely economic questions. Protest was also in response to efforts to destroy the unions, and ultimately their political and social power, in Troy. Two lengthy strikes, and the attendant violence, suggest as much.

Aggressive employer behavior continued after 1873, when such tactics as time cards, a black list, and discharge papers already had failed, owing to worker resistance. This entrepreneurial assault on the union movement had its impact on working-class political life as well. After all, strike violence often overflowed into the city streets, bringing together the political and social worlds of the police and politicians, as well as those of workers and ironmasters. Workers reorganized politically to meet this challenge from management. In July, 1875, the city's trade unions organized the Industrial Council of Troy. They elected the president of the Troy iron molders' union, John J. Grace, as council president, and proclaimed their intention to help unions in difficulty with management, to sustain workingmen's candidates, and to bind weaker labor organizations to the strong ones.[48]

In November, 1875, Troy workingmen rallied under the leadership of familiar faces from the molders' union and again nominated their own candidate for the state legislature. The meeting was chaired by their 1866 candidate, George Thompson, and the main speaker was Dugald Campbell, the fiery Scot. John J. Grace, a reform candidate representing the Tilden wing of the Democratic party, was their choice. In this return to politics, the Troy Working Men's party garnered 16 percent of the vote and Grace came in third.[49]

During the next years, molders and puddlers continued to be placed on the Industrial Council of Troy. Working with the state convention of trades' assemblies, the council sought to form an umbrella group that would unite the labor organizations into a national federation. Its members also campaigned and testified before the state legislature for an eight-hour law, and against convict labor in the stove and the shirt-and-collar trades.[50] For the 1876 legislative elections they endorsed, apparently without much enthusiasm, two candidates: the Democratic candidate from the Troy district, and Aaron P. Williams, a Greenback shoemaker from Green Island, in the neighboring Albany County district. Williams received only 2 percent of the vote, and the Democratic party candidate won handily.[51] In February, 1877, the general committee of the Working Men's party met to consider the two

Democratic candidates for mayor: the incumbent, Edward Murphy, or the "reform" candidate, Thomas Norton. Its choice was relatively easy. Norton was a one-time molder and alderman who had led and encouraged their strikes, but later, as "mediator" during the 1874–75 puddler lockout, he had betrayed the union. The committee supported Murphy, and explained their position: ". . . Norton having counselled and encouraged the workingmen to strike for their rights, and having preceded a procession of them in the streets of this city . . . in this most trying hour of their distress this man Norton deserted their ranks and became an ally to their foes, gaining for himself the profits of the overseer of a work shop and the disdain of every honest man."[52] Being endorsed by the Working Men's party, Mayor Murphy was easily reelected. Since the mayor appointed the police board, Murphy's reelection turned out to be an integral part of the continuing conflict between ironworkers and their employers.

Employer-employee relations remained subdued for most of 1874, as the mills and foundries frequently closed or ran on a part-time schedule; however, protest entered a new, more militant stage before the year was out. Late in September, when work resumed, steelworkers were informed that their wages would be based on tonnage, not on the work day. Anxious for work, they accepted the new pay system without protest—but the ironworkers did not. When the ironworks posted notice of a 22 percent wage decrease, the puddlers resisted. Advised by President Harris of the National Forge that their reduced salary would put them far below the rest of the country, and convinced that the wages would be impossible to live on, the puddlers, "generally favor[ing] arbitration," asked management to meet with them at Molders' Hall. The ironmasters, however, refused to negotiate so long as Harris was present. No ironmaster appeared, although Chester Griswold offered to meet with the men in his office anytime. Consequently, even before the struggle commenced, the manufacturers had in effect refused to recognize the Vulcans or to negotiate with them.[53]

Supported by other iron mill workers, the 258 members of the Sons of Vulcan in the five Troy area forges determined to strike rather than accept the wage reduction, submission, and impoverishment. The heaters joined them, and the Troy iron mills and Bessemer Steel Works were forced to close. Many strikers then hired out to harvest potatoes and apples and immediately left town. By November the puddlers and their helpers had begun to receive funds from the International union. Except for small amounts used for the return fare of imported would-be Troy puddlers and for the traveling expenses of the fund-raising committees, the money was divided among strikers. Single men received a few dollars a month less than married men, and helpers received substantially less. The strike lasted thirty-one weeks; during that time, a married puddler received perhaps $40 and a single man about $25.[54] Unfortunately, the walkout affected those other than unionized puddlers and heaters. In mid-November, most hands at the Bessemer Steel Works accepted the 20 percent reduction and returned to their jobs.

Since the mill could not operate unless the six striking heaters agreed to work, John A. Griswold, proprietor of both the steel works and the Rensselaer Iron Works, decided to take action. On November 24, 1874, he started up the Bessemer works, using helpers to replace the striking heaters, and the next day he resumed work at one of the Rensselaer mills with mostly "green hands"—untrained, non-union labor.[55] Five years earlier, at the 1870 annual convention of the Sons of Vulcan, the National Forge president had warned puddlers of "employers' violence." When workers resisted a wage reduction, the employer as landlord, grocer, and whiskey dealer (the "store system") could thrust the mother and her baby "out of the shanty which the employer had erected."[56] Similarly, non-union workers thrust out union men. The ironworkers responded immediately and forcefully. "Two [non-union] Sons of the 'Emerald Isle' " quit on their first day at work, influenced by the advice of their wives, who warned that they would surely be murdered if they stayed on.[57] Threats filled the air. Two foremen were stoned and, two days later, seven policemen had to be stationed at the steel works to protect the hired hands.[58] The manufacturers now began to organize, and the battle for the survival of the puddlers' union started.

The puddlers at the nail factory had rejected a sliding scale— that is, a wage advance of ten cents for every puddled ton of iron when iron prices advanced one-tenth cent on the pound. But, at the beginning of the new year, the heaters and rollers accepted a

20 percent salary cut. Since production could not resume until the puddlers returned, the Burdens decided to replace their puddlers with non-union labor. At the same time, Corning's Albany Iron Works also resumed with non-union puddlers, thereby becoming Troy's last ironworks to adopt this tactic. By mid-January, 1875, a concerted effort was underway to crush the puddlers' union.

The manufacturers pushed forward with all the political and social pressure they could muster. Rumors spread that Corning's striking puddlers would be evicted from the company tenements.[59] The Burdens moved to convert their warehouse into a dormitory for the non-union puddlers, and a month later the Rensselaer Iron Works opened a boardinghouse for its scabs.[60] The firms began to place advertisements in New York and Philadelphia newspapers for non-union puddlers. Those who came—some themselves striking puddlers from Bridgeton, New Jersey—were then forced to sign "yellow dog" contracts pledging that they would have nothing to do with the union.[61] The manufacturers turned their iron mills into garrisons guarded by twenty city police and eight "specials"—armed guards imported from New York City and elsewhere.[62] These "specials," not being residents of Troy, only further alienated the local community when they brandished their guns. On one occasion the Burdens had to disarm and send back to New York two of the "specials," who had been arrested. "These 'worthies' had gotten drunk and amused themselves by perambulating the street, looking for striking puddlers to fight them, indecently exposing their persons, and firing off their pistols to the great danger of the lives of the people in the vicinity."[63]

The predominantly Irish ironworkers responded vigorously to the use of scabs—not unlike their forefathers in Ireland only thirty years earlier. Shortly after Corning's and Burden's mills resumed work, non-union puddlers found themselves the targets of stonings and assaults by gangs of teenage boys and unemployed or striking ironworkers. Throughout the winter and spring, attacks were a daily occurrence. In one incident, five shots were fired down at the puddlers from Scotch Hill.[64] Another time Edward Cough, an expelled member of the puddlers' union who turned scab, had to have a police escort back to the mills and had to be protected from a hostile and threatening crowd of 200 people.[65] (Ironically, the previous year's lockout had been fought in Cough's behalf.) Violence became a daily fact of life in south Troy.

The protest extended to the entire community and demonstrated the importance of the existing network for worker support. Wives of several non-union puddlers complained that strikers' wives intimidated, annoyed, and even assaulted them at every opportunity.[66] When a man who had been mistaken for a non-union heater was shot, the police could only obtain "evasive answers" about the affair from iron ward residents.[67] Furthermore, iron manufacturers complained that some puddlers were receiving public relief. Management alleged that the "leaders in the strike in this city obtained money by subscription from the politicians and office holders."[68] Indeed, the striking puddlers were supported financially by their community; contributions to their cause included $300 from the Troy iron molders' union, $100 from the Troy stove mounters' union, $50 from the Troy machinists' and blacksmiths' union, and, most significantly, $510.75 from local fund-raising events and general contributions.[69] Benefit picnics provided one means of financing strikes and labor organizations. Held on an island in the Hudson River, such picnics involved extra horsecars, boats, or trains to transport the large and enthusiastic crowds. These all-day affairs included food, parades, athletic contests (from baseball and boxing to three-legged races), bonfires, fireworks, and speeches by state and area union leaders.

Money collected at such affairs went toward support of the puddlers' strike, which continued into the spring of 1875. President Harris encouraged Troy's Vulcans by reminding them that spring orders would put additional pressure on manufacturers to submit. In addition, the union expected a favorable settlement of another major strike in Pittsburgh; it felt that settlement there would further improve the bargaining position of Troy's puddlers.[70] Then, on April 16, word came that the Pittsburgh strike had ended with what the *New York Times* reported as "a victory for the puddlers."[71] Within a week and a half, negotiations quietly began between the Burdens and a committee of union puddlers. By May 5 the wage dispute between all the ironmasters and the puddlers had ended. The latter, who in October had faced a reduction from $4.80 to $3.75 per ton (the helper received one-third of this wage), now accepted $4.47½ per ton with a 12½ cents per ton increase for the helpers. Thus the original 22 percent decrease was held to about 8 percent.[72]

But two important questions had not been resolved: Would the non-union puddlers now be dismissed, and would the union rules be followed? On these issues the manufacturers remained adamant. Negotiations suddenly ended on May 8 and, according to the local papers, a "reign of terror," a "saturnalia of crime," including incendiarism, followed in south Troy. Non-union puddlers were attacked or stoned. In one incident, after a union and a non-union puddler were arrested for fighting, an angry crowd of 2,000 men and women gathered. Stones were thrown; the union man was freed, and the scab was attacked. "Even the women in the crowd were calling out for blood," stated one account. In the end, the scab was arrested, fined $25, and jailed for two months; the union puddler went unpunished.[73]

Non-union men could not walk through the ironworker community without fear of attack, and, as the 1873 worker sympathy parade for the police had foreshadowed, Troy's police and courts were unsympathetic to their plight. In the police court, they claimed, "a union man has been fined $3 for a serious offence and allowed to go on credit, while a non-union man would be fined $25 for a trivial offence."[74] Company officials finally reached an accord with the puddlers: they agreed not to interfere with the union, but still would not dismiss the non-union men. Having been on strike for thirty-one weeks and unemployed for almost fifty consecutive weeks, the puddlers agreed. On May 18, 1875, their walkout officially ended.

Their victory was incomplete as long as non-union puddlers remained in Troy, so intimidation of scabs continued. On May 19, the first group quit the Albany Iron Works under police escort. A crowd whistled the "Rogue's March" and threw stones at them. A few weeks later, Rensselaer's scab boardinghouse closed, most of the remaining non-union men left town, and the "reign of terror" ended. The puddlers and the ironworker community had preserved their union, maintained their integrity and power in the industry, and demonstrated surprising social and political power.

The puddlers' victory did little for Troy's molders. Since the 1866 lockout, the molders' union and the stove manufacturers had worked out an arbitration procedure that had settled the more recent disputes. Management and union officials each chose two representatives to constitute an arbitration committee, and those four agreed upon a fifth member. In June, 1873, for example, such a committee satisfactorily settled a labor-management dispute at Giles's Foundry.[75] However, when trouble arose early in 1875 over a wage reduction at Foxell and Jones' Foundry, the two sides could not agree on a fifth man. A lockout followed, and the firm immediately hired non-union molders.[76] Thus, while the Troy Vulcans were locked in their struggle against the use of non-union men, Troy's molders' union confronted a similar threat. Again violence erupted. Ironically—and in a commentary on ironworker mobility—one of the proprietors, James Foxell, had been a "most valued union molder" in the Clinton Foundry during the 1866 lockout.[77]

In mid-February, 1875, Foxell and Jones placed a notice in the *Troy Daily Times* stating that they would protect their new molders and not employ old ones. They also published some of the wages of union molders for the past year. The workmen saw the announcement as a challenge and the salary list as an unjustifiable exposure of their private affairs. Consequently, a scab was attacked by three union molders when he bragged to them that he held one of their jobs. But the company felt Troy courts were too lenient and pro-union, and it obtained arrest warrants for the three molders in the village of Lansingburgh.[78]

A few days later gunfire erupted in another confrontation. After work on February 19, Michael Jones, the co-owner of Foxell and Jones', and seven of his armed employees left the foundry by sleigh. They encountered some two hundred hooting schoolboys, a few of whom tried to hitch rides on the back of the sleigh. The company men panicked. Fearing an attack, they fired into the crowd, wounding a boy as well as a union molder innocently walking along the street. Jones and one of his non-union hands were subsequently arrested and released on $2,000 bail each. As a result of this incident, management hired special police to guard its foundry. The Rensselaer County grand jury, hearing conflicting testimony, handed down no indictments, but all concerned had learned the price of violence. Until the spring of 1876, the molders and their adversaries remained noticeably subdued.[79]

In April, 1876, two drunken non-union men paraded through south Troy bragging that they were employed in Filley's Foundry on Green Island. They had evidently just been hired in that village west of Troy, located on a large island in the Hudson River, and the news of their hiring created a stir among the molders. A few incendiary attempts at the foundry failed. Then came the attack, described above, of fifty to one hundred masked and armed "Molly Maguires" on the boardinghouse next to Filley's, where fifteen non-union molders and four special policemen were living.[80] Denouncing the attack, the molders' union denied all knowledge of it. Indeed, as subsequent events demonstrated, molders were not the only ones threatened by the use of scabs.

Troy's entire ironworker community depended on the strength and vitality of the molders' union—as became clear a few days later when Halsey Alexander, a non-union molder from Filley's, unwisely visited a south Troy tavern on Saturday night. Alexander's father, a temperance lecturer, also ran a scab boardinghouse. After being threatened by several men, Alexander and two others escaped, ducking into a cigar store. A crowd of several thousand soon surrounded the store. Though Alexander was under police escort, presumably for his own safety, bricks and stones began to rain down; then Alexander shot into the crowd, someone shot back, and a union molder, William Sheehan, was fatally wounded.[81] At the inquest, one policeman termed the crowd "desperate"; another witness, a molder, insisted it had been orderly until Alexander fired. The jury reached a verdict of innocent after the coroner demonstrated that the fatal bullet had not been fired from Alexander's gun.[82] The working-class community, however, had already honored its own: 2,000 trade unionists from Troy and Albany had joined 400 members of the Troy molders' union at Sheehan's funeral procession five days earlier. Five to ten thousand sympathizers lined the streets, with others on rooftops and at windows.[83] Once more violence was sobering, and quiet returned for a brief time.

The fall of 1876 arrived with notices of impending wage reductions, and with company talk about leaving for non-union cities where wages were lower,[84] so molders again prepared to defend their interests. A new dispute began when, complaining of "great competition in the stove trade," the stove founders posted announcements of wage decreases ranging from 10 to 30 percent, to start December 4. A replay of the 1874–75 puddler strike followed. The molders took their tools home with them and refused to work; the large Clinton Foundry reacted immediately, and was joined by a few of the smaller firms. They would open as scheduled and employ scab labor if necessary. The union molders first tried to open negotiation for an equitable and reasonable settlement. Union president John J. Grace wrote to George C. Burdett, one of the owners, requesting a meeting with management which would take up the economic plight of all concerned.[85] Burdett, in turn, asked the other manufacturers to join him for a discussion of Grace's letter, but not one appeared. They would no longer have anything to do with the unions, the founders declared, and with unintended irony proclaimed that "they will treat these men hereafter as men and not machines in the hands of others."[86]

In January, 1877, at the sixth annual National Stove Manufacturers' Association convention in Albany, a Troy manufacturer named Charles Eddy alluded to the firm stand of the founders on the issue of labor's right to fix wages. What he left unsaid, however, was readily apparent to the molders: the founders threatened to emasculate the union's power—its ability to protect its membership and the community that relied on it. The manufacturers fully understood what was at issue. As one stated a few months later, "This conflict, it is claimed relates not so much to wages as to the control of the business. The molders limit the number of apprentices to one for each eight men. . . . The rules allow no molder to work who is not a member of the union. The union claims the right to regulate the wages at any time."[87] Thus the confrontation: using their political and social connections in the working-class community, union molders defended their influence over their living and working conditions; mobilizing vast financial resources and power, the founders attacked the union.

The conflict again resulted in disorder. In mid-February, 1877, a fire mysteriously broke out at the Clinton Foundry. The firm posted a $1,000 reward, but no arsonist was identified. Then unknown assailants attacked three non-union employees at the Clinton Foundry and shot one in the leg.[88] When, increasing the pressure on the union, another Troy foundry opened in mid-March with non-union molders, violence erupted in south Troy. It increased over the last two weeks in March, as scab molders were stoned, jeered, chased, assaulted, and shot. Crowds of a thousand or so—men, women and boys—gathered nightly outside the Clinton Foundry to intimidate non-union hands who tried to escape back to their homes. Only a "large force" of police could contain the trouble. Then an Albany founder announced the signing of a five-year contract with Sing Sing prison to have the inmates make stoves. It was also reported that a Troy firm planned to employ convict labor for work at the Clinton prison.[89] By employing convicts, management threatened both the wage system and the regulation of apprentices, elements central to union power. As the founders had broadened their attack, the molders intensified their response.

From March 24 to 26, 1877, a "reign of terror" again existed, according to the *Troy Daily Times*. Large crowds gathered near the foundries, hooting, stoning, and generally trying to intimidate the non-union men as they left work. They did not disperse until two molders were arrested.[90] Even then they did not quit, however; they only changed their tactics. Through much of April, covert but violent intimidation replaced the public demonstrations. Teams of men ambushed and tried to shoot non-union molders on quiet and deserted alleys and streets. Every day scabs were stoned or assaulted; as has been suggested, the violence resembled the tradition of Irish peasant resistance embodied in the terrorist tactics of the Molly Maguires.

Protests against management policies took other forms as well. Members of the Industrial Council of Troy heard Dugald Campbell call the non-union molders "Benedict Arnolds," and they protested attempts by local newspapers (the *Times* and the *Whig*) to turn public opinion against the molders. One council resolution, supported by the iron molders, also publicly opposed the violence because it "only serves to aid the employers by alienating public sympathy."[91] But individual molders and their hungry brethren did not heed this disavowal. Moreover, the disputes affected not just the union, but also the entire ironworker community. When the Republican *Troy Daily Times* (whose editor, John M. Francis, was the brother of a leading ironmaster) complained that police "inefficiency" prevented apprehension of the troublemakers, it also hinted at community involvement and Irish working-class solidarity.[92] Between 1874 and 1877 manufacturers had mounted a drive to discipline the workforce, and police had been called upon to enforce order. Seeking to crush the union movement, they had imported scab labor. Resistance had prompted the police in November, 1874, to station seven officers at the steel works to protect non-union workers, and by January, 1875, the ironworks had become an armed camp, with guards recruited and imported by management.[93] Again, when scab laborers were almost daily assaulted, the police could only obtain "evasive answers" from iron ward residents.[94] The police appeared powerless, thought the *Troy Daily Times*, and the newspaper had a point: in the last few weeks of the violence in 1875, for example, only one puddler was convicted in the courts, and he was fined only $10.[95]

Many were assaulted in 1876, and five were wounded and one killed (a union molder) in shooting incidents relating to renewed ironworker political protest.[96] By this time manufacturers had hired armed guards to do what the regular city police seemed unable to do: maintain law and order. As the depression deepened and the violence increased, they had found the police increasingly ineffectual; during a bitter lockout of molders in 1877, Troy was characterized as an "assassin's carnival."[97] At this time, the *Times* complained, "outrages" continued while "inefficient" police "ignored" them. Furthermore, prosecution was hindered by community opinion, which rested with the molders. According to the *Times*, "the police find it very difficult to obtain the slightest evidence against union molders from any of the residents of south Troy in this or other cases of a similar nature."[98] Finally, as the *Press* observed in reporting an assault upon a non-union molder: "the strangest part of the affair is that citizens who were looking on urged the pursuers on to the cowardly attack."[99]

The business community's campaign for an effective police network took on new significance during these labor struggles of 1876 and 1877. The violence accompanying them confirmed fears that Irish police would act in collusion with Irish workers. Again violence escalated, although no assailants, or even witnesses, could be found. The local press charged police negligence and implied collusion with law-breaking molders or their supporters. Such charges laid bare the issue of criminality within the context of nineteenth-century urban, industrial dislocations: Who, indeed, were the criminals? What was the function of the police?

It has been possible to obtain the names of thirty-nine people arrested for assaulting non-union ironworkers during labor-related protest between 1874 and 1884 (Table 6.1). Virtually all were skilled workers, molders or puddlers trying to "convince" other workers not to scab. Not everyone could be tracked down in census records, for they were likely to be more transient than most, perhaps jumping bail for work elsewhere. "The aggressors seem to be privileged," the *Times* lamented. "If arrested, they are either fined $3 or admitted to bail, and that is the last of the case."[100] Only thirteen were traceable through newspaper accounts to census records or the city directory. Young males of Irish background, they were often single or newly married with no children. Only one, a stove-mounter in 1884, seems to have been over thirty years old. Those involved in the 1883 killing of a twenty-eight-year-old union molder, William Hutchinson, were more typical. His assailants, aged eighteen and nineteen respectively, also wounded Arthur Imeson, who was twenty-three, and Joseph Winestone (no age available). Two brothers arrested for charging the police in order to lynch Hutchinson's assailants were twenty-two and twenty-three years old.[101] Interestingly, most of these militant molders, puddlers, and mounters lived not in south Troy, but among the more respectable skilled working class in wards slightly north or uphill (east) of the central business district. Moreover, like Troy's puddlers and molders generally, they were overwhelmingly of Irish extraction.

These thirty-nine represented only those protestors who engaged in violence and were apprehended. Almost daily during 1875–77 and 1883–84 there were protests by crowds. Between 1875 and 1876, for example, when the ironworks, then described as like a "military fort," were guarded by a hundred men, newspaper accounts reported protesting crowds of "two hundred schoolboys," or "two hundred men," or "teenage gangs of boys and unemployed and striking iron workers," or "two thousand

TABLE 6.1. Militants Arrested for Assaulting Non-Union Labor During Troy's "Reigns of Terror," 1874–84

Name	Arrest date	Occupation	Age	Ethnicity	Marital status	Disposition	Resid (Ward
Joe Malone	11–19–74						
Joseph Murray	12–9–74	puddler				$500 bail	
Albert Pryor	2–15–75	molder					
John "Forty" O'Connors	2–15–75	molder					
John Moulton	2–15–75	puddler					
Thomas Kerwin	2–15–75	molder					
Mary Welch	2–24–75	puddler's wife			m		
Edward Burke	3–8–75	puddler				$2,000 bail	
Michael Connolly	4–6–75	puddler					
Patrick Keating	4–16–75	puddler				2 mos. in jail	
Dennis Walsh	5–10–75	puddler	30	Irish	m	freed by crowd	12th
James Ross	9–26–76	molder				freed	
Thomas "Butter" Kelly	3–28–77	molder	30	Irish	m	forfeits bond	10th
Charles Buras	4–2–77	ex-molder and ex-policeman	28	Irish	m, no child	$5,000 bail	10th
Owen Mangler	4–13–77	molder					
Roger Nailor	4–13–77	molder				$2,000 bail	
John "Wacker" Meehan	4–13–77	app. molder	25	Irish	s	$2,000 bail	
	4–30–77					10 yrs. jail	
William J. Boyle	5–5–77	molder				not guilty	
John Monahan	5–8–77	molder				$25 fine and 3 mo.	
John Flynn	6–4–77	iron laborer					
Cornelius Dorsey	6–4–77	iron laborer					
Daniel T. Delaney	6–5–77	molder	25	Irish	m, no child	$3,000 bail	8th
Charles Laundrey	6–13–77					not guilty	
Patrick McGrath	3–19–80	molder	26	Irish	s		11th
John Flanigan	3–19–80	molder					
Robert Reynolds	3–19–80	molder	36	Irish	m		12th
Joseph Winestone	5–2–83	molder				$1,000 bail	
Theodore Law	5–2–83	molder	22	USA	s	hung jury; re-tried 6 mos.	5th
Arthur Imeson	5–2–83	molder	23	English	s		2nd
Peter Rankon	5–29–83	molder				dismissed	
William Ryan	5–29–83	molder				dismissed	
Harry E. Vanyea	12–21–83	molder					
Thomas Allen	1–7–84	molder					
Charles Dwyer	1–7–84	molder					
Fred Low	1–7–84	molder	26	English	s		5th
Frank Canfield	6–5–84	stove mounter	36	Irish	m	$60 or 60 days	10th
Joseph Larkin	6–5–84	stove mounter	27	Irish	s	$60 or 60 days	10th
Patrick Ryan	7–1–84	molder	29	Irish	m, no child	$250 and 1 yr.	10th
Thomas Farley	7–1–84					$250 or 6 mos.	

men and women," and "several thousand."[102] Small groups of boys and striking workers also gathered daily to insult and intimidate non-union laborers going or returning from work.

These crowds had two obvious characteristics: they were youthful, and they supported the worker community. Newspaper reports, as noted above, repeatedly described the corner gangs as "boys." Though no statistical portrait of the crowd can be drawn, participants seemed to have been generally younger than those apprehended.[103] But, with the exception of the crowd's youthfulness, assaulting molders and puddlers were indistinguishable from them. The voices of militants would be lost in the "hootings of a mob of Irish women and men."[104] Law-breaking workers and their support community were both young, Irish, and working class, remarkably like the larger criminal population arrested during these years. The similarity complicated police work.[105] Moreover, crowds did not give merely passive support to striking workers; rather, as in the case of William Hutchinson, they tried to mete out vigilante justice to non-union labor and to protect union members. Striking ironworkers received community support from women, children, family, friends, and neighbors. One case may serve as an example. Joseph Murray, a puddler, had been arrested in December, 1874, during a labor dispute. Subsequently, Murray apparently joined the Troy police force, and six months later he was called upon to settle a fight between a union puddler, Dennis Walsh, and a non-union puddler, William McCloskey. He arrested both men, but a crowd of about two thousand gathered to free Walsh and attack McCloskey. Stones were thrown, and police reserves were called in to prevent a riot. McCloskey, who had been drunk, was fined $25; Walsh went free.[106]

The cordial relationship between Irish police and Irish workers, reinforced by the Irish community's refusal to aid the authorities, forced employers to turn to other authorities, namely, the courts and the National Guard. Their success in bringing assault charges against three molders before the Rensselaer County grand jury finally defeated the union. The first and most celebrated case involved John "Whacker" Meehan, a twenty-five-year-old apprentice molder accused of shooting a non-union molder. He was tried by a jury overwhelmingly rural and Protestant in composition,

which included eight farmers and four carpenters. Only one carpenter came from Troy, and the sole molder called up was dismissed. During the trial, witnesses insisted that the scab had fired
first, but, to the spectator's dismay, Meehan was convicted. The
judge, in sentencing him, admitted, "There was a serious conflict in
the evidence in your case. . . ." But then, noting that similar
crimes in Troy had become "alarmingly prevalent," he prescribed
the maximum term: ten years at hard labor. Violence which had
begun in order to protect working-class rights had ended in a trial
with political overtones. Though evidence was lacking, both judge
and jury apparently chose to make Meehan an example to those
supporting the molders' cause. The judge sentenced Meehan, but
the jury convicted the entire Irish ironworker community.[107]

Though the second molder jumped bail and the third was exon-
erated by a new jury, the union seems to have lost its
impetus[108]—after all, a union molder had been given a ten-year
sentence, while scabs continued to work. On May 30, 1877, the
Albany iron molders' union suspended its constitution and by-
laws for six months; on June 21, as "a tactic" for winning back
their jobs, the Troy iron molder's union conceded to the founders. It, too, suspended all union rules for six months and declared
all shops open.[109]

After 1873, then, aggressive employer behavior was the dominant factor. Such attempted controls as time cards, the ton system, and the use of non-union and convict labor threatened to
impose rigid discipline and to sacrifice the independence of
skilled workmen upon the altar of efficiency and control. In the
industrializing world, craftsmen gradually lost the personal satis-
faction, dignity, and sense of achievement once known to the independent artisan. This danger was especially apparent to the
molders and puddlers, who still had a distinct work subculture
with pre-factory work rhythms. Aggressive management behavior
threatened their very skills and, ultimately, their standard of living and world of work. The workforce reacted militantly, with
strikes and violence, and employers appealed to the political
authorities—the police, the mayor, or the courts—to preserve order
and to discipline the workers.

But local politics had changed radically since mid-century.
Troy's ironmasters, often mayors themselves, had controlled polit-

ical patronage and, with it, appointments to both the courts and the police force. Since the war, however, they had lost their leverage, as two Irish mayors were elected with the support of the Working Men's party. In response, employers generally led a Republican effort to replace the city police with the county force. Their effort had failed, but the relationship between the police and the labor struggles became more explicit after 1873 and illustrated two major themes. First, worker protest must be viewed within its broader social and political context. Second, having lost local political control, Troy's industrialists utilized regional and national resources, and they appealed to the state for assistance in destroying working-class community control. We have two examples: the Harmony Mills' emphasis on national markets, and the stove manufacturers' recourse to a national founders' association and to a county grand jury. That the National Guard was called in to avert trouble during the great railroad strike of late July, 1877, serves as a further example. Significantly, two companies of the 10th Regiment, composed almost entirely of molders, were deliberately not activated.[110]

The stove founders managed temporarily to blunt the power of Troy's molders and, given their leadership role, of the labor movement in general. The molders had defeated at least one company, Foxell and Jones', the first to have hired non-union molders. But then its management rented the premises at the Auburn State Prison for the manufacture of stoves and announced that it would leave Troy.[111] Its departure did not portend well for Troy's ironworkers. Their one victory had been costly and illusory, and the Age of Resistance had scarcely begun.

NOTES

1. Foner, *History of the Labor Movement*, I, 417–20.

2. Andrews, "Nationalisation"; Commons, *History of Labor in the United States*, II, pt. 5, pp. 55–56. The death in 1869 of William Sylvis, the champion of the cooperative movement, should not be minimized, either.

3. *Troy Daily Times*, November 14, 1874.

4. Eleventh Census, 1890, *Census Reports*, Vol. 6; *Manufacturing Industries*, pt. 2, *Statistics of Cities*, gives wages for Cohoes's Harmony Mills. The low wage differential for female spinners probably relates to the introduction of ring-spinning in the 1880s. See also Lars S. Sandberg, "American Rings and English Mules; The Role of Economic Rationality," in *Technological Change: The United States and Britain in the Nineteenth Century*, ed. S. B. Saul (London, 1970).

5. This reference appears in a UAW newspaper, *Ammunition* (1949), quoted in Loren Baritz, *The Servants of Power: A History of the Use of Social Science in American Industry* (New York, 1960).

6. *Cohoes Cataract*, May 9, 1857.

7. Ibid., December 10, 1864.

8. Ibid., July 21, 1860, December 10, 1864.

9. Ibid., October 4, 1856.

10. Ibid., June 22, 1867, April 4, 1868, October 11, November 1, 1873.

11. *New York Herald*, quoted ibid., November 8, 1873.

12. *Troy Budget*, quoted ibid., November 29, 1873.

13. Ibid., April 24, 1875.

14. Ibid., October 23, 1875.

15. "A Constant Reader" to the editor, *Cohoes Daily News*, October 26, 1875.

16. *Troy Daily Times*, November 1, 1875.

17. *Cohoes Daily News*, May 24, 1876.

18. *Cohoes Cataract*, May 27, 1876.

19. *Cohoes Daily News*, June 6–7, 1876.

20. *Cohoes Cataract*, September 30, 1876, February 10, 1877.

21. Ibid., April 6, 20, 1867.

22. See ibid., March 9, 1872, March 7, 1874, March 6, 1875, March 11, 1876, March 10, 1877, March 9, 1878. In November 1874, in the gubernatorial election, Tilden (Democrat) carried the first ward, 454 to 243. In the March 1874 mayoral election, which he lost, David J. Johnston (Republican) carried it 460 to 294.

23. Ibid., November 7, 1877, January 25, 1878. Le Boeuf had been a Cohoes justice of the peace in 1871.

24. Tenth Census, 1880, *Statistics of Wages*, p. 361; *Cohoes Cataract*, January 11, March 1, 1879.

25. *Cohoes Cataract*, March 8, 1879.

26. *Troy Daily Times*, November 25, 1865, contained long articles on the Albany and the Rensselaer works. The Burden works are discussed briefly.

27. These were annual affairs, and each was duly reported. The fullest descriptions include those in *Troy Daily Times*, August 23, 1858, and *Cohoes Cataract*, September 10, 1864.

28. Judith R. Walkowitz, " 'We Are Not Beasts of the Field': Prostitution and the Campaign Against the Contagious Diseases Acts, 1864–86" (Ph.D. dissertation, (University of Rochester, 1974).

29. Cardoze, *The Police Department of Troy*.

30. *Troy Daily Times*, February 3, 1865.

31. *Troy Directory, 1865*, and *Albany Directory, 1865*.

32. *Troy Directory, 1857* and *1865*. No occupation could be found for one alderman from south Troy in 1857.

33. Cardoze, *The Police Department of Troy*, p. 40. Unfortunately, Cardoze does not recount the details of this transfer of power, though presumably the city never relinquished its right to withdraw from the Capital Police District.

34. *Troy Directory, 1865*.

35. Cardoze, *The Police Department of Troy*.

36. The pattern of police living among those whom they are expected to supervise is discussed in a study of English common prostitutes in Plymouth and Southampton: Judith R. Walkowitz, "The Making of an Outcast Group: Prostitutes and Working Women in Nineteenth-Century Plymouth and Southampton," in *A Widening Sphere*, ed. M. Vicinus (Bloomington, Ind., 1977).

37. *Troy Daily Press*, January 23, 1873; *Troy Daily Times*, January 15–30, 1873.

38. *Troy Daily Times*, May 5, 1873; *Troy Daily Press*, May 6, 1873.

39. *Troy Daily Times*, August 7–November 13, 1873.

40. *Troy Daily Press*, August 8, 1873.

41. National Forge of the Sons of Vulcan resolution, quoted ibid., August 9, 1873.

42. *Vulcan Record*, no. 12 (August 1873):55–56.

43. Ibid., pp. 54–55, 75–76.

44. *Troy Daily Times*, October 4, 1873. "A Workingman" to the editor, *Troy Daily Press*, October 4, 1873, confirmed this report, although Burden subsequently denied it.

45. *Troy Daily Times*, December 5, 1873.

46. *Vulcan Record*, no. 13 (December 1873):15.

47. Ibid., p. 5.

48. *Troy Daily Times*, July 13–14, 1875.

49. Ibid., November 2–3, 1875. Grace received 1,393 of the 8,801 votes cast for assemblyman. In comparison with the voting for secretary of state in the same wards, one-third of Grace's voters appeared to have voted Republican, either to bolt the Democratic "ring" or to vote their usual preference. See also *Troy Morning Whig*, November 3, 1875.

50. *Troy Daily Times*, January 22–28, March 25, December 20, 1876, February 16, 1877; *Troy Daily Press*, December 27, 1876.

51. *Troy Daily Times*, October 23–November 8, 1876.

52. General Committee of the Troy Working Men's party resolution, quoted in *Troy Daily Press*, February 9, 1877. See also *Troy Daily Times* of that date.

53. *Troy Daily Times*, September 26–October 15, 23, 1874; *Troy Daily Press*, October 6–7, 1874.

54. *Vulcan Record*, no. 16 (August 1875):45–46, 79–83; *Troy Daily Times*, November 6, December 1, 1874.

55. *Troy Daily Times*, November 19–25, 1874; *Troy Daily Press*, November 18–24, 1874.

56. J. O. Edwards, "Have We the Right to Organize," *Vulcan Record*, no. 5 (January 1870).

57. *Troy Daily Times*, November 25, 1874.

58. Ibid. and *Troy Daily Press*, both November 27, 1874.

59. *Troy Daily Times*, January 6, 1875.

60. Ibid., January 12, 1875; *Troy Daily Press*, March 15, 1875.

61. *Troy Daily Press*, February 13, 1875, quotes an advertisement from the *Philadelphia Press*; *Troy Daily Times*, February 17, 1875, quotes a report from the *New York World* on the Bridgeton, N.J., puddlers. *Troy Daily Times*, February 9, 1875, reported that Corning would require all puddlers "to forswear their allegiance to the union." Other firms followed suit.

62. *Troy Daily Times*, January 12, 1875; *Troy Daily Press*, February 6, 1875.

63. *Troy Daily Press* and *Troy Daily Times*, both February 6, 1875.

64. *Troy Daily Times*, April 13, 1875.

65. Ibid., February 15, 24, 1875.

66. Ibid., January 26, 1875.

67. Ibid., February 3–4, 1875.

68. Ibid., February 9, 20, 1875.

69. *Vulcan Record*, no. 16 (August 1875):45–46, 79–83.

70. *Troy Daily Press*, March 22, 1875.

71. *Troy Daily Times*, April 27, 1875, quoting the *New York Times* sometime earlier in April. See also *Troy Daily Press*, April 16, 1875.

72. *Troy Daily Press*, April 29–May 4, 1875.

73. *Troy Daily Times* and *Troy Daily Press*, both May 10, 1875.

74. *Troy Daily Times*, May 24, 1875; *Troy Morning Whig*, May 12, 1875.

75. *Troy Daily Times*, June 11–12, 1873.

76. Ibid., January 26–February 12, 1875.

77. Ibid., February 16, 1875.

78. *Troy Daily Press*, February 20, 1875; *Troy Daily Times*, February 15, 1875. No record of the men's arrest could be found.

79. *Troy Daily Press*, February 20, 1875; *Troy Morning Whig*, February 20, March 19, 1875.

80. *Troy Daily Times* and *Troy Daily Press*, both April 25, 1876.

81. *Troy Daily Times* and *Troy Daily Press*, both May 8, 1876.

82. *Troy Daily Times*, May 16–18, 1876.

83. Ibid. and *Troy Daily Press*, both May 13, 1876.

84. *Troy Daily Times*, March 4, August 23, 1876.

85. *Troy Daily Press*, December 2, 1876.

86. Ibid. and *Troy Daily Times*, both December 6, 1876.

87. *Albany Argus*, quoted in *Troy Daily Press*, March 26, 1877.

88. *Troy Daily Times*, February 19, March 5, 1877.

89. *Albany Argus*, quoted in *Troy Daily Press*, March 26, 1877.

90. *Troy Daily Times* and *Troy Daily Press*, both March 23–April 3, 1877.

91. Industrial Council of Troy resolution, quoted *Troy Daily Times*, May 4, 1877.

92. Ibid., April 9, 1877.

93. *Troy Daily Times*, January 12, 1875; *Troy Daily Press*, February 6, 1875.

94. *Troy Daily Times*, February 3–4, 1875.

95. Ibid., May 24, 1875.

96. *Troy Daily Press*, February 20, 1874, April 25, May 8, 1876; *Troy Daily Times*, April 25, May 8, 1876.

97. *Troy Daily Press*, March 23–April 3, 1877.

98. *Troy Daily Times*, April 30, 1877.

99. *Troy Daily Press*, March 22, 1877.

100. *Troy Daily Times*, May 6, 1875.

101. See Donald H. Coleman, "Patterns of Labor Violence: Troy, New York, 1883" (mimeographed; University of Rochester, May 1968), p. 21; *Troy Daily Press*, June 12, 1883.

102. *Troy Daily Press*, February 13, 20, 24, May 10, 1875, May 8, 1876; *Troy Daily Times*, February 17, 24, April 13, May 10, 1875, May 8, 1876.

103. Those arrested were older than those apprehended, for two possible reasons. First, older, more established men were more likely to be recognizable to the police. Second, people were less likely to be arrested in crowds than in more isolated incidents in which the older skilled hands, in defense of their jobs, would participate.

104. *Troy Daily Times*, March 26, 1875.

105. Crime statistics during these years are scattered, but all draw a similar portrait of the average person arrested: an immigrant working-class Irish male between the ages of 15 and 35. See, e.g., First Annual Report of the Capital Police District for the year ending November 30, 1866, in *Troy Daily Times*, December 16, 1866, or annual Troy reports in *Troy Daily Times*, February 9, 1874, December 14, 1876.

106. *Troy Daily Times*, December 7–9, 1874, May 10, 1875.

107. *Troy Daily Times* and *Troy Daily Press*, both May 24–25, 1877.

108. *Troy Daily Times*, June 13, 1877.

109. Ibid., May 31, June 22, 1877.

110. Ibid., July 25, 1877.

111. Ibid., August 6, 1877.

CHAPTER 7

The Final Debacle, 1880–84

DURING THE EARLY 1880s, strikes erupted among the Cohoes cotton workers which were much like the lengthy, bitter, and sometimes violent ironworker conflicts of the previous decade. French Canadians had by this time begun to settle into the Harmony Hill community and to unite with Irish workers against the extensive control and influence of the company. Meanwhile, textile and iron manufacturers everywhere attempted to reduce wages, break up new unions, and otherwise dominate the industries. The union movement developed new tactics to meet such attacks, and working-class resistance became widespread in both industries. Politics became a major arena for protest between labor and management, with the latter using state government and national market conditions to suit its purposes. Legislative action, court battles, and election contests became a conscious and extensive weapon for both sides in their struggle for control of the workplace, the community, and ultimately the city. Finally, by the mid-1880s, a few far-sighted employers and workers had a vision of the future of the cotton and iron industries. It was not a pretty sight: developments within each industry and city discouraged further investment, and neither Troy nor Cohoes would continue to grow. Entrepreneurs thereafter sought safer investments in non-union southern and western towns near new markets and raw materials.

COHOES

By 1880, some of the Harmony Mills paternalism had been shattered by a growing worker self-consciousness, and the cotton hands organized to resist further wage reductions. Two factors especially influenced the timing of their new organization. First, French Canadians had by now adapted to their new surroundings on Harmony Hill. Their large community had grown more stable in the previous five or six years as mill expansion ceased and immigration slowed. The French-Canadian Catholic Church flourished; a local French newspaper kept residents informed; social and political organizations, such as the French-Canadian Political Club or the Atheneum, strengthened ethnic bonds; and a French-Canadian labor leader, Samuel Sault, emerged. Second, textile labor was family work. The French-Canadian and Irish working-class families sent many of their number into the mills; family members and neighbors lived and worked together, and their prospects were interrelated. When such labor organized and protested, it relied on strong family, kinship, and neighborhood cohesion, which moved fluidly between the worlds of work and the home.

In contrast to Troy, Cohoes's cotton workers organized in a dramatic and rapid fashion. In 1878 the cotton mule-spinners formed a union. Simultaneously, Joseph P. McDonnell, a socialist Irishman from Paterson, New Jersey, founded the short-lived International Labor Union (ILU). It became a union of mostly textile workers, though McDonnell meant to organize all unskilled labor.[1] Meanwhile, in March, 1879, the Harmony Mills cotton hands suffered their fourth wage reduction in five years. During the mid-1870s they had convened some mild protest meetings and conferences with the Johnstons, and they experienced their most dramatic "success" in the 1878 elections when the Greenback-Labor candidate received 25 percent of the total vote. Late in 1879, the company raised wages 10 percent; the workers' optimism was shattered, however, when management followed up that raise with a proportionate increase in the number of yards of cloth to be cut. (The workers were paid piece rates.) Management also imposed a new policy whereby weavers were docked for every imperfectly woven piece of cloth. The net effect reduced wages further.

Disappointed and disgusted, the women weavers at Harmony Mill No. 1 struck in February, 1880. They sought a 10 percent wage increase, a lengthening of their lunch break from forty minutes to one hour, and an end to the "docking system." Their walkout, significantly, was not due to wage fluctuations; rather, it was as if their threshold of toleration had been breeched. They had accepted three successive salary cuts for the security of relatively steady and full employment and some of the emoluments of paternalism—low-cost housing and a few social amenities. Real wages may not have declined (nor real income), but textile workers seemed more aware of the actual reductions than of their effects on living standards. Moreover, as noted above, French Canadians had adapted by 1880 and, with the predominantly Irish cotton workers, had organized cohesive ethnic neighborhoods with kinship, workplace, and associational ties that could sustain protest. And protest they did. A day after it began, the February, 1880, strike became general throughout Harmony Mills as the nearly 5,000 cotton hands—men, women, and children—unanimously resolved to walk out. Unfortunately, local accounts only hint at the mechanism of trade union organization, but the workers' response suggests considerable spontaneity. Their action also indicates the centrality of family labor in households headed by the more skilled weavers and mule-spinners. Within two days the male mule-spinners had joined the female weavers in organizing three committees to run the strike. A committee on organization consisted of six men; one on finances consisted of two men and three women; and another to negotiate with management consisted of seven female weavers. A month earlier, cotton-worker organization had been limited to benevolent associations, such as the Mule Spinners' Sick and Burial Benevolent Association.[2]

Textile workers organized and strengthened their position during the walkout. Pressure from below—from female weavers—initiated the strike, inevitably producing rank-and-file leaders who exclusively staffed the negotiating committee. But the walkout was led by men—in particular, by two ex-weavers: Samuel Sault, now editor of the *Regulator*, a Cohoes labor paper; and Mark Deurden, the proprietor of a newsroom on the Hill. Even the *Cohoes Daily News*, usually unsympathetic to labor, agreed that the entire community supported the strikers.[3] The ironworkers at the Cohoes rolling mill offered $100 per week to sustain the cotton workers, and speakers such as George Gunton, the editor of the *Fall River Labor Standard*, addressed strike rallies of thousands of workers.[4] To elicit sympathy, hundreds of raggedly dressed Harmony Hill children paraded through the city, carrying banners such as "Pity our Hard Fate, No Time to Play in God's Sunshine."[5] By the time the strike had ended, after nine days, the Weavers' Union had recruited over 1,700 members and the Mule-Spinners' Association had organized all but six of Cohoes's mule-spinners. In addition, the Card Room Union had enrolled almost 300 members, and the cotton-twisters had also begun to organize.[6] The cotton textile workers had won the 10 percent wage advance, gotten their lunch break extended ten minutes, and obtained an agreement that would restrict the docking system. Most important, the workers had revealed unusual collective power.[7]

Their unions, however, won the enmity of management. Within two weeks the mule-spinners learned that the union treasurer had been given two weeks' notice for his persistence in collecting funds for a sick friend during working hours.[8] The spinners' committee decided to seek an immediate meeting with company officers to discuss the matter. One overseer refused to allow a committee member to leave work for the meeting, even though a substitute was available. The worker went anyway and was also promptly discharged. When word of this second dismissal spread, spinners throughout the mill began to walk out, and a general strike of the cotton mule-spinners followed. They demanded that the overseer be fired and that no union members be blacklisted, but the Johnstons maintained that they would "not allow anyone else to attempt to tell . . . [them] what to do."[9] The underlying issue, of course, was the continued existence of the new union.

Two days later, the weavers reversed the scenario of the earlier strike and offered support to their union brothers. The section hands likewise voted to strike against the limited docking system which was still in effect. In response, the company mobilized its power. Spinners were given thirty days' notice to vacate the company tenements; those in company boardinghouses were told that no food would be provided while the strike lasted. Management docked the strikers two weeks' back pay for not giving two weeks' notice before they struck.[10] The company also tried intimidation by having a detachment of police patrol the mills; it announced recruitment of Canadian non-union labor, and it exerted pressure on mill families by discharging non-striking maintenance men whose children were out on strike.[11]

Such pressures were partially successful, but they also disclosed another side to paternalism. Some workers returned to work; with help from overseers and their assistants, production resumed, with 21 of 140 mules and almost a third of the looms operating. But all the spinners and most of the weavers and carders remained firm. Daily crowds gathered at the mills and hooted at those who entered. Support, meanwhile, came from the Massachusetts textile centers of Lawrence and Fall River, and the revived Troy iron molders' union promised $500 per week. Then Joseph P. McDonnell, released from jail only two days earlier, arrived from Paterson to direct the strike. At a massive rally on April 3, 1880, he argued that the overseer was only a catalyst to the strike and urged that the workers not insist on his dismissal. The real issue, he declared, did not involve an unjust overseer so much as it concerned three other grievances against management: its attempts to crush the union, its use of the blacklist, and its retention of the workers' back pay.[12] McDonnell's influence was felt almost immediately. A few days later, the spinners issued a new list of resolutions, emphasizing the rights of the union and asking only that the overseer be "restrained" in the future. With this change in emphasis, McDonnell's International Labor Union and area labor leaders such as Samuel Sault, who had been unenthusiastic in their support of the strike, now gave it unqualified approval.[13]

Management adamantly continued to assert its right to fire whomever it pleased. The workers then resorted to the courts and sued the company for their back pay. On April 9, Sault announced that lawyers would file claims for the "no notice" pay. Six days later, a West Troy justice served company superintendent D. J. Johnston with 414 summonses "to show cause why the two weeks pay returned by the company should not be refunded." In a related development that same day, management received a joint committee of spinners and weavers and, for the first time, treated them with civility.[14] On April 21, the very day on which litigation was to commence, a committee of spinners met with the Johnstons. Representing the Spinners' Benevolent

Union, so they declared, they proved anxious to end their strike, even with victory apparently at hand. Obviously delighted with the conversion of the trade union into a "benevolent" union, D. J. Johnston said, "Now you talk like men." The two sides quickly reached an agreement that "no trade union will or shall be recognized," that management would not blacklist or interfere with the spinners' "society," and that the "no notice" money would be returned to the workers. For their part, the hands conceded that two especially impertinent weavers would not be rehired.[15] The compromise was ratified that same day, and the month-long strike came to an end. Thus the cotton workers had organized themselves and won a 10 percent wage advance, in addition to resisting an attempt to blacklist them and modifying company rules on docking and hours. Management also agreed to settle the "no notice" suit out of court. Although at the end they had clothed their union in the garb of a "benevolent" association, labor had reason to feel proud. After years of acquiescence, within a mere two months it had organized, twice walked out, and won victories over one of the nation's largest and most powerful corporations.

Almost two years passed before there was any further major labor trouble at the Harmony Mills. During these years, weavers' union president Samuel Sault had incurred severe financial losses; after losing his newspaper, the *Regulator*, he left Cohoes for Des Moines, Iowa.[16] Moreover, Mark Duerden, the newsdealer whose back room had served as a secret command post during the 1880 strikes, was shot by a special company policeman. It was a personal incident, however, unrelated to the earlier strikes.[17] With Duerden's death and Sault's departure, cotton-worker leadership fell onto the shoulders of Joseph Delehanty, who had become increasingly visible in the Irish and worker communities since the mid-1870s. When management posted notice on April 6, 1882, that, "owing to the depressed condition of the market," wages would be reduced about 10 percent, he quickly became one of the strike leaders. Throughout the bitter four-month strike, the cohesive working-class ethnic neighborhoods on Harmony Hill withstood, under unusual financial hardship, two separate management attempts to reopen the mills. Before the conflict ended, it demonstrated how social, political, industrial, and ethnic dimensions of working-class culture shaped labor protest.

When the 10 percent wage reduction announcement was posted, the cotton workers immediately gave two weeks' notice that they would quit rather than accept the pay cut. In this way, the "no notice" controversy of two years earlier was avoided. The *Cohoes Daily News* reported that many workers had saved some money for just such an emergency and were pleased to have the opportunity now to "vacation" and tend their small tenement gardens.[18] Few workers, however, saved much on meager textile wages, and after two months the reports of destitution became commonplace.[19] Consequently, as often occurred earlier, labor tried to avoid a bitter third strike by first offering what they thought might be reasonable alternatives to a wage reduction. The spinners organized a committee on April 16 and proposed two separate solutions to the problem of overproduction: shutdown of the mills for a month or two, or running operations on a three-quarters work schedule for a few months. The dominant *laissez-faire* ethic espoused by management might rationalize monopolistic developments, but it did not sanction any socially planned regulatory policy; nor could local adjustments solve national market problems. D. J. Johnston rejected both suggestions, insisting that the other large eastern cotton manufacturers would not agree to them and consequently would profit at his expense. In July management also rejected an attempt at mediation by Robert Blissert, the representative of the New York City Central Labor Union.[20] Left with no alternative to the wage reduction, the cotton workers organized for a strike.

For various reasons, the unions had disbanded after 1880. Most textile workers were adolescents and females who only expected to work in the mills a few years. Moreover, the long workday and low wages provided little time or money for union organizing. Possibly as important, workers were still too imbued with paternalistic attitudes and had not yet seen the need for more permanent organization. In any case, the weavers, spinners, and carders now reorganized their unions and began to investigate the possibility of a "combination union for the future."[21] Committees were formed; funds came in which would sustain striking cotton-worker families and permit some to seek temporary employment in other cities. By early May, one out of every fourteen company tenements had been vacated. Meanwhile, hundreds of cotton hands found work in the woolen mills. By the time the conflict had ended, from a third to half of the Harmony Mills workforce had either left Cohoes or found other work in the city.[22] Then, in late July, the cotton workers began to transform their trade unions into an assembly of the Knights of Labor.[23]

These textile workers' strikes were a community action, as noted above, and not simply a labor protest. The 1882 walkout directly involved about 10,000 people—more than half of the Cohoes population—and indirectly affected everyone. Weekly rallies occurred on Saturday evening at Willow and Vliet Streets. Thousands gathered to hear state and national leaders such as John Swinton, Robert Blissert, and Samuel Gompers, as well as local labor chiefs like Joseph Delehanty and Dugald Campbell— all of whom attacked the Harmony Mills and encouraged resistance. Picnics and vaudeville benefits regularly raised funds for the striking families. About $2,300 in donations enabled the newly established workers' supply store to remain well stocked. The largest contributions came from iron molders: the Troy local (which included the Cohoes molders) gave $500, and the Albany Iron Molders' International Union No. 8 sent $100, the next largest amount.[24] In addition, non-strikers also made significant contributions. At least one local merchant offered the striking cotton hands a 5 percent discount until such time as they defeated the 10 percent reduction, and many merchants gave money. The sense of community and regional social activities played a central role in developing solidarity among the Irish and French-Canadian workers. Mass meetings were often addressed in both French and English. When New York's Central Labor Union urged state labor to aid the Cohoes cotton workers, Blissert, the CLU head, asked that contributions be sent to the *Irish World*.[25] Delehanty's ties to the Irish community were well known. Furthermore, both French Canadians and Irish considered the Johnstons "outsiders" on two counts: they were English and Protestants. When management imported Swedish strikebreakers, it directly threatened the strikers' ethnic culture. Praising the Swedes for possessing the traditional Protestant virtues, the *Cohoes Daily News* found them "orderly, well-behaved strangers."[26]

Management made a frontal assault on the working-class community by attacking its cohesiveness. It sought to break the community bonds that joined the women and allowed them to resist outside interference. For example, one woman complained that her family, which was working, had been persecuted by the family in the apartment above her and that one of them had hit her on the head with a bottle. A second woman refused to work, citing social pressure on the part of her neighbors. Management paternalism, however, had controlled much in their lives, and now it mobilized its financial, social, and political power in an attempt to reimpose control. Six weeks after closing down, the mills quietly reopened, hoping to attract tired and hungry strikers now ready to accept the wage reduction. The bells were not rung "for fear of creating too much excitement." Only one adult and two children appeared on the job, so the mills closed again. The next week the company tried once more, but the workforce still comprised only twelve hands, five strikers and seven section bosses.[27] The Johnstons then placed additional pressure on the community. In mid-July they announced that arrangements had been completed to bring fifty Swedish families to Cohoes. These workers, management declared, would replace families that had left the city for work elsewhere. To the workers, however, this new development threatened job security, ethnic community bonds, and the working class generally.[28] In addition, at the time of the announcement regarding the Swedish workers, eviction notices were served on 14 strike leaders and 150 women who lived in company boardinghouses.[29] Management heretofore had feared that evictions would arouse public support for the workers, and they apparently wanted to threaten the workers' sense of security—no more!—in order to force them back into the mills. But the notice was served, and Delehanty, perhaps intentionally, became the first and only tenant ejected for non-payment of advance rent. (Until this walkout, management had always collected rent two weeks after occupancy.) By his refusal to pay and his subsequent eviction, Delehanty turned the company threat into a psychological victory: he had become a martyr, and his vindication prompted further resistance.[30]

Such tactics, however, were not the major sources of company power; rather, those proved to be time and money. On August 4, fifteen weeks after the first shutdown, the Harmony Mills reopened for the third time and the struggle intensified. Each day for the next three weeks, management fought to break the community's solidarity and to entice strikers back to work. It charged the cotton-workers' union with corruption. It sought to intimidate non-striking relatives who worked in the mills, such as carpenters, painters, or laborers. And, as a last resort, it again began to send eviction notices to many strikers who lived in the tenements.[31] In response, workers' resistance hardened. Each day crowds gathered at the mill to hoot at or otherwise intimidate those returning to work. Management then hired five deputy sheriffs to guard the mills, and the contest entered the political arena. In contrast to the "gentlemanly" regular police, the *Troy Press* reported, the special police "act disgracefully and by their strutting about seem inclined to get up a row if possible."[32] But the workers' protest remained mostly non-violent intimidation. Striking workers continued to "bulldoze" non-striking neighbors. Union committees watched the morning trains and streetcars and paid the return fare of prospective cotton workers. Finally, the union published a blacklist of sixteen "rat spinners" who had returned to work.[33]

Intimidation by the strikers counterbalanced company threats. Between hammer and anvil stood impoverished cotton-worker families. As early as July, Troy's pro-labor *Press* had reported that many strikers were discouraged by the insufficient relief funds.[34] Accounts of near starvation increased in August, and workers began to feel the pressure of hungry families. Gradually the number working grew, and neighborhood solidarity dissolved. On August 16, management began to serve eviction notices to all striking residents, ostensibly to make room for the Swedish laborers then en route to Cohoes. Destitute and demoralized after four months of resistance, the strikers collapsed; on August 26, they voted to return to work under the wage reduction.[35] The walkout, management later admitted, ended only after neighborhood unity was broken.[36]

The operatives had lost, but out of the battle came a permanent association and preparations for further resistance. At the same meeting at which they decided to return to work, they also resolved to join a new national labor movement and to continue their struggle against the Harmony Mills. In their own words:

"*Resolved*, That we do not consider it a defeat neither do we consider the question of capital and labor settled in Cohoes. We have shown this corporation that they under-estimated the strength and intelligence of their work people. . . . *Resolved*, [we shall] join and unite in that grand phalanx of labor that is known as the Knights of Labor."[37] Increased militancy and a political consciousness had come to Cohoes cotton workers. Predictably, violence flared when the Swedish workers arrived and entered the mills. Crowds gathered before the tenements of the newcomers and threw stones through the windows and, during the day, tried to intimidate the occupants.[38] Then came the fall elections and a major political victory for the cotton workers. Owing to his strike leadership and his eviction, Delehanty was a celebrity. After the walkout ended, he became a leading figure in the state labor movement, chairing the state labor convention meetings that September in Buffalo. Carrying the banners of the Democratic party, the Albany County Trades' Association, the Anti-Monopolists, and the Cohoes Working Men's party, he was elected to represent Cohoes as the state assemblyman from Albany County's Fourth District.[39]

By the end of 1882, the cotton workers could claim mixed results. They had lost a lengthy, bitter, and costly strike to a corporate giant. Many had been out of work or only partially employed for four months, and their already low wages had declined even further. But they had organized an assembly of the Knights of Labor and had elected their leader to public office. After the election returns were in, assemblyman-elect Delehanty and Troy's Dugald Campbell led the Hill residents in celebration. Their evicted martyr had been vindicated.[40]

TROY

Following their defeat in the 1877 Clinton Foundry strike, the Troy molders' union had suspended its by-laws for six months in order to allow its members to return to the foundries. Over the next four years management maintained a workers' benevolent association as an alternative to the union. By October, 1881, however, the molders were restored to power in the iron industry, and after a one-week strike the Clinton Foundry again became a closed shop.[41] How molders regained their former prominence remains unclear, but in the 1880s ironworkers and entrepreneurs both continued their efforts to control mill work and urban social and political power. A protracted molder dispute with the Malleable Iron Company between December, 1882, and March, 1884, again involved the police and illuminates the resolution of these competing efforts.

The fortunes of the ironworker community rose and fell with the success or failure of the molders' union, which remained the largest and most influential union in Troy. At the quadrennial convention of the Iron Molders' International Union in July, 1882, Troy's local was represented by eight members, the largest delegation. Since the International permitted one delegate for each hundred members, the local evidently contained over 800 workers.[42] But other ironworkers failed to develop powerful autonomous unions. The Sons of Vulcan—the puddlers—joined with the Associated Brotherhood of Iron and Steel Heaters and the Iron and Steel Roll Hands' Union in 1876, forming the National Amalgamated Association of Iron, Steel, and Tin Workers. All five Troy-area puddler forges had disbanded by 1880, however. In their stead, an amalgamated union—the Hogan Lodge—organized, with 134 members at Burden's Iron Works in 1883,[43] and a city-wide Metal Workers' Association surfaced in 1886. But these unions never developed much power, and no others formed in the ironworks at this time.[44]

Different forms of work organization in stove foundries and rolling mills begins to explain the greater organization of skilled foundry workers—molders and mounters. The iron mills averaged 882 employees, three-quarters of whom were unskilled. Large numbers were also adolescents with low salaries; often transient, they lacked the experience and wherewithal to sustain successful unions. In contrast, foundries averaged 84.5 employees, most of whom were skilled craftsmen. Their relatively small size and high percentage of more financially secure skilled workers facilitated craft unionization in foundries.

A more likely explanation exists for the relative quiescence of the skilled puddlers: rolling mill hands received four wage advances in 1880 alone. They experienced some decline in wages in subsequent years, but employment usually remained full. Fur-

thermore, mill management established benevolent associations
as alternatives to the unions. The Burdens, the *Times* declared,
set the tone for a more harmonious relationship with the hands.
For instance, half the 3,000-man workforce at the Albany and Rensselaer works were unemployed in December, 1883, yet Burden's workers unanimously voted to accept a 10–12 percent wage
decrease, offering three cheers for the company administrator,
James Burden.[45] Relative improvement in the iron trade since the
1870s, as well as some worker economic advancement and job
security, probably contributed to industrial calm in the rolling
mills. But the depression and violence of the mid-seventies were
probably as important in educating the workers to the virtues of
order and financial security. Not just affluence, but fear of reprisals also motivated the millhands' search for security and order. In
contrast to the *Times* report of harmonious worker-management
relations, the Hogan Lodge stated that it had disbanded at Burden's mill in 1883 "from fear of the employers."[46]

Fear undoubtedly encouraged ironworkers to combine in more
secretive labor organizations, such as the Knights of Labor. Unfortunately, there is inadequate and contradictory evidence about
the early history of the Troy Knights. According to one historian,
the Knights developed such strength in Troy and vicinity in the
late 1870s "that trade unions were almost submerged."[47] A
contemporary report, however, dates the first Troy Knights' Assembly in 1882. The sixty-eighth district encompassed Troy and
the four-county area north of the city; by 1886, "about thirty"
assemblies supposedly existed within the city's limits, including
the Rensselaer, Alpha, Cigarmakers, Ferguson, Victor, Trojan,
Joan of Arc, Star, Trowel, and John Swinton assemblies.[48] Such
references to local and national labor leaders, local foundries or
mills, geographic regions, militant heroines, crafts, and familiar
symbols suggest the diverse membership, competing interests,
and complex structure of the Troy Knights. They also published a
newspaper, established a circulating library, purchased the old
Armory for use as a meeting hall, and supported political candidates. But when the organization tried "to sink the identity of the
trade unions in the Knights of Labor by coercion . . . [it]
brought the revolt which established the American Federation of
Labor in 1881."[49] Delegates from various Troy unions met in

Mayor Murphy's office on April 13, 1882, and organized the Workingmen's Trades' Assembly. The organization changed its name to the Central Labor Council in 1886, and to the Central Federation of Labor in 1893, in order to distinguish it more completely from the district assembly of the Knights of Labor.[50]

During the early 1880s, competing Troy labor organizations frustrated union solidarity. Many skilled foundry workers—in the molders' union, the Stove-mounters and Pattern-makers' Union, the Polishers' Union, or the Tinsmiths' Union—also joined the Knights. These trade unions retained their separate identities, however, and participated in the Federated Trades' Assembly. Hands in the iron mills, who were mostly unskilled or semi-skilled, may have joined one of the local Knight assemblies.[51] Additional information concerning this important transition period in the Troy labor movement, if available at all, lies hidden in the histories of other area unions. One union, however—the molders' union—retained its prominent position in Troy. When labor trouble erupted, the working-class community, fearfully seeking a secure and ordered existence, continued to look to the molders for leadership.

Mediation procedures settled most disputes between management and ironworkers, but foundrymen still complained that high molder wages made competition with western manufacturers impossible.[52] On November 1, 1882, they *asked* the molders' union to approve a 30 percent wage decrease. Molders had received three wage increases totaling 40 percent over the past six years, and founders insisted that a price decline and fewer orders required a major cutback. The union refused, and the foundries shut down. Six weeks later, management offered to reopen with a 15 percent reduction. This, too, was rejected, and in late February the foundries reopened at the old rates—all except the Malleable Iron Company, which resolved to fight the molders' union.[53] Management posted notices in early December that thereafter molders would have to give two weeks' notice before quitting or forfeit two weeks' pay. The shop's molders rejected this rule, and when their union denied the founders' February request for a wage decrease, the Malleable Iron Company shut down and locked out its molders.[54]

Malleable primarily cast accessory parts for railroad cars,

locomotives, horsecars, carriages, and agricultural machinery and implements.[55] Three men owned the foundry, but two lived out of state. Management therefore rested with William Sleicher, Jr., the one local proprietor. The plant lay on Ida Hill, the bluff overlooking the city's center, in a ward of ironworker "aristocrats"— molders and mounters who worked the area foundries. Operating at full capacity, the foundry employed about 300 men, though at the time of the lockout it was employing only 140. When Sleicher started the works a week later with fifteen scab molders, he incurred the union molders' wrath. Furthermore, when the non-union men turned out to be predominantly German and Italian, he had to confront the anger of the entire Irish working-class community.

The Malleable lockout of Troy Iron Molders' International Union No. 2 extended over more than sixteen months. Extreme violence during this struggle ultimately provoked the establishment of a molders' patrol and a Law and Order League, and caused a series of court battles. In addition, the dispute overlapped with political campaigns to elect labor candidates, and with legislative fights to end contract labor. Finally, it coincided with renewed efforts to repeal a "reform," anti-labor police act initiated by the entrepreneurial interests in 1881.

During the early 1880s, while the molders rebuilt their union, the business community continued its efforts to "reform" the police system. Republicans finally pushed a new Troy police bill through the state legislature in May, 1881, and the battle of a decade earlier resumed. A new police force was chosen, called the "reform" police by the anti-labor *Times* and the "alleged" police by the pro-labor *Press*. In contrast to 1873, however, the police issue was now intricately connected to a labor-management dispute. The city editor of the *Times* was the brother of William Sleicher, Jr. Mayor Murphy, who had been elected three times with the support of the Working Men's party, was owner of the Troy Press Company, publisher of the *Press*.[56]

According to the 1881 legislation, the new police would be chosen one at a time by each of four commissioners, with each prospective policeman needing the support of two commissioners. Mayor Murphy quickly neutralized the effect of the bill: after its

passage, he promptly suspended one of the two Republican commissioners, E. W. Hydorn, for pocketing $346 collected from
license fees. (Hydorn, one of the wealthiest men in the city,
claimed he intended to deposit the money when he had completed his collections.) The Democratic commissioners proceeded
to elect a full complement of police. The Republicans, meanwhile, ignoring the suspension, elected half of another force and
appealed to the governor to impeach Murphy. The governor refused to judge the mayor, however, and the Democratic (or "old")
force remained in power.[57]

After almost eight years in office, and facing a possible split
within his own party over his controversial decision, Mayor Murphy declined to stand for reelection in 1882. He would later become a senator from New York and a power in state and national
politics.[58] With Murphy out of the race, the Democrats did split,
and an "Independent" Democrat, Edmund Fitzgerald, was
elected mayor with Republican endorsement. Like Murphy,
Fitzgerald was an Irishman and a brewer, but unlike the former
mayor, his decisions more often favored the city's business interests. Soon after taking office, the new "reform" mayor appointed a
reform police board. Fitzgerald reinstated Hydorn as police
commissioner and replaced one of the old "ring" Democrats with
an Independent Democrat.[59] In the context of Troy's labor unrest, this "reform" movement focused less on civic and moral corruption than on political, social, and industrial power. Criminality
was an ambiguous term that depended on one's perspective or
social context. "Reform" pitted entrepreneurial interests—a
wealthy-born Protestant establishment, increasingly augmented
by a rising ethnic bourgeoisie—against the mores, values, and institutions that helped to sustain the working-class community.
This Troy "reform" movement resembled the Progressive movement at the turn of the century: it was a conservative effort by
older manufacturing interests to regain power from new ethnic
city bosses.[60] Not only older manufacturers, however, supported
"reform"; many second-generation Irish professionals and businessmen also joined the cause.

As discussed earlier, a sizable Irish professional and
entrepreneurial class emerged by the early 1880s, creating a new
political balance. (See Table 7.1.) Responding to Troy's recent

urban violence, members of this class argued that good business demanded social order and industrial harmony. Sympathetic to business demands for law and order but traditionally Democratic, the ethnic bourgeoisie could easily support an Independent Democratic caucus free of labor control. Since the mid-sixties, when the Working Men's party demonstrated that it held the balance of power in local elections, the Democrats had chosen candidates who could win labor endorsement. In the 1870s Democrats supported labor, and labor reciprocated. The Democratic party provided patronage for aspiring working-class (thus usually Irish) politicians. Even when a brewer such as Edward Murphy was elected mayor, he identified with and supported labor. The common council created public work for destitute laborers during the depression, and ex-molders regularly won appointments to a sympathetic police force.

Democrats like ex-molder Hooley, campaigning for an end to contract prison labor, continued to receive Democratic support in the eighties. Nevertheless, Irish entrepreneurs and professionals remained party loyalists and continued patronage for the Irish as Independent Democrats, simultaneously shifting the party's allegiance away from the workingmen and re-creating a traditional, non-class, all-encompassing political machine. Unlike Murphy, a consummate ethnic politician and businessman who cultivated labor support, these men were entrepreneurs who sought ethnic political support. Irishmen, not workers, would now be served by the party, but potential political mobility would remain an important working-class Irish ambition.

Three examples illustrate the opportunities which workers found in business, and their shifting priorities and associations. George Mead, former president of Local No. 15 of the Cigar Makers' International Union, later operated a hotel. A Troy alderman, he was also vice-president of the National League of Democratic Clubs and a member of the Young Men's Catholic Literary Association. Joseph Broderick, a boilermaker who became a cigar manufacturer, was "essentially a businessman." His biographer declared: "His social position is high, and his future is bright with promise."[61] Finally, there was Denis J. Whelan. Born in Ireland in 1846 (he arrived in Troy four years later), Whelan worked as a plumber until 1876. He then began the manufacture

TABLE 7.1. Occupations of Troy's Seventy Leading
Young Irish-Americans, 1889

	Holding political office[a]	N
Professionals	6	19
Manufacturers	4	12
Agents, dealers, and shopkeepers	8	30
Skilled workers	4	5
Police officials	0	4[b]
Total	22	70

[a] All were Democrats.
[b] Three were formerly molders.
SOURCE: E. H. Lisk, *Representative Young Irish-Americans of Troy, N.Y.* (Troy, 1889).

of soda water, a temperance drink. Elected alderman from south Troy's eleventh ward in 1880, Whelan was president of the common council in 1882 when the old police force was thrown out. The legislature gave him the power to appoint a new force, and evidently he did the job in an even-handed manner. In 1885, this one-time plumber was unanimously reelected council president, with the Republican minority supporting him "most heartily."[62] So, while the Democratic party retained substantial Irish involvement, these ethnic and political allegiances no longer served working-class interests alone.

The election of Independents like Whelan and Mayor Fitzgerald changed the political balance of power in favor of entrepreneurial interests, but the resolve of the old police and their worker supporters only hardened. After the reform police board appointed a new force to enforce "order" more "efficiently," the old police promptly reconstructed the barricades and refused to hand over the station houses. The ensuing struggle resembled the contest of a decade earlier, with one modification: "reform" now charged not just the police, but the entire Democratic "ring" and its supporters, with corruption. The old police remained "prisoners" in their own stationhouses for almost four months, awaiting a court decision. Meanwhile, the Malleable strike raged.

The dispute actually involved two distinct phases. The first began when management posted its order requiring two weeks' notice before quitting. The molders' refusal to accept the 15 percent wage reduction only exacerbated the conflict. When management reopened with imported non-union molders in late February, 1883, tension mounted. A crowd gathered each day near the works to protest the action; after a week of protest without any discernible effect, and with its patience exhausted, it grew angrier. When the scabs left work on the evening of March 2, nearly a thousand angry union sympathizers pursued them. Although they were guarded by five or ten "reform" policemen, the crowd threatened them. Then, as the scabs boarded the train for home, a shot was fired at them. The police rushed in reinforcements, and quiet was soon restored. No one had been hurt, but the confrontation apparently frightened all involved. The "reform" police removed their shields during the protest to avoid recognition, no one was arrested, and no major incident occurred for nearly two months thereafter.[63]

Additional non-union molders arrived late in March, and the union tried a new tactic: it planted a spy among the more than fifteen newcomers, most of whom came from out of town. Three Troy union molders had gone to Albany, sought out an Albany union leader, William Hogan, and convinced him to return with them "to get the workings" of the Malleable operation.[64] Hogan discovered that Sleicher had armed the scabs and had encouraged them to use their weapons against union men. On March 29, less than an hour after he had been uncovered and fired, Hogan swore out a statement against the manager, alleging that Sleicher had offered the non-union hands a bounty for shooting a union molder or two. Sleicher allegedly had stated: "Now you men, when you go upon the streets, will be met by Union molders, who will be standing about the corners and throughout the city. Don't let them get within three feet of you. If you see them raise a hand (they may do so under pretense of blowing their noses) shoot them at once. If you kill a couple of them that will frighten the rest. I will give you $5 or $10 for each Union molder you shoot."[65] Hogan also charged that the firm promised to "spend its last dollar in defending him or any other men in their employ."[66] Formal charges were not immediately pressed, however, and management's new militance continued. It next hired twenty Pinkertons, fully equipped with their own revolvers and nightsticks. Quartered inside the foundry, they gave the plant "the appearance of a busy military headquarters."[67] Finally, the company rented a nearby old church and parsonage and a row of four tenements for boarding its fifty non-union workers.

From late April to mid-June, 1883, a series of assaults occurred in which union molders attacked non-union hands. The Court of Appeals had ruled the new "reform" police legal in mid-March, ending the contest between the rival forces. Arrests had followed,[68] but convictions had not, for non-union men were afraid to press charges. For example, two union molders, Arthur Imeson and Joseph Winestone, were arrested for assaulting scabs, but charges were not pressed against either. Charges of disorderly conduct against two others were dropped. Only one molder was convicted of assault, and he required two jury trials. The first could not reach a verdict and was dismissed; when the second convicted him, he was sentenced to six months in jail. The outcome is unknown, but he was released on $500 bail pending an appeal.[69] By the end of May, with assaults becoming increasingly frequent, both sides girded themselves for an intensive struggle.

Outside the foundry, the Workingmen's Trades' Assembly gathered in Molders' Hall on May 23 for the first of a series of biweekly meetings to perfect their organization. Leading Knights of Labor men from the area spoke, including Troy's Robert H. Ferguson and Cohoes's Joseph Delehanty. Delehanty criticized working-class political behavior and urged more active resistance: "It is time the workingmen stopped making resolutions and commenced to act. It has been the custom for the workingmen to make resolutions 364 days in the year and break the whole of them on the 365th—election day."[70] Two days later, a large hole was discovered beneath the church boardinghouse, suggesting that someone intended to dynamite it. Within twenty-four hours the nervous non-union hands vacated the building for temporary accommodations inside the foundry.[71] Nothing more came of the plot, however, and a strange quiet settled over Ida Hill. A hostile working-class community surrounded the scabs, and the foundry became their prison.

The first phase of the Malleable lockout culminated with the killing of a union molder on June 11. Early that evening, while two young non-union men, Sanford C. White and Thomas Camfield, walked just a few blocks from the foundry, a stone struck White from the rear. Both turned and exchanged angry words with Arthur Imeson, the above-mentioned molder (who had been previously arrested for assault), and William Hutchinson, a union molder employed at the Cooperative Stove Foundry. Then the non-union men pulled revolvers and began firing. Hutchinson fell dead, a bullet in his heart. Someone in a nearby house handed Imeson a gun, but he was wounded in the thigh and fell. A friend of Hutchinson's, Joseph Winestone, tried to head off the two retreating scabs, but he, too, was wounded, while White and Camfield ran to the foundry for refuge. At the evening's end, two union molders lay seriously wounded, and another was dead.

An angry crowd quickly gathered, demanding that the two non-union hands be arrested. A squadron of police and detectives went to the foundry and took the men into custody. But the crowd was not satisfied; cries of "lynch the scab" filled the air. Two brothers then charged the police, and the detectives had to pull their guns to hold back the crowd. The brothers were arrested. The two non-union men were held by the police pending the outcome of a coroner's inquest, and a warrant was issued for the arrest of the Malleable Iron Company's manager and part-owner, William Sleicher, Jr. On the testimony of the union spy, William Hogan, and the Troy molder who had "hired" him, Sleicher was charged with aiding and abetting the murder of William Hutchinson.[72]

The trials of Sleicher and the two non-union molders ended the first phase of the Malleable lockout. Troy stove manufacturers recognized that the outcome of Sleicher's trial could affect their own future dealings with labor, and several immediately started a defense fund. Affidavits from a local hardware dealer proved that the manager had purchased fifty-four revolvers during the past few months, but Sleicher denied urging his men to shoot union molders or promising rewards if they did. The police court judge chose to believe Sleicher rather than Hogan, and the manager was released.[73] During the inquest into the death of William Hutchinson, the coroner impaneled a jury of twelve men. After examining nearly fifty witnesses, the jury determined that White, aided by Camfield, had killed Hutchinson. But in their verdict eleven jurors ruled the death an unjustifiable homicide, while one ruled it justifiable. Since they had been unable to reach a unanimous verdict, the jury was dismissed and the two scabs were released.[74] Thus ended the first phase of the Malleable dispute. Sleicher's aggressive tactics had succeeded, the journal of the militant cigarmakers' union indignantly exclaimed, and he would now "continue to accumulate wealth, and the comforts of life, from the slave labor of his scabs!"[75]

The molders' union had not been destroyed, however, and during the next few months the ironworkers—like Cohoes's cotton mill operatives—continued to organize. Mobilizing the worker communities, both prepared for the fall's state elections. Five thousand workers from Troy and Albany attended a Knights of Labor mid-summer picnic. In the fall, James P. Hooley was elected state assemblyman from Troy by one of the largest margins in the city's history. In Cohoes, Joseph Delehanty lost his bid for reelection—but only by sixty-five votes. Albany County Democrats had refused to endorse his candidacy and ran a third candidate, who placed a poor third in the election but attracted just enough votes to insure Delehanty's defeat. Delehanty rolled up an almost two-to-one margin over the Republican candidate in Cohoes, but he lost heavily in the rest of the county. Finally, a Troy referendum opposing convict labor won overwhelmingly, 8,000 to 148.[76] Labor had lost some of its influence in the mayor's office, but on certain specific issues it could still rally considerable support.

Important labor developments also took place inside the foundry. Union molders had gradually infiltrated the Malleable works. One by one, they took jobs at the foundry without disclosing that they belonged to the union. Once inside, they quietly signed up many of the non-union molders. On December 11, 1883, when management rejected their demand for higher wages, about two-thirds of the molders walked out and officially joined the union.[77] Thus began the second phase of the Malleable dispute.

This phase intensified quickly. The company imported new scabs, including Germans and Italians. To the Irish ironworker community, these newcomers represented a further threat to their ethnic-based solidarity. Within a week, according to the *Times*, another "reign of terror" existed. Assaults and shootings occurred daily, and arsonists attempted to burn the old church that housed non-union families. But since Sleicher had previously armed his scabs and a molder had been killed, the union decided to take preventive action. First, it voted to provide relief funds for the striking molders—$5 a week for single men and $7 a week for married ones.[78] Second, it rented a house a block from the foundry to serve as a base of operations for a molders' patrol—a thirty-man platoon headed by an ex-police sergeant. This patrol would walk around the foundry in teams of two or three, "to take the workers aside and talk to them."[79] They disapproved of violence, the molders declared. Nonetheless, violence erupted almost daily, as angry crowds regularly attacked and shot at the non-union laborers and the eight policemen who guarded the plant. No one was seriously wounded, but after several weeks of this siege about twenty Malleable employees asked Mayor Fitzgerald for more protection. The mayor explained that no additional police were available and that the company would have to hire its own guards.[80]

So management turned its attention to the molders' patrol. At a mass meeting on January 30, 1884, prominent Troy manufacturers, bankers, and merchants demanded that the patrol be stopped—before Malleable was forced to leave the city. "We have been strongly solicited," Sleicher warned, "to remove our business to cities where protection would be guaranteed us."[81] Mayor Fitzgerald responded in a contradictory fashion. He publicly defended the patrol, and then saw its members arrested. Several leading citizens, he pointed out, had never seen the patrol commit a crime or prevent anyone from walking the streets. In fact, "to a considerable extent," he continued, the non-union men, instead of the union molders, were causing the trouble. Sleicher himself had steadfastly refused to swear out a warrant against any patrol member.[82] Despite the mayor's public statement, that evening seven molders who were walking about the Malleable works were arrested, supposedly for being on patrol. Six more were arrested two days later on a similar charge.[83] With the expressed intention of prosecuting the patrol, Troy manufacturing interests then promptly met and organized a Law and Order

League. Some uninvited molders attended the organizational
meeting: after all, said one, we "propose to be law-abiding citizens." Why, they asked, did the League not protest Sleicher's
arming of his "tramp molders"? Finally, when assemblyman
Hooley tried to get the floor, the chairman adjourned the meeting.[84]

The trial of the fourteen molders began a week later in police
court. Outside the courthouse, molders and their supporters
awaited a verdict; inside, the Law and Order League pressed for
the patrol's conviction, and the molders' union president swore
out a warrant against the three Malleable proprietors for blockad-
ing the street in front of their foundry with pig iron. The battle
was adjourned a few days later, when the patrol case was referred
to the county grand jury. Meanwhile, each molder was released
on $200 bail, management was forced to remove the public nui-
sance, and each side mobilized its supporters.[85] The Law and
Order League hired an attorney to prosecute the molders, and
several unnamed Catholic and Protestant clergymen publicly endorsed their suit. Against the entrepreneurial and religious establishment stood Troy's workingmen, who rallied late in February
to oppose the League's attack. Hooley, Delehanty, and John S.
McClellan, a Knights of Labor spokesman from New Jersey,
urged the men to unite and boycott the churches whose ministers
had spoken against the patrol.[86] On the surface, the trial contested the legality of the molders' patrol. Underlying the lengthy
contest, however, were more basic issues: the survival of Troy's
labor movement, and the power of the predominantly Irish ironworker community. The trial made this clear.

During the jury selection, the prosecution challenged all citizens from Troy's Irish working-class wards. The jury ultimately
chosen included eight men from outlying rural areas—six farmers,
a merchant, and a village laborer—and four from other parts of
the city—two carpenters, a machinist, and a harness-maker.[87] Before the trial ended, the ethnic side of the contest became apparent: both the defense and the prosecuting attorneys alluded to the
ethnic background of the competing workforces during their
summations. For management, the destruction of the molders'
union and their political and social influence could be achieved by
replacing the Irish union workers with a new, and therefore less

threatening, community of German and Italian workers. The defense attorney concluded: "The Germans say they were stopped. By whom? Not the defendants. . . . The Italians do not swear to anything against the defendants."[88] Similarly, the prosecuting attorney summed up his remarks by ridiculing a molder witness who did not know his age: "It is characteristic of Irishmen not to know their own age." To drive home his point, he stated that a drunken man who "might have been Irish" had told him that he could not possibly hope to convict the molders because they had "four jurors with them for sure."[89] The Malleable lockout resembled the long 1882 Harmony Mills strike, where imported Swedish operatives replaced the Irish and French-Canadian strikers. In Troy, predominantly Irish union molders opposed imported German and Italian non-union molders. The scabs were surrogates for management in the contest, of course, and a logical union target. But, ironically, the ironworkers' struggle to defend their union, their community interests, and their ethnic-based class culture only produced inter-class violence between working-class ethnic groups.

The verdict confirmed the ethnic and political nature of the contest: the jury split eight to four and was dismissed. All eight rural jurists had voted against the molders.[90] And so, sixteen months after it began, the union's contest with the Malleable Iron Company ended in a stalemate. The union had not ended the lockout, but it had withstood the manufacturers' combined legal pressure. Neither side vanquished the other; yet ironworkers, led by the molders, managed to sustain Troy's union movement and to continue for a time their dominance over much of the industry.

One tragic irony, however, remained. The ironworkers' success in maintaining high local wages cost many workers their jobs. Two days after the trial ended, Simon F. Mann, the first molders' union president and the present superintendent of the Cooperative Stove Foundry, noted that stove manufacturers had begun to leave the city two years earlier. Two problems had beset Troy foundrymen: high wages and the "reign of terror." According to Mann, "Troy manufacturers paid 20–30 percent more than is paid elsewhere. . . . Thus, we cannot even bring men from outside who are willing to work at the wages we offer for there is a 'reign of terror' here."[91] The bulk of the business, he prophesied, "is destined to leave Troy."[92] The molders' union had successfully resisted the manufacturers, but within the framework of laissez-faire capitalism in nineteenth-century America, they had won a Pyrrhic victory. Responding to Mann's complaint, the union immediately agreed to the founders' request for a city-wide 20 percent wage reduction.[93] Nevertheless, compromise had come too late. High wages and union militance continued and were aggravated by depression, expanding western markets, and Troy's relatively poor access to raw materials. Local stove foundries began stagnating, shutting down, or moving. Similarly, the iron mills began a long period of stagnation in the mid-1880s, as ironmasters were reluctant to make the large investments necessary for full conversion to steel production, especially in a city so far from coal reserves and with such a turbulent labor history. By the time of another depression during the 1930s, there was little left of Troy's iron industry.

For similar reasons, Cohoes's mammoth Harmony Company was also in trouble.[94] Ring-spinning using cheap, unskilled female labor was introduced in the 1880s, displacing the well-paid and well-organized male mule-spinners. Employment in the mills declined from 4,800 in 1880 to 3,200 in 1887. In the early 1890s David and Robert Johnston, the two men who had so closely guided the company for the previous forty years, died. Unable to meet the competition from non-union western and southern manufacturers, production at the mills rapidly declined. The knitting mills, too, began to leave Cohoes. By the 1930s, the city's textile industry had virtually disappeared. The Cohoes textile and Troy iron industries had fulfilled Simon Mann's prophesy: the workers might have won the battles, but they had lost the war. The industries had moved elsewhere.

NOTES

1. Andrews, "Nationalisation," pp. 222, 304–6. The ILU folded in 1882.
2. Cohoes Daily News and Troy Daily Press, both February 26–27, 1880.
3. Cohoes Daily News and Troy Daily Times, both March 8, 1880.
4. Ibid.
5. Troy Press claims the parade consisted of 1,000 children and was a "sad sight"; Cohoes Daily News insisted that only 150 boys paraded and had a "fine time." (Both March 6, 1880.) These views of the participants are not, however, completely contradictory: the children may have been poor but enthusiastic. On the crowd estimate, both are partisan accounts and the actual number of children could have been anywhere between the two.

The *Press* was openly pro-labor; the *News* was partial to management.

6. *Cohoes Daily News*, March 8, 1880; *Troy Press*, March 2, 1880.

7. *Troy Press*, March 8, 1880.

8. Ibid., March 25, 1880; *Cohoes Daily News*, March 25–27, 1880.

9. *Cohoes Daily News*, March 26, 1880.

10. Ibid.; *Troy Press*, April 9, 1880.

11. *Cohoes Daily News*, March 30–April 1, 1880.

12. Ibid., April 5, 1880.

13. Ibid., April 8–12, 1880.

14. Ibid., April 16, 1880.

15. *Troy Press*, April 22, 1880; *Cohoes Daily News*, April 21–23, 1880.

16. *Cohoes Daily News*, November 4, 1880.

17. Ibid., August 23, 1881. Duerden was shot and killed by officer Patrick Glynn after Duerden remonstrated the policeman's sister for harboring a drunken boy who was supposed to be at work in Duerden's store. Governor Alonzo B. Cornell of New York offered a $500 reward for Glynn's capture. The funeral was held at Harmony Hall under the direction of D. J. Johnston, the Harmony Mills superintendent.

18. Ibid., April 25, May 10, 1882.

19. Ibid., July 28, 1882; *Troy Press*, July 22, 1882.

20. *Cohoes Daily News*, April 17–18, July 19, August 3, 1882; *New York Tribune* and *New York Times*, both July 23, 1882; *Troy Press*, July 19–20, 1882.

21. *Troy Press*, April 26, May 6, 1882.

22. *Cohoes Daily News*, April 26, May 10, July 27, 1882; *Troy Press*, April 27, May 18, June 13, July 6, 28, 1882.

23. *Troy Press*, July 19, 1882; *Cohoes Daily News*, July 26, 1882.

24. *Cohoes Daily News*, April 24–August 28, 1882; *Troy Press*, June 24, 1882.

25. *Cohoes Daily News*, August 10, 19, 22, 1882.

26. Ibid., September 19, 1882.

27. *Cohoes Daily News*, June 5, 12–24, 1882; *Troy Press*, June 5, 12–14, 1882.

28. *Cohoes Daily News*, July 15, 1882.

29. *New York Times* and *Cohoes Daily News*, both June 17, 1882.

30. *Cohoes Daily News*, July 26–27, 1882; *New York Times*, July 26, 1882.

31. *Cohoes Daily News*, July 28, August 9–23, 1882; *Troy Press*, August 10–16, 1882.

32. *Troy Press*, August 10, 1882.

33. *Cohoes Daily News*, August 9–22, 1882; *New York Times*, August 16, 1882.

34. *Troy Press*, July 22, 1882.

35. *Cohoes Daily News*, August 16–18, 1882.

36. Ibid., August 16, 22, 1882.

37. Cohoes cotton workers, quoted in *Troy Daily News*, August 28, 1882.

38. *Cohoes Daily News*, September 18–19, 1882.

39. Ibid., September 14, October 3, 6, 16, 30, November 8, 1882.

40. Ibid., November 9, 1882.

41. *Troy Daily Times*, September 10, 1880, October 3–10, 1881; *Troy Press*, October 3–11, 1881.

42. *Iron Molders' Journal* (Cincinnati, Ohio), July 31, 1882. See also Coleman, "Patterns of Labor Violence," p. 2.

43. National Amalgamated Association of Iron, Steel, and Tin Workers of the United States, Annual Proceedings and Records, 1876–86.

44. *Troy City Directory, also Cohoes*, 1880–89.

45. *Troy Daily Times*, December 12, 1883.

46. Iron, Steel and Tin Workers, *Proceedings*, ninth annual convention, August 5–13, 1884, pp. 1, 328.

47. John M. O'Hanlon, quoted in Rutherford Haynor, *Troy and Rensselaer County, New York* (New York, 1925), II, 444–45. O'Hanlon published the *Legislative Labor News* from 1911 to 1917.

48. Weise, *City of Troy*, p. 184.

49. Ibid., and Haynor, *Troy and Rensselaer County*, pp. 444–45.

50. *Troy Press*, April 13, 1882.

51. Ibid., September 28, 1883. Representatives from the different labor organizations attended a workingmen's convention to nominate an iron molder, James P. Hooley, for the state legislature. The R. H. Ferguson Assembly may have limited its membership to painters, but, considering the relatively small number of painters in Troy, this seems unlikely.

52. *Troy Daily Times*, February 23, April 19, June 6–22, 1880, June 22, 1881, July 12–13, 1882; *Troy Press*, March 9, 1882.

53. *Troy Daily Times*, November 1, December 20, 1882, January 24, February 8, 14–16, 1883.

54. Ibid., November 1, December 20, 1882, February 22, March 2, 1883.

55. Weise, *City of Troy*, p. 302.

56. *Troy Daily Times* and *Troy Daily Press*, both November 16–28, 1883.

57. *Troy Daily Times*, May 25–28, December 20, 1881.

58. Rezneck, *Profiles out of the Past of Troy*, pp. 181–84.

59. *Troy Daily Times*, November 16, 1882.

60. See Samuel P. Hays, "The Politics of Reform in Municipal Government in the Progressive Era," *Pacific Northwest Quarterly* (October 1964):157–69.

61. Lisk, *Representative Young Irish-Americans*, p. 229.

62. Ibid., pp. 9–10.

63. *Troy Daily Press* and *Troy Daily Times*, both March 2, 1883.

64. *New York Times*, June 14, 1883.

65. William Sleicher, Jr., quoted in *Iron Molders' Journal*, June 30, 1883.

66. Ibid.

67. *Troy Daily Press*, March 13, 1883.

68. Ibid., March 16, 1883.

69. *Troy Daily Times*, April 23, May 2–31, 1883; *Troy Daily Press*, May 2–31, 1883.

70. Joseph Delehanty, quoted in *Troy Press*, May 24, 1883.

71. *Troy Daily Times*, May 26, 1883.

72. *Troy Daily Press* and *Troy Daily Times*, both June 12, 1883; *Progress*, June 23, 1883.

73. *Troy Daily Press* and *Troy Daily Times*, June 13–17, 1883; *Progress*, June 23, 1883.

74. *Troy Daily Times* and *Troy Daily Press*, both June 14, July 16, 1883.

75. *Progress*, June 23, 1883.

76. *Troy Daily Times*, August 7, September 8, November 7, 1883; *Troy Daily Press*, November 7, 1883.

77. *Troy Daily Press*, December 11–12, 1883; *Troy Daily Times*, December 11, 1883.

78. *Troy Daily Times*, December 12, 1883.

79. Ibid., December 17, 1883.

80. *Troy Daily Press*, December 24, 1883.

81. William Sleicher, Jr., quoted in *Troy Daily Times*, January 30–31, 1884.

82. *Troy Daily Times* and *Troy Daily Press*, both January 31, 1884.

83. *Troy Daily Times*, January 31, February 2, 1884.

84. *Troy Daily Times* and *Troy Daily Press*, both February 6, 1884.

85. *Troy Daily Times*, February 8–11, 1884.

86. *Troy Daily Press*, February 26, 1884. No minister or priest in the city had publicly endorsed the patrol.

87. *Troy Daily Times*, March 30, 1884.

88. *Troy Daily Press*, March 26, 1884.

89. Ibid.

90. *Troy Daily Times* and *Troy Daily Press*, both March 26, 1884.

91. Simon F. Mann, quoted in *Troy Daily Times*, April 1, 1884.

92. Ibid.

93. Ibid., April 16, 1884.

94. Rezneck, *Profiles out of the Past of Troy*, p. 9; Clark, "Economic History of the Harmony Mills."

Conclusion

PROTEST AGAINST THE emergent structures associated with the social reorganization of work took many forms in the industrializing American city, but we have been primarily concerned with collective action, especially by the working class. To be sure, individual workers challenged the equity of their salaries and fought industrial regimentation by pilfering goods or, for example, absenting themselves on Saint Monday.[1] But entrepreneurial organizations such as the Law and Order League also constituted an important form of industrial protest to control these same structures. When higher productivity and profits required more intensive work discipline, and when management-labor relations broke down, management sought alternative labor controls—to dissolve unions, or to destroy or neutralize their power through company unions, anti-labor legislation, or social and political "reform." Management expected workers to think and act from management's own perspective, and organizations such as Sabbath Schools, temperance clubs, and the Law and Order League reflected its hierarchical and sober social and moral values. It believed unions and violence were "irrational," and that workers had to develop greater understanding and respect for the rights of property. Failing this, workers had to be controlled by tougher law enforcement or by "special" police. Such entrepreneurial responses both reflected and stimulated a high level of worker protest against industrial capitalism.

Timing

The study of collective protest has had two foci: social and economic conditions that influenced the timing of protest; and the attitudes, values, and traditions that encouraged or hindered its

247

emergence. The timing of protest in Troy and Cohoes followed the pattern identified by Shorter and Tilly in French strikes; their strike statistics, as my introduction has noted, predicted greater worker agitation in the iron than in the textile industry, in the poly-industrial city than in the company town, and only after immigrant adaptation had been completed.[2] Omitted from their general discussion were the "particular mentalities" which informed protest—intellectual characteristics most effectively studied at the local level. Their aggregate data necessarily had to ignore the detailed historical context of agitation in which values, social institutions, and the adaptive process interrelated with the size of a city, the work situation, and the market economy. The social histories of Troy and Cohoes illustrate these interrelationships and suggest how workers within different social contexts responded to the problems of a maturing industrial capitalist society. While a comparison of their histories cannot provide a definitive model for worker protest, it does illuminate various social and economic variables that influenced the distinct timing and pattern of protest in each city.[3]

Why did protest and violence occur in each city, and why did it erupt earlier in Troy? Both cities underwent simultaneous and comparable industrial growth, and manufacturers confronted many similar problems. During the postwar years, a fluctuating economic market and the demands of increased competition compelled iron and cotton manufacturers to cut costs—to make their operations more efficient, and hence to introduce new methods or procedures into the mills. Industrial capitalism was a dynamic process, continually requiring cost reductions (often involving wage decreases) and production increases. The 1873–77 depression affected durable goods such as stoves and iron rails more than it affected cotton cloth; moreover, advanced technology permeated work in the textile industry, while the iron industry remained unmechanized and labor intensive. Finally, in contrast to the skilled male workforce of the iron industry, textile labor was substantially female, adolescent, and unskilled. Such distinctions presented management with different options and shaped the history of each industry and city.

Troy had a diversified economy based on expanding iron, laundry, and shirt-and-collar industries. Led by molders, workers organized a strong trade union movement in the 1860s, wielding considerable political and economic power. Possessing a vital work subculture and distinct lifestyle, molders earned high wages and had valued skills not easily subject to technological displacement. Civil War veterans returned from military duty with a sense of their rights as soldiers in the new industrial army and soon reorganized their molders' union. Puddlers, meanwhile, with a similar work experience, initiated the union movement in the rolling mills. In the new cooperative spirit of the age, labor began to build a "worker city." An ethnic working-class community united behind them, ready to support labor's economic, political, and industrial claims. Finally, an emergent working-class leadership cadre helped unions—most notably the molders and puddlers—defend their individual and collective gains during the intense turmoil of the mid-1870s. Ironworker achievements were assaulted by management then, as employer associations formed to break the unions and assert control over the workforce. Ironmasters tried to control working conditions with time cards and apprenticeship regulations, and to destroy the unions with imported non-union labor. At the same time, under-employment, lengthy lockouts, and layoffs created wild wage fluctuations, jeopardizing the stability and living standards of families dependent on mill and foundry employment. Ironworkers saw their achievements threatened by these conditions and reacted forcefully.

Explanation for the later unionization and protest among Cohoes cotton operatives rests in the timing and coincidence of particular social and economic conditions there. A fourth wage cut in seven years precipitated the 1880 walkout, and that protest developed *after* the initial settlement and adaptation of French Canadians at the Harmony Mills. Cohoes, a company town, was early dominated by that one large, paternalistic textile corporation. Protest remained negligible during the 1870s, although salaries were reduced three times. Cotton hands, however, remained fully employed, and real wages did not decline. Moreover, low-paid adolescents and women, especially those in fatherless families dependent on the multiple labor of family members, were usually more difficult to organize. Troy's female laundresses and tailoresses, who had the support and leadership of the molders behind them, organized as early as the 1860s, but Cohoes labor lacked a comparable male leadership cadre at the time. Not until the 1870s did French-Canadian immigrants arrive to work for the expanding cotton company; consequently, they did not develop the urban associational life and esprit de corps that could sustain an extended strike until late in the decade. By 1880 they had adapted to their new environment and, like the Irish cotton hands, established cohesive family, kin, and religious bonds in coherent ethnic neighborhoods. In addition, by that time the Cohoes operatives may have learned the lessons of militance from other worker communities which had organized in preceding decades. Textile hands in Fall River and Paterson and various workers in neighboring Troy had organized and walked out in the 1870s.[4] The place of any of these factors in protest cannot be determined, of course, but by 1880, when the fourth reduction was announced, Cohoes operatives clearly had exhausted their limits of tolerance, and the Harmony Hill worker community had adapted sufficiently to back up and sustain their grievances. Following the announcement, the millhands walked out.

Attitudes, Values, and Traditions

The question of protest timing cannot be separated from that of worker attitudes, values, and traditions—that is, from the question of working-class consciousness. Local urban and industrial conditions provided a social context for protest, helping to shape the grievances—wage reductions, income fluctuations, or labor intensification—that would stimulate worker reform or reaction. But values, attitudes, and traditions informed expectations and demands. Certain traditions and experiences supported particular types of protest, but workers either had to perceive the changing social and economic conditions as oppressive, or they had to possess a vision of a better life and feel that they had been deprived of their right to it.

The predominantly English and native-born leadership cadre that organized both industries in the antebellum years had had important earlier experiences with trade unionism and evangelical Protestantism. Skilled English mule-spinners, molders, and puddlers had had some trade union experience before emigrating to America. Many early Troy union leaders—men like Henry Rockefeller, George Thompson, and Mark Smith—were born in Britain, and many Cohoes cotton spinners, even some who were of Irish parentage, had once worked in English textile mills. Moreover, evangelical Protestantism infused labor leadership with a reform spirit. A convert like Dugald Campbell stimulated radical social reforms such as trade unionism and temperance, giving these movements a messianic enthusiasm.

But resistance and the great rank-and-file protest and organization among molders and puddlers also rested in the unique work situation of these particular laborers. In contrast to work in textiles, their labor had remained unmechanized. Both molders and puddlers worked daily "heats" or "pourings" with the molten metal—perhaps forty-minute stints of strenuous, hot, and dangerous labor—and then rested. Between stints they might retire to the neighborhood saloon for fortification and comradely relaxation. Work rhythms resembled those in pre-factory iron production, and were part of an admired and distinctive work subculture in the industrial world. The native-born molders and puddlers inherited artisanal traditions of labor's dignity and rights from the early Republican experience and passed them on to immigrants who were learning these crafts in the 1850s and 1860s. The continuing pre-factory work routine in the iron mills and foundries then reinforced these traditions.

Molding and puddling required a long apprenticeship, great strength, and substantial skill. Both crafts were well paid, and families of such "labor aristocrats" enjoyed a relatively affluent lifestyle. If employment was regular, children did not have to work, and the family could afford some better furniture and more entertainment. Furthermore, alternative employment possibilities—perhaps as a policeman, labor organizer, politician, or shopkeeper—occasionally opened to such workers. But molders' and puddlers' expectations, raised by relatively high salaries and social achievements, were threatened by layoffs and imported scab labor during the depression. Management, moreover, continually made efforts to mechanize their crafts. Skilled ironworkers recognized these dangers and, knowing their rights and potential power, organized industrially and politically to defend their interests.

Violent molder and puddler protest in the 1870s was not solely a function of distinctive work experience. By then, such workers were overwhelmingly Irish, and associational traditions of resistance which had been carried over from Ireland also shaped their militance. By the 1880s puddlers in the vast rolling mills were being made redundant through the conversion to open-hearth furnaces and steel production; their unions ultimately dissolved. In the 1870s, however, and for molders even into the next decade, work traditions intersected with Irish resistance traditions, producing Troy's "reign of terror."

By way of contrast, in Cohoes, where protest erupted later and remained more orderly, cotton operatives lacked a distinctive work subculture. Equally important, French Canadians did not have a militant resistance tradition like that of the Irish. Artisanal work traditions had been substantially lost in the mechanized cotton mills by the Civil War. In addition, Irish immigrants, followed later by the French Canadians, displaced native-born operatives, breaking any ties with pre-factory production methods. Only woolen spinners, who were still mostly English or native-born, walked out in the mid-1860s, and they worked in the knit goods factories, which were smaller and easier to organize. Ring-spinning always threatened to displace the mules, and the spinners remained quiescent until the 1880s.

To summarize, local industrial and urban conditions stimulated early, frequent, and intense protest in Troy, a poly-industrial city with diverse political and economic opportunities. Immigrant Irish workers had settled in by the mid-sixties, developing a cohesive and supportive community with extensive political connections. In addition, associational traditions aided trade union organization. Evangelical Protestantism provided a reform spirit for the English and native-born trade union leaders in both cities, but, most important, rank-and-file molder and puddler militance could be traced to two coincident associational traditions: continuing artisanal work rhythms in a distinctive work subculture and lifestyle, and Irish traditions of resistance to authority. Extreme wage fluctuations in the iron industry coupled with management's introduction of non-union labor in the 1870s to jeopardize the unique social and industrial position of these men, and to stimulate their traditional response: militant resistance.

Militance, however, is not necessarily radicalism, and in neither city did the labor movement sustain the cooperative perspective of the "worker city" into the 1880s. A radical vision of a fundamentally reorganized society did not motivate labor after the depression. Rather, workers increasingly fought defensive battles or struggled for limited gains. American social and political experiences as well as dominant cultural attitudes transformed the cooperative industrial, social, and political vision into a pragmatic economism: pure-and-simplism. The causes of this transformation are complex, raising important questions of class consciousness— of the nature of shared attitudes and values throughout the working class.[5]

Class Consciousness: Mobility versus the Ballot Box

Two relevant alternative arguments have generally been put forth to explain the American working class's failure to build and sustain a broad-based socialist movement: social mobility, and the American democratic political experience. Stephan Thernstrom's pioneer work on occupational and property mobility in Newburyport, Massachusetts, found that few laborers moved into skilled employment or entrepreneurial positions. Labor did not typically rise from rags to riches but, Thernstrom argued, the gains of a few provided ample role models to stifle collective protest.[6]

More recently, Alan Dawley has persuasively argued that electoral politics, not social mobility, constituted the "main safety-valve of working-class discontent."[7] Workers did unionize and protest, he properly reminds us, but the ballot box and the American political party experience co-opted militant workers (Lynn shoemakers, in his study) into classless parties. Although Dawley claims that the Working Men's party was no different from the Democratic or Republican parties, his blanket dismissal of the former is not quite fair; after all, it did hold distinctly pro-labor positions, independent views which the Democrats certainly tried to pre-empt. To be sure, the Working Men's party was eventually co-opted, but Dawley fails to explain why the Working Men did not press greater class claims in the political arena against the Democrats. Why were workshop issues not regularly raised by worker political representatives on the common council? And why did workers continue to support the Democrats into the 1880s? Explanations for these positions and the dissolution of the cooperative vision, however, do not require choosing between the hypotheses regarding social mobility and electoral politics. Rather, the dominant liberal social and political ideology of progress undermined labor's class consciousness, while social mobility and the political process both provided experiences that confirmed that ideology.

First, limited social mobility did exist, especially among Troy molders; it was the experience of the skilled, of politicians and the police, and of the growing ethnic entrepreneurial class. Social mobility needs to be measured both objectively and subjectively, however. The squalor and destitution of famine Ireland and impoverished Quebec provided the long-term standard against which these immigrants measured their American experience. They did not find gold on the streets; in fact, the nineteenth-century industrial city was a challenging, harsh environment. Working-class families often lived in an unhealthy and dangerous environment, in or on the brink of poverty. Technology constantly threatened to reduce skills, intensify labor, or absorb jobs completely, and depressions, company paternalism, seasonal employment, and other such conditions kept most families in a continual state of dependence. Still, people measure achievements in terms relative to their prior experience, and while worker ambitions may have soared, their relative expectations were met rather easily in the industrial boom. Consequently, Irish and French-Canadian immigrants could still be pleased with their new homes. They found ample employment for themselves and their children; they achieved some status through occupational mobility into the skilled trades; they managed to keep their families intact. Furthermore, they sustained a significant network of labor, social, and political institutions. Finally, Irish workers in particular accumulated some property, and by the second generation an Irish professional and entrepreneurial class had emerged. From the perspective of these workers and their families, the iron and cotton industries had provided success, status, and even some security.

Second, the right to vote in America was no doubt prized by the large British immigrant population, disenfranchised in its mother country. But voting was more than a political act; it was participation in a social convention. The dominant political tradition celebrated political, and not economic, democracy. Economic competition was to be fought in the marketplace, rather than in the ballot box. In *The Federalist* Madison had urged support for the federal constitution on just this basis. Divisive economic interest groups would be neutralized in broad-based political appeals;[8] hence economic inequalities were considered natural and desirable. This political philosophy relied, however, on the continuing existence of equal opportunity. Since immigrant social mobility seemed to confirm the "openness" of American society, the limited but nonetheless real possibility of social mobility coincided with a traditional republican political ideology, ultimately informing both local working-class political consciousness and labor protest. In this ideological context, failure was thought to be due to personal shortcomings, rather than to social injustice, and the political arena was an improper place for contesting class issues.

Still, class concerns were not entirely divorced from working-class politics in Troy and Cohoes. The Working Men's party did express class interests, supporting labor candidates, the Short-Hour Movement, and the cooperative movement. In the 1870s it petitioned Troy City Hall for public works projects for the unemployed, and it steadfastly fought contract labor. Since the mayor appointed the police, whoever controlled the mayoralty held considerable power during the labor violence of these depression years. Mayor Murphy was elected as a Democrat, but only after he could claim the support of the Working Men. Reelected four times, he was careful to retain their allegiance.

When the Working Men's party made its political muscle felt in local elections, the Democrats sought to undermine its political base. On a daily basis, the Democrats continued—much like the Republicans—to be concerned with patronage and with government as usual;[9] urban social institutions were not fundamentally altered. Murphy, moreover, may have been more than the Working Men had bargained for. He was a consummate Irish politician, using his office to establish a statewide and national political base. But he always maintained his links with labor—even as he established himself within the financial community.[10] The Working Men's party *was* substantially co-opted, but it received Democratic support on some major issues and continued to endorse Murphy's reelection.

By the early 1880s the Working Men's party had dissolved, and the Democratic "ring" had been taken over by the "Independents." Labor had had considerable political influence in the

1860s and 1870s, and both the Working Men's and Democratic parties responded to worker interests, albeit in limited ways. The success myth and traditional political ideology emphasized that politics was meant only to insure that the individual's struggle for survival would be "fair," not that parties would serve class interests. Labor was manipulated by politicians such as Murphy, but as an interest group its needs were served well, especially in the context of previous anti-labor administrations.[11] In the 1880s, though, Irish entrepreneurs and professionals gained control of the city's political apparatus and further circumscribed class politics. Irish politicians still provided an important symbol of immigrant mobility, success, and power, while Democratic assemblymen like James Hooley continued to lead the ultimately successful fight to end state contract prison labor. But the Democrats forsook their working-class ties for traditional bourgeois political interests: an umbrella party with continuing ethnic patronage.

Mobility also encouraged working-class acceptance of a dynamic hegemonic political ideology—of attitudes that were continually growing more sophisticated about encompassing the industrial world. Social Darwinism and the Gospel of Wealth, for example, both emerged in the Gilded Age, insisting that "the opportunity to get rich," as the Reverend Russell Conwell reminded his listeners, was "within the reach of almost every man and woman."[12] Easy geographical mobility for some—a vast subject, little understood—made it possible for workers to seek employment elsewhere during strikes, to establish new careers in the burgeoning West, or to earn supplementary cash in seasonal farm labor.[13] In fact, relatively few moved West; but the possibility existed, and so the myth of opportunity remained for others.[14] Social mobility also existed for some, since well-paid skilled labor was in short supply.[15] A significant minority, especially among the second-generation Irish, became professionals, dealers and traders, or police and politicians. Most Irish in the 1850s and 1860s were working class, and their ethnic and political associations reinforced their class identity. By the 1880s, however, an Irish bourgeoisie and "independent" political machine had emerged. Workers had always adhered along ethnic lines—as seen in the residential neighborhoods—but the ethnic base of class allegiances was now steadily eroding.

Immigrant social and political experiences reinforced working-class acceptance of hegemonic values. In this regard, one institution in particular—the Catholic Church—should also be mentioned. The Church exerted a basically conservative influence on its parishioners, sponsoring attitudes that coincided with hegemonic values. To be sure, the Irish and French-Canadian Church provided a center for ethnic neighborhood organization as well as an important cultural symbol. But it celebrated hierarchical, deferential values and certainly never encouraged resistance to the wage system.

After the decline of the cooperative movement in the 1870s, working-class political consciousness grew increasingly economist, supporting craft unionism pure and simple. Politics was not seen as another arena in which workshop grievances could be fought. So Troy, the Worker City, came to inherit an industry-specific identity as the Collar City. That identity was based on the city's developing soft industry, not on the heavy industry that had first attracted capital and labor to the area. As in Cohoes, class struggles still filled the streets, but no one saw any classes there. Instead, molder, mounter, and operative interest groups were seen—self-respecting or lawless, depending on one's perspective, rather than representing any particular class.

The Irony of Progress

It is important to appreciate labor's achievements and vision in their historical context. Labor organization and militance confronted unremitting governmental and entrepreneurial hostility during this era. Management had at its disposal a vast surplus of unskilled labor, and new technologies, with tremendous productive capacities, always threatened to displace skilled workers. Finally, the national market was traditionally unregulated and unstable. In the nineteenth-century world of *laissez-faire* individualism, some workers had created radical institutions. Unionism and the Cooperative Movement, for example, both emphasized collectivism and united individuals for the welfare of all. In Troy, led by the molders, men and women had joined to build the Worker City in the 1860s. Against the tremendous financial resources of some powerful corporations and industrial capitalists, workers in both Troy and Cohoes had resisted lengthy lockouts and gained political power. When workers asked to work part-time rather than have their wages reduced, they understood that the country's economic problems involved national and not purely local decisions. If the problem was overproduction, the solution lay in reduced work, not in reduced wages. While local workers could do little to affect complex and distant markets, they could hope to control local conditions.

Faced with continued management encroachment on worker achievements and union power, labor—with the support of the working-class communities in both cities—eventually resisted. The Harmony Mills management did not import non-union labor until the 1882 lockout was virtually over, and labor resistance never became particularly violent in Cohoes. But workers in both cities applied available pressures in order to preserve some control over their work, and thus over their lives. Management, therefore, was continually confronting short-lived but strong labor organizations which were integrated on various ethnic, social, political, and economic levels. A strong union movement, effective Irish-dominated political machines, cohesive Irish and French-Canadian working-class communities, and militant and well-organized Irish nationalist groups such as the Fenians and the Clan na Gael presented serious obstacles to uncontested entrepreneurial urban authority. Before management could fully dominate its workforce and improve its competitive position in the industrial world, it had to restore order within the city.

Workers struggled not so much to gain more power as to preserve the achievements and advantages they had already won. One aspect of the violent and near-violent protest is important: it sought to defend the newly achieved status of workers and their families. Whole segments of the community participated in the effort, although in different ways. Women, whether they were cotton workers or the wives of working men, regularly joined the crowds that intimidated non-union labor; indeed, often they vociferously led the throngs. But while many in the community demonstrated their sympathy with labor protest and even helped create an atmosphere of intimidation, gangs of boys and young bachelors committed most of the assaults and shootings. These were men without families of their own to support. Neighborhoods united men and women in protest, whereas the family's role varied according to the stage of protest, the economic independence of the family members, or its internal hierarchical sex-role divisions. Early in protest, family and kinship ties sustained workers and helped them organize, but as a strike extended and pressures of hunger mounted within the family, the trend back to work would increase. In addition, dependent wives and children would be less likely to initiate independent strike action than would their fathers and brothers, or widows.

While Troy's militance was often deliberate and systematic (as with the city's erstwhile Molly Maguires in 1876 and 1877), the protest was not based on a new vision of society. Even the cooperatives had quickly become devices for worker investment rather than alternatives to the profit system. The violence was a defensive tactic, a holding action born of anger and fear; it was not designed to fulfill a program. Most often workers in both cities fought for short-range, wage- and job-conscious goals. When they saw their accomplishments threatened by management, they resisted, drawing on traditions from their world of work and ethnic experience. They did, for a time, establish a postwar Worker City in Troy and create an enduring union movement—impressive achievements that should not be minimized. But by the 1880s radicalism was truncated, at best; it was the legacy of the Worker City, though, part of a tradition that would reappear in the Knights of Labor and the American socialist movement. Bourgeois cultural values of individual status and achievement held increasing sway within the worker community and labor movement, however, and those values shaped working-class protest.

Encouraged by the relative success of a few, workers had always set their sights on the good life. In the 1880s, the "good life" was defined differently from what it had been in the "Worker City"; nonetheless, the life that most workers *were living* throughout this period, with meager wages, unsanitary and cramped living conditions, and child labor, remained unembellished and unchanging. Consequently, twin ironies in these iron and cotton workers' achievements illuminated a larger theme in America's industrial history: the decline in the early twentieth century of first-generation urban industrial cities in the North Atlantic states. First, social mobility for some also meant the

development of an ethnic middle class with ties to the city's commercial interests. Instead of the few *petit bourgeois* Irish shopkeepers (grocers and saloonkeepers) who were traditionally men
of the worker community, a new middle class had emerged which
consisted of professionals and entrepreneurs, or men of commerce. The latter's domination of the Democratic party, and their
continued involvement with workers in French-Canadian and
Irish ethnic clubs and nationalist movements, began to diminish
the working-class base within the ethnic community and to shift
ethnic allegiances to an inter-class axis.[16] Second, the success of
the union movement compelled iron and cotton manufacturers to
close their mills and look for "safer" and more economical labor
markets elsewhere. Relatively high wages, a strong union movement, and the development of new western markets and coal reserves encouraged manufacturers to limit further investment in
these facilities. Thus the final irony: under a vision of progress
that considered the future of a city and its workforce more
expendable than profit levels, both the Worker City and the
Company Town ultimately became industrial wastelands. While
managements left Troy's iron and Cohoes's cotton industries to
die, the legacy of the cooperative vision and worker resistance
remained alive—a spark ready to ignite labor's struggles
elsewhere.

NOTES

    1. See Thompson, "Time, Work-Discipline, and Industrial Capitalism," and Gutman,
"Work, Culture, and Society in Industrializing America."
    2. Shorter and Tilly, *Strikes in France*.
    3. Sewell, "Marc Bloch and the Logic of Comparative History."
    4. Herbert G. Gutman, "Social Structure and Working-Class Life and Behavior in an
Industrial City: Paterson, New Jersey, 1830–1905," an unpublished manuscript which the
author kindly allowed me to read.
    5. Lenin, in *What Is to Be Done?*, labeled "Economism" as the "tendency to reduce
revolutionary politics to the level of trade-union struggles." See Jean Monds [pseud.],
"Workers' Control and the Historians: A New Economism," *New Left Review* 97 (May-
June 1976):81–100. This important article defines the emerging historical debate on the
Anglo-American literature on working-class consciousness and behavior.
    6. Thernstrom, *Poverty and Progress*.
    7. Dawley, *Class and Community*.
    8. James Madison, "The Federalist, No. 10," in *The Federalist Papers* by Alexander
Hamilton, James Madison and John Jay, ed. C. Rossiter (New York, 1961), pp. 77–84.
    9. Minutes of the Common Council of the City of Troy, March 1873–February 1877,
1880–82, 1886–87. Minutes for the other years between 1855 and 1885 were reprinted in
the *Troy Daily Times* exactly as they appeared in the extant minute books.
    10. For a biographical sketch of Murphy, see Rezneck, *Profiles out of the Past of Troy*.

The discussion of the Working Men's party and working-class politics has benefited considerably from my many conversations with Barbara Abrash, an astute student of Troy's labor and political history.

11. The Know-Nothings controlled local politics in the late 1850s, and conservative businessmen and entrepreneurs dominated the Common Council and filled the mayoralty until 1868.

12. Russell H. Conwell, *Acres of Diamonds* (New York, 1905), p. 15. Social Darwinism received its fullest American articulation in the writings of William Graham Sumner.

13. Local newspapers regularly carried stories of former area residents who were leading successful careers in the West, including Troy's Thomas Norton and Cohoes's Samuel Sault. In addition, iron and cotton workers frequently moved out of town for work during a strike. Undoubtedly, many did not return.

14. James P. Shannon, *Catholic Colonization on the Western Frontier* (New Haven, 1957), pp. 125–53.

15. H. J. Habbukuk, "The Economic Effects of Labor Scarcity," in *Technological Change*, ed. S. B. Saul (London, 1970), pp. 23–76.

16. Several recent articles illuminate this transition. Arno Mayer sees a second *petite bourgeoisie* emerging in European commercial centers at the end of the nineteenth century. This lower middle class possessed two especially important characteristics that affect urban protest: it had a predisposition against revolutionary confrontation, and it developed remarkable social coherence during crises. In another conceptually important article, John Alt roots this transition in the economic and political crises of the New Deal. The working-class experience, Alt argues, is superseded by a socially private existence mediated by consumerism. Alt associates this shift with the end of capitalism's competitive phase and development of monopoly capital in the 1930s. I would date this transition— especially for antebellum immigrants like the Irish—much earlier, although the process clearly accelerates for others later. See Arno J. Mayer, "The Lower Middle Class as Historical Problem," *Journal of Modern History* 47, no. 3 (September 1975):409–36; Jonathan M. Weiner, "Marxism and the Lower Middle Class: A Response to Arno Mayer," *Journal of Modern History* 48, no. 4 (December 1976):666–71; John Alt, "Beyond Class: The Decline of Industrial Labor and Leisure," *Telos* 28 (Summer 1976):55–80. Howard Green very kindly gave me these references.

Appendix: Subsistence Data

COST-OF-LIVING ESTIMATES are available for the United States, but data used in chapters 4 and 5 are based on wages and prices in Troy and Cohoes. Since I am trying to measure the degree of poverty, I have been as generous as possible with the data: for example, estimates use lowest prices, alternative purchases when costs seem high (e.g., lard instead of butter), and the barest subsistence budget (primary poverty—minimal food, clothing, heat, and shelter only).

For comparative purposes, I have borrowed the methodology utilized by John Foster (*Class Struggle and the Industrial Revolution* [1974]) in his analysis of English poverty. Foster uses B. Rowntree's (*Poverty* [1902]) subsistence diet for one adult male workhouse inmate for a week, substituting a small quantity of meat for some of the cheese to accommodate new consumption information. I have further modified this diet slightly, adding some beans to meet both U.S. Department of Agriculture minimum nutrition estimates and what seem to be typically available working-class budget expenditures. (See R. L. Chapin, *The Standard of Living among Workingmen's Families in New York City* [1909] and L. B. More, *Wage-Earners' Budgets* [1907]. The Department of Agriculture "Report on Nutrition Investigation" is appendix 6 in Chapin. Written by Frank P. Underhill, the report is based on tables in U.S. Department of Agriculture Bulletin 28, rev. ed. [1899].) Converted to more familiar American quantities, the diet for one week reads: 4 loaves bread, 1 qt. milk, ½ lb. lard, 2 qts. potatoes, ½ lb. cereal, ½ lb. bacon, 1 lb. meat, 1 qt. beans, 3 eggs, ½ lb. sugar, ¼ lb. coffee. Clothing costs, based on the budget studies noted above, have been estimated at 25 percent of food costs. Rent costs are based on the lowest rents charged in the tenements and boardinghouses, assuming that the poor lived in the most meager accommodations (Census *Reports*, 20, and local newspaper sources). The total costs per adult male have then been determined for family members, using weights assigned by A. Bowley (*Livelihood and Poverty* [1915]) and adopted by Foster: man over 18 = 100; woman over 16 = 80; boy over 14 = 85; girl over 14 = 70; child over 5 = 50; child under 5 = 33; anyone over 60 = 60. Finally, model families are then constructed using Foster's model of the family life cycle:

Stage One: man and/or woman, below 60, without children
Stage Two: man and/or woman, below 60, with half the children below age 10 and no earning relative
Stage Three: man and/or woman, below 60, with half the children between ages 10–19 and no earning relative
Stage Four: man and/or woman, below 60, with children and an earning relative or child over 18
Stage Five: man and/or woman, over 60, without an earning relative or child

Several interesting and related aspects of this problem are only hinted at in the text—for instance, the distribution of the budget among family members, and the various strategies adopted by families to deal with economic pressures. Such questions merit more extended treatment elsewhere and, I hope, will engage the attention of other historians. For a fuller discussion of the relative degree of poverty among families in distinct stages of the family life cycle, see the books by Foster and by Michael Anderson (*Family Structure in Nineteenth Century Lancashire* [1971]). Although tentative attempts to investigate the relationship between family life cycle and protest patterns have been made, this relationship also merits further study.

Finally, these data have two important qualifications. First, economizing strategies adopted by families entailed child labor, the use of boarders, the wife's paid labor at home or in the factory, and other forms of multiple incomes. A full study of the family's income beyond formal wage levels would have permitted closer estimates of actual poverty in these cities. Such a formidable task exceeded the present limits of my data and was not undertaken. The data do, however, permit assessment of the changing stress, or lack of stress, which workers in particular trades might have felt during these years. Second, most available wage data were provided to the Census Bureau by manufacturers, and I have calculated income data based upon the number of months during which mills were supposedly open in a given year. The social history of these cities clearly indicates that mills, especially in the iron industry, often ran at less than full capacity. Absenteeism, under-employment, and unemployment are not reflected in the data. Thus, while one of my conclusions is that even skilled workers experienced vast income fluctuations and might have to adapt various strategies to economize during periods of stress, the data have been biased toward high wages and low subsistence costs.

Bibliography

UNFORTUNATELY, FREQUENT FIRES swept the wooden houses of America's industrial cities, destroying valuable records. Troy, in particular, had a series of such conflagrations—in 1820, 1848, 1854, and 1862. Moreover, many local documents remain lost or buried in dusty basements. The Harmony Mills records have either been lost or destroyed, and the Burden and Corning papers do not contain relevant mill records for the period under investigation. Similarly, reports of only a few sermons exist, and church baptismal or marriage records have not been uncovered for the relevant Troy and Cohoes churches.

Moreover, neither city completed substantial social investigations of its laboring poor. The lack of such data reflects the state of social science in nineteenth-century America. In England, for example, local statistical societies and parliamentary commissions had begun to stimulate systematic studies of social conditions, but such interest was only just emerging in the United States, and then only in cities such as Boston, Philadelphia, and New York. Similarly, highly centralized authorities in some European countries, such as France, efficiently collected police and political records. Troy and Cohoes authorities were less efficient, however, and their only known reports were regularly reprinted in the local press. Finally, while police reports were detailed in the daily newspapers, Troy experienced no social investigations, and Cohoes had only one: a thin but useful 1882 New York legislative assembly report on conditions affecting child labor in the Harmony Mills.

The most serious problem involved in any study of an "inarticulate" group—the lack of documentary evidence on worker attitudes—was especially apparent in smaller cities such as Troy and Cohoes. The relationship between attitudes and social protest has been of central concern, of course, and has had to be carefully considered. Still, source limitations have required that the discussion of worker perceptions—the impact of religious life and the pre-immigrant experience in particular—be suggestive rather than conclusive. Local workers did not leave personal accounts of their thoughts or feelings, and consequently there is little information concerning those traditions or prior experiences on which they drew. But there are national labor newspapers, the *Iron Molders' International Journal*, and national trade union reports. These records complemented the virtually complete files that also exist for five daily newspapers in Troy and Cohoes. The importance of the rich local newspaper archives, which reflect differing political perspectives, can not be overemphasized. Too much of the recent social history of the working class has focused narrowly on social mobility and family life and has been excessively dependent on statistical sources, often unsatisfactorily resulting in functionalist accounts. Absent has been the social context, the historical behavior in which empirical data come alive. Newspapers permitted examination of such a context. They provided a remarkably detailed account of local social and political developments, especially since the common council in each city granted one of the local newspapers the authority to report the minutes of its meetings as well as the official daily and monthly police reports. Furthermore, both Troy and Cohoes possessed numerous city and county histories that focused on area entrepreneurs, the establishment of financial, business, and charitable institutions, and the development of religious, fraternal, and civic organizations. Finally, besides the federal and state population and manufacturing censuses, annual city directories facilitated the tracing of individuals and gave useful lists of the officers in fraternal and civic clubs of both Troy and Cohoes, while fairly extensive census *Reports* provided social statistics on living conditions as well as on area manufacture. Thus not only could the social profile of workers in each city be drawn, but that profile could then be placed in the context of three decades of historical development.

It is not possible to list all the secondary sources that have informed this study, and the following bibliography focuses on those that bear most directly on my argument.

PUBLIC DOCUMENTS AND DIRECTORIES

Cohoes, New York. Common Council. *The laws and ordinances of the city of Cohoes, including the revised charter, acts of the Legislature relating to the city of Cohoes, together with certain general statutes and parts of statutes of the state of New York, applicable to said city, besides other useful matter pertaining to its government.* Compiled, annotated, arranged, and indexed by Edgar B. Nichols. Cohoes, 1901.

Directory of Albany, N.Y. Albany, 1865, 1875, 1885.

England. Irish Office. "Secret Societies in England and America." 32 pp. April 9, 1889. Balfour Papers.. Ireland Misc. Reports, etc., 1889.

Gazetteer and Business Directory of Albany and Schenectady County, New York, for 1870–1871. Compiled and published by Hamilton Child. Syracuse, 1870.

C. L. MacArthur's *Troy City Directory.* Troy, 1854–57. Becomes *The Troy Directory, also Cohoes and Waterford, Watervliet and Green Island, N. Y.* Boston, 1890.

Massachusetts. Bureau of Labor Statistics. *Third Annual Report, 1880.* "The Canadian French," p. 75. Boston, 1882.

New York. Bureau of Statistics of Labor. *Second Annual Report, 1884.* Legislative Assembly Document no. 26 (1882). "Establishing the Fact of the Existence of Child Labor in the State," pp. 60–362. Albany, 1885.

————. *Third Annual Report, 1885.* Albany, 1886.

————. *Fourth Annual Report, 1886.* Albany, 1887.

————. *Fifth Annual Report, 1887.* Albany, 1888.

New York. Census Office. *The 1855 New York State Census of Population.* For Town of Watervliet, Albany County. Original unpublished returns.

————. *The 1865 New York State Census of Industry and Commerce.* For Town of Watervliet, Albany County. Original unpublished returns.

Troy, New York. Association for Improving the Condition of the Poor. *1st Annual Report, 1848.* Troy, 1848.

Troy, New York. Chamberlain. *Annual Report to the Common Council*, vols. 23–24, 27–28, 31–33, 36, 38, 40. Troy, 1848–49, 1852–53, 1856–58, 1861, 1863, 1865.

Troy, New York. Common Council. *Minutes* (weekly). Troy, 1866–67, 1873–77, 1880–82.

Troy, New York. Comptroller. *Annual Report to the Common Council.* Troy, 1874–76, 1878–84, 1886, 1900.

Troy, New York. Law and Order League. *Constitution and By-Laws.* Troy, 1884.

Troy, New York. Orphan Asylum. *Annual Report.* Troy, 1836–37, 1839, 1856, 1858–61, 1865, 1882–88, 1905.

Troy, New York. Rensselaer County Historical Society. "Official Report, 10th Brigade, 3rd Division—N.G.S., N.Y.: Services of the Brigade during certain riotous proceedings by railroad employees and others, July 23d–28th, 1877." Troy, 1877.

Tuttle's City Directory. Troy, 1846, 1847.

United States. Bureau of Labor Statistics. *Reports, 1886–90* (annual). Washington, 1887–91.

United States. Bureau of the Census. *Census Monographs 9: Women in Gainful Occupations, 1870 to 1920.* Washington: Government Printing Office, 1929.

———. Thirteenth Census, 1910. *Reports of the Census of Manufactures, 1909.* Vol. 9. Washington, 1910.

United States. Census Office. Eighth Census, 1860. *Statistics of the United States (including mortality, property, etc.) in 1860.* Compiled from the original returns and being the final exhibit of the eighth census, under the direction of the secretary of the interior. Washington, 1866.

———. Eighth Census, 1860. *Manufactures in the United States in 1860.* For Cohoes, Albany County, New York, and Troy, Rensselaer County, New York. Original unpublished returns.

———. Eighth Census, 1860. *Population of the United States in 1860.* For Cohoes, Albany County, New York, and Troy, Rensselaer County, New York. Original unpublished returns.

———. Ninth Census, 1870. *Manufactures in the United States in 1870.* For Cohoes, Albany County, New York, and Troy, Rensselaer County, New York. Original unpublished returns.

———. Ninth Census, 1870. *Population of the United States in 1870.* For Cohoes, Albany County, New York, and Troy, Rensselaer County, New York. Original unpublished returns.

———. Tenth Census, 1880. *Manufactures in the United States in 1880.* For Troy, Rensselaer County, New York. Original unpublished returns.

———. Tenth Census, 1880. *Census Reports, Tenth Census. June 1, 1880.* Vol. 1, pt. 2. *Statistics of the Population, embracing extended tables of the population of states, counties, and minor civil divisions, with distinctions of race, sex, age, nativity, and occupations, together with summary tables, derived from the census reports, relating to newspapers and periodicals; public schools and illiteracy; the dependent, defective, and delinquent classes, etc.* Ed. Francis A. Walker and Henry Gammett. Washington, 1883.

———. Tenth Census, 1880. *Census Reports, Tenth Census. June 1, 1880.* Vol. 18. *Social Statistics of Cities.* Comp. George E. Warring, Jr. Washington, 1887.

———. Tenth Census, 1880. *Census Reports, Tenth Census. June 1, 1880.* Vol. 20. *Statistics of Wages in Manufacturing Industries; with supplementary reports on the average retail prices of necessaries of life; and on trade societies, and strikes and lockouts.* Comp. Joseph D. Weeks. Washington, 1888.

————. Eleventh Census, 1890. *Compendium of the Eleventh Census, 1890*. 3 vols. Washington, 1892–97.

————. Eleventh Census, 1890. *Report on Statistics of Churches in the United States*. "Denominations by Cities," pp. 112–13. Washington, 1893.

————. Eleventh Census, 1890. *Census Reports*. Vol. 6. *Manufacturing Industries*. Pt. 2. *Statistics of Cities*. Washington, 1895.

————. Eleventh Census, 1890. *Report on the Population of the United States*. Vol. 1. Washington, 1895.

————. Twelfth Census, 1900. *Census Reports, Twelfth Census, 1900*. Vols. 1–2. *Statistics of Population*. Vol. 9, pt. 3. *Manufactures*. Washington, 1905.

United States. Commissioner of Labor. *Annual Report*. "Working Women in Large Cities." Washington, 1888.

United States. Department of Agriculture. "Report on Nutrition Investigation." By Frank P. Underhill. *Bulletin* 28, revised. Washington, 1899.

United States. Immigration Commission. *Reports of the Immigration Commission to Congress*, 1910. Vols. 8–9, pt. 2, and Vol. 10, pt. 3. *Immigrants in Industries*. Washington, 1911.

NEWSPAPERS AND JOURNALS

Cohoes Cataract (weekly). January 1, 1855–December 31, 1879.

Cohoes Daily News. January 1, 1874–December 31, 1883; 1883–1887 *passim*.

Fincher's Trade Review, An Advocate of the Rights of the Producing Classes (weekly). Philadelphia, June 6, 1863–March 31, 1866.

Iron Molders' International Journal (monthly). Cincinnati, 1864–74. Becomes the *Iron Molders' Journal* (monthly): Cincinnati, 1874–95.

John Swinton's Paper (weekly). Fall River, Mass., 1884–85 *passim*.

Legislative Labor News (weekly). Troy, 1911–17 *passim*.

"Minutes." Iron Molders' International Union No. 2, of Troy, New York: April 28, 1858–March 29, 1866.

National Amalgamated Association of Iron, Steel, and Tin Workers of the United States. *Annual Proceedings and Records*. 4 vols. Pittsburgh, 1876–86.

National Convention of Iron Molders. *Annual Proceedings and Records*. Cincinnati, 1859–70.

New York Times (daily). April 7–September 13, 1882.

New York Tribune (daily). April 7–September 13, 1882.

272 WORKER CITY, COMPANY TOWN

Progress (Cigarmakers' Progressive Union, weekly). New York, June 23, 1883.
Troy Daily Press. August 8, 1863–December 31, 1866; January 1, 1873–December 31, 1877. Becomes the *Troy Press* (daily): January 1, 1880–May 11, 1883. Becomes the *Troy Daily Press*: May 12, 1883–December 31, 1884.
Troy Daily Times. January 1, 1855–December 31, 1860; January 1, 1864–December 31, 1866; January 1, 1873–December 31, 1877; January 1, 1880–December 31, 1884.
Troy Daily Whig. January 1, 1858–December 31, 1859; January 1, 1864–December 31, 1866; January 1, 1873–October 26, 1873. Becomes the *Troy Morning Whig* (daily): October 28, 1873–December 31, 1877.
Vulcan Record, devoted to the interests of the Puddlers and Boilers in the United States (semi-annual). Proceedings of the National Forge of the United States United Sons of Vulcan. Pittsburgh, 1868–75.
Workingman's Advocate, devoted to the Interests of the Producing Classes of the Northwest (weekly). Chicago, 1864–68. Philadelphia, 1869–71. Chicago, 1871–72.

SECONDARY SOURCES

Articles, Papers, and Theses

Adams, E. L. "History of the Harmony Mills." Typewritten MS in Troy Public Library. Cohoes, October 15, 1932.
Alt, John. "Beyond Class: The Decline of Industrial Labor and Leisure." *Telos* 28 (Summer 1976):55–80.
American Academy of Arts and Science. "Historical Population Studies." *Daedalus* 97, no. 2 (1968).
Andrews, John B. "Nationalisation (1860–1877)." In *History of Labor in the United States.* Ed. John R. Commons. Vol. 2, pt. 5. New York, 1918.
Ashton, T. S. "The Standard of Life of the Workers in England, 1790–1830." *Journal of Economic History,* Supplement 9 (1949):19–38.
Beattie, J. M. "The Pattern of Crime in England, 1660–1880." *Past and Present* 62 (February 1974):47–95.
Bloch, Marc. "Toward a Comparative History of European Societies." [1925] In *Enterprise and Secular Change.* Ed. Frederick C. Lane and Jelle C. Riemersma. Pp. 494–521. Homewood, Ill., 1953.
Brumbach, Will; Evansohn, John; Foner, Laura; Meyerowitz, Laura; and Naison, Mark. "Literature on Working-Class Culture." *Radical America* 3, no. 2 (1969):32–33, 36–37, 39–55.

Clark, Edward Joseph. "An Economic History of the Harmony Mills of Cohoes, New York." Master's thesis, Siena College, 1952.

Coleman, Donald H. "Patterns of Labor Violence: Troy, New York, 1883." Mimeographed. University of Rochester, May, 1968.

Conk, Margo. "The U.S. Census and the New Jersey Urban Occupational Structure, 1870–1940." Ph.D. dissertation, Rutgers University, 1977.

Dawley, Alan, and Faler, Paul. "Working-Class Culture and Politics in the Industrial Revolution: Sources of Loyalism and Rebellion." *Journal of Social History* 9, no. 4 (Summer 1976):466–80.

Dublin, Thomas. "Women, Work, and the Family: Female Operatives in the Lowell Mills, 1830–1860." *Feminist Studies* 3, nos. 1/2 (Fall 1975):30–39.

Dyer, George. "Edmund Jones." *National League Journal* (London), October 1, 1877, pp. 3–5.

Dyos, H. J. "The Slums of Victorian London." *Victorian Studies* 11 (September 1967):5–40.

Faler, Paul. "Working-Class Historiography." *Radical America* 3, no. 2 (1969):56–68.

Feldberg, Michael. "The Crowd in Philadelphia History: A Comparative Perspective." *Labor History* 15, no. 3 (Summer 1974):323–36.

Garraty, John. "The Workingman." In his *New Commonwealth, 1877–1890*. Pp. 128–78. New York, 1968.

Gatrell, V. A. C., and Hadden, T. B. "Criminal Statistics and Their Interpretation." In *Nineteenth-Century Society: Essays in the Use of Quantitative Methods for the Study of Social Data*. Ed. E. A. Wrigley. Pp. 336–96. Cambridge, 1972.

Goubert, Pierre. "Local History." *Daedalus* 100, no. 1 (1971):113–27.

Graham, Hugh, and Gurr, Ted. "Introduction." In their *History of Violence in America: Historical and Comparative Perspectives*. Pp. i-xxxvi. New York, 1969.

Gutman, Herbert G. "Class, Status, and Community Power in Nineteenth-Century American Industrial Cities—Paterson, New Jersey: A Case Study." In *The Age of Industrialism in America*. Ed. Frederic Cople Jaher. Pp. 263–87. New York, 1968.

———. "Labor's Response to Modern Industrialism." In *Main Problems in American History*. Ed. Howard H. Quint, Dean Albertson, and Milton Cantor. Vol. 2, pp. 83–105. Rev. ed. Homewood, Ill., 1968.

———. "Protestantism and the American Labor Movement: The Christian Spirit in the Gilded Age." *American Historical Review* 72, no. 1 (October 1966):74–101.

————. "Work, Culture, and Society in Industrializing America, 1815–1919." *American Historical Review* 78, no. 3 (June 1973):531–88.

Habbukuk, H. J. "The Economic Effects of Labor Scarcity." In *Technological Change*. Ed. S. B. Saul. Pp. 23–76. London, 1970.

Hareven, Tamara. "Women's Time, Family Time and Industrial Time: The Interaction between Immigrant Families and Industrial Life, Manchester, New Hampshire, 1900–1940." *Journal of Urban History* 1, no. 3 (May 1975):365–89.

Hartwell, R. M. "The Rising Standard of Living in England, 1800–1850." *Economic History Review* 13 (April 1961):397–416.

Hays, Samuel P. "The Politics of Reform in Municipal Government in the Progressive Era." *Pacific Northwest Quarterly* (October 1964):157–69.

Hobsbawm, Eric J. "The British Standard of Living, 1790–1850." *Economic History Review* 10 (August 1957):46–68.

————. "From Social History to the History of Society." *Daedalus* 100, no. 1 (1971):20–45.

Kessler-Harris, Alice. "Where Are the Organized Women Workers?" *Feminist Studies* 3, nos. 1/2 (Fall 1975):92–110.

Lane, Roger. "Urbanization and Criminal Violence in the Nineteenth Century: Massachusetts as a Test Case." *Journal of Social History* 2, no. 1 (December 1968):156–63.

Langer, Elinor. "Inside the New York Telephone Company." *New York Review of Books* 14, no. 5 (1970):17–24.

————. "Women of the Telephone Company." *New York Review of Books* 14, no. 6 (1970):14–22.

Laurie, Bruce. "Fire Companies and Gangs in Southwark: The 1840s." In *The Peoples of Philadelphia*. Ed. Allen F. Davis and Mark H. Haller. Pp. 71–88. Philadelphia, 1973.

Le Goff, T. J. A. "The Agricultural Crisis in Lower Canada, 1802–1812: A Review of a Controversy." *Canadian Historical Review* 15, no. 1 (March 1975):1–31.

Lemisch, Jesse. "The American Revolution Seen from the Bottom Up." In *Towards a New Past: Dissenting Essays in American History*. Ed. Barton J. Bernstein. Pp. 3–45. New York, 1968.

————. "Jack Tar in the Streets: Merchant Seamen in the Politics of Revolutionary America." *William and Mary Quarterly*, 3rd ser., 25 (July 1968):371–407.

Lerner, Gerda. "The Lady and the Mill Girl: Changes in the Status of Women in the Age of Jackson." *Midcontinent American Studies Journal* 10 (April 1969):5–15.

McLaughlin, Virginia Yans. "Patterns of Work and Family Organization:

Buffalo's Italians." *Journal of Interdisciplinary History* 2, no. 2 (Autumn 1971):111–26.

Mayer, Arno J. "The Lower Middle Class as Historical Problem." *Journal of Modern History* 47, no. 3 (September 1975):409–36.

Middlekauff, Robert. "The Ritualization of the American Revolution." In *The Development of an American Culture.* Ed. Stanley Coben and Lorman Ratner. Pp. 31–43. Englewood Cliffs, N.J., 1970.

Mintz, Sidney W. "Foreword." In *Afro-American Anthropology, Contemporary Perspectives.* Ed. Norman E. Whitten, Jr., and John F. Szwed. New York, 1970.

Monds, Jean [pseud.]. "Workers' Control and the Historians: A New Economism." *New Left Review* 97 (May-June 1976):81–100.

Montgomery, David. "The Shuttle and the Cross: Weavers and Artisans in the Kensington Riots of 1844." *Journal of Social History* 5, no. 4 (Summer 1972):411–46.

Pleck, Elizabeth. "The Two-Parent Household: Black Family Structure in Late-Nineteenth Century Boston." *Journal of Social History* 6, no. 1 (Fall 1972):3–31.

Rezneck, Samuel. "Cohoes: The Historical Background, 1811–1918." In *A Report of the Mohawk-Hudson Area Survey.* Comp. Robert M. Vogel. Pp. 121–23. Washington, 1973.

———. "Office Building, 1881, Burden Iron Company, Troy: Historical Information." In *A Report of the Mohawk-Hudson Area Survey.* Comp. Robert M. Vogel. Pp. 73–94. Washington, 1973.

———. "The Rise and Early Development of Industrial Consciousness in the United States, 1760–1830." *Journal of Economic Business History* 4 (1932):784–811.

———. "The Social History of an American Depression, 1837–1843." *American Historical Review* 40 (July 1935):662–87.

Sandberg, Lars S. "American Rings and English Mules: The Role of Economic Rationality." In *Technological Change: The United States and Britain in the Nineteenth Century.* Ed. S. B. Saul. Pp. 120–40. London, 1970.

Sewell, William. "Marc Bloch and the Logic of Comparative History." *History and Theory* 6, no. 2 (1967):208–18.

Skotnes, Andor. "Irish Peasant Political Culture in the Prefamine Era." Unpublished MS, Rutgers University, March 1974. 200 pp.

Stearns, Peter N. "National Character and European Labor History." *Journal of Social History* 4, no. 2 (Winter 1970):95–124.

———. "Working Women in Great Britain." In *Suffer and Be Still.* Ed. Martha Vicinus. Pp. 100–120. Bloomington, Ind., 1971.

Thernstrom, Stephan. "Urbanization, Migration, and Social Mobility in

Late Nineteenth-Century America." In *Towards a New Past: Dissenting Essays in American History*. Ed. Barton J. Bernstein. Pp. 158–75. New York, 1967.

———. "Working-Class Social Mobility in Industrial America." In *Essays in Theory and History: An Approach to the Social Sciences*. Ed. Melvin Richter. Pp. 221–38. Cambridge, Mass., 1970.

Thompson, Edward P. "The Political Education of Henry Mayhew." *Victorian Studies* 2 (September 1967):41–64.

———. "Time, Work-Discipline, and Industrial Capitalism." *Past and Present* no. 38 (December 1967):56–97.

Tilly, Charles. "Collective Violence in European Perspective." In *The History of Violence in America: Historical and Comparative Perspectives*. Ed. Hugh Graham and Ted Gurr. Pp. 4–44. New York, 1969.

Vandercar, E. J. "An Outline History of Cohoes, New York, from 1869 to 1890." Mimeographed. Cohoes, 1969.

Wade, Richard C. "Violence in the Cities: A Historical View." In *Urban Violence*. Ed. Charles U. Daly. Pp. 7–26. Chicago, 1969.

Waite, Diana S. "Number 3 ('Mastodon') Mill, 1868 and 1872: Harmony Manufacturing Company, Cohoes." In *A Report of the Hudson-Mohawk Area Survey*. Comp. Robert M. Vogel. Pp. 99–106. Washington, 1973.

Wallot, Jean Pierre. "Religion and French-Canadian Mores in the Early Nineteenth Century." *Canadian Historical Review* 52, no. 1 (March 1971):51–94.

Walkowitz, Daniel J. "Statistics and the Writing of Working-Class Culture: A Statistical Portrait of the Iron Workers in Troy, New York, 1860–1880." *Labor History* 15, no. 3 (Summer 1974):416–60.

———. "Working-Class Culture in the Gilded Age: The Iron Workers of Troy, New York, and the Cotton Workers of Cohoes, New York, 1855–84." Ph.D. dissertation, University of Rochester, 1972.

———. "Working-Class Political Culture." *Newsletter on European Labor and Working-Class History* 7 (May 1975):13–18.

———. "Working-Class Women in the Gilded Age: Factory, Community and Family Life among Cohoes, New York, Cotton Workers, 1860–1880." *Journal of Social History* 5, no. 4 (Summer 1977):464–90.

Walkowitz, Judith R. "The Making of an Outcast Group: Prostitutes and Working Women in Nineteenth-Century Plymouth and Southampton." In *A Widening Sphere*. Ed. Martha Vicinus. Pp. 72–93. Bloomington, Ind., 1977.

———. " 'We Are Not Beasts of the Field': Prostitution and the Campaign Against the Contagious Diseases Acts, 1864–86." Ph.D. dissertation, University of Rochester, 1974.

————, and Walkowitz, Daniel J. " 'We Are Not Beasts of the Field':
Prostitution and the Poor in Plymouth and Southampton under the
Contagious Diseases Acts." *Feminist Studies* 1, no. 3 (Winter 1973/
74):73–106.
Weiner, Jonathan M. "Marxism and the Lower Middle Class: A Response to Arno Mayer." *Journal of Modern History* 48, no. 4 (December 1976):666–71.

Books

Abbott, Edith. *Women in Industry: A Study in American Economic His-
tory*. New York, 1910.
Anderson, Michael. *Family Structure in Nineteenth-Century Lanca-
shire*. Cambridge, 1971.
Andrews, John B., and Bliss, William P. *History of Women in Trade
Unions*. 61st Congress, 2nd session. Senate Document 645, 1909–10.
Vol. 10: *Report on the Condition of Women and Child Wage Earners*.
Washington, 1911.
Ariés, Philippe. *Centuries of Childhood: A Social History of Family
Life.* Trans. Robert Baldick. New York, 1962.
Baker, Elizabeth F. *Technology and Woman's Work*. New York, 1964.
Baldwin, George Colfax. *Notes of a Forty-one Years' Pastorate*.
Philadelphia, 1888.
Banks, Joseph A. *Prosperity and Parenthood: A Study of Family Plan-
ning among the Victorian Middle Classes*. London, 1954.
Baritz, Loren. *The Servants of Power: A History of the Use of Social
Science in American Industry*. New York, 1960.
Bean, William. *The City of Cohoes: its past and present history, and
future prospects. Its Great Manufactories*. Albany, 1873.
Berthoff, Rowland Tappan. *British Immigrants in Industrial America,
1790–1950*. Cambridge, Mass., 1953.
————. *An Unsettled People: Social Order and Disorder in American
History*. New York, 1971.
Bezucha, Roberta. *The Lyon Uprising of 1834*. Cambridge, Mass., 1974.
Bird, Caroline, and Briller, Sara Welles. *Born Female*. New York, 1968.
Bowley, Arthur L., and Hurst, A. R. B. *Livelihood and Poverty; A
Study in the Economic Conditions of Working-Class Households in
Northampton, Warrington, Stanley and Reading*. London, 1915.
Braverman, Harry. *Labor and Monopoly Capitalism: The Degradation
of Work in the Twentieth Century*. New York, 1974.
Bridenbaugh, Carl. *Myths and Realities: Societies of the Colonial South*.
New York, 1963.
Brody, David. *Steelworkers in America: The Nonunion Era*. Cambridge,
Mass., 1960.

Broehl, Wayne G., Jr. *The Molly Maguires.* Cambridge, Mass., 1964.

Brown, Thomas N. *Irish-American Nationalism: 1870–1890.* Philadelphia, 1966.

Burden Iron Company. *Burden Iron.* Advertising pamphlet. Rensselaer County Historical Society. Troy, 1920.

Campbell, Helen S. *Women Wage-Earners.* Boston, 1893.

Cardoze, Frederic T. *History of the Police Department of Troy, N. Y. from 1786 to 1902.* Troy, 1902.

Chapin, Robert Coit. *The Standard of Living among Workingmen's Families in New York City.* New York, 1909.

Clapham, John. *Economic History of Modern Britain.* 3 vols. Cambridge, 1926–38.

Clark, Victor S. *History of Manufacturers in the United States.* 3 vols. New York, 1929.

Cochran, Thomas C., and Miller, William. *The Age of Enterprise: A Social History of Industrial America.* Rev ed. New York, 1961 [1942].

Commons, John R., and associates. *History of Labor in the United States.* 4 vols. New York, 1918–35.

Conwell, Russell. *Acres of Diamonds.* New York, 1905.

D'Arcy, William. *The Fenian Movement in the United States: 1858–1886.* Washington, 1947.

Dawley, Alan. *Class and Community: The Industrial Revolution in Lynn.* Cambridge, Mass., 1976.

Destler, Chester McArthur. *American Radicalism, 1865–1901.* New London, 1946.

Devoy, John. *Devoy's Post Bag, 1871–1928.* 2 vols. Ed. William O'Brien and Desmond Ryan. Dublin, 1953.

Dubofsky, Melvyn. *Industrialization and the American Worker, 1865–1920.* New York, 1975.

Erickson, Charlotte. *Invisible Immigrants: The Adaptation of English and Scottish Immigrants in Nineteenth-Century America.* Coral Gables, Fla., 1972.

Ernst, Robert. *Immigrant Life in New York City, 1825–1863.* New York, 1949.

Fancher, Irving E. *A History of the Troy Orphan Asylum, 1833–1933.* Troy, 1933.

Fels, Rendig. *American Business Cycles, 1865–1897.* Chapel Hill, N.C., 1959.

Flexner, Eleanor. *Century of Struggle: The Woman's Rights Movement in the United States.* Cambridge, Mass., 1959.

Foner, Philip S. *History of the Labor Movement in the United States*. 4 vols. New York, 1947.

Foster, John. *Class Struggle and the Industrial Revolution*. London, 1974.

Frisch, Michael. *Town into City: Springfield, Massachusetts, and the Meaning of Community, 1840–1880*. Cambridge, Mass., 1972.

Funchion, Michael F. *Chicago's Irish Nationalists, 1881–1890*. New York, 1976.

Fyrth, H. J., and Collins, Henry. *The Foundry Workers: A Trade Union History*. Manchester, 1959.

Gillespie, W. Nelson. *History of Apollo Lodge, No. 13, Free and Accepted Masons, Troy, N.Y.* Troy, 1888.

Gitelman, Howard M. *Workingmen of Waltham: Mobility in American Urban Industrial Development, 1850–1890*. Baltimore, 1974.

Goode, William J. *World Revolution and Family Patterns*. New York, 1963.

Gosden, Peter H. J. H. *The Friendly Societies in England, 1815–1875*. Manchester, 1961.

Gramsci, Antonio. *Selections from the Prison Notebooks*. Ed. and trans. Quintin Hoare and Geoffrey N. Smith. London, 1965.

Green, Constance McLaughlin. *The Rise of Urban America*. London, 1965.

Greven, Phillip. *Four Generations: Population, Land and Family in Colonial Andover, Massachusetts*. Ithaca, N.Y., 1970.

Grob, Gerald. *Workers and Utopia: A Study of Ideological Conflict in the American Labor Movement, 1865–1900*. Evanston, Ill., 1961.

Grossman, Jonathan. *William Sylvis, Pioneer of American Labor*. New York, 1945.

Habakkuk, H. J. *American and British Technology in the Nineteenth Century: The Search for Labor-Saving Inventions*. Cambridge, 1962.

Hammond, John L., and Hammond, L. Barbara. *The Town Laborer, 1760–1832*. London, 1917.

Handlin, Oscar. *Boston's Immigrants, 1790–1865: A Study in Acculturation*. Cambridge, Mass., 1941.

———. *Race and Nationality in American Life*. Boston, 1957.

———. *The Uprooted: The Epic Story of the Great Migrations That Made the American People*. New York, 1951.

Harrison, Brian. *Drink and the Victorians*. London, 1971.

Havermans, Peter. *Golden Memories*. Troy, 1880.

Haynor, Rutherford. *Troy and Rensselaer County, New York*. 3 vols. New York, 1925.

Henry, Alice. *Women in the Labor Movement*. New York, 1923.

Henry, Jules. *Culture Against Man*. New York, 1963.

Hewett, Margaret. *Wives and Mothers in Victorian England*. London, 1958.

Hillman, Joseph. *The History of Methodism in Troy, N.Y.* Troy, 1888.

Hobsbawm, Eric J. *The Age of Revolution, 1789–1848*. New York, 1962.

————. *Laboring Men: Studies in the History of Labor*. New York, 1964.

————. *Primitive Rebels: Studies in Archaic Forms of Social Movement in the Nineteenth and Twentieth Centuries*. Manchester, 1959.

Hoggart, Richard. *The Uses of Literacy: Changing Patterns in English Mass Culture*. London, 1957.

Howell, George Rodgers, and Tenney, Jonathan. *History of the County of Albany, N.Y., from 1609 to 1886*. New York, 1886.

Hutchinson, Edward P. *Immigrants and Their Children, 1850–1950*. New York, 1956.

Jenkins, Brian Arthur. *Fenians and Anglo-American Relations during Reconstruction*. Ithaca, N.Y., 1969.

Josephson, Hannah. *The Golden Threads: New England's Mill Girls and Magnates*. New York, 1949.

Judson, H. P. *History of the Troy Citizens Corps*. Troy, 1884.

Knights, Peter. *The Plain People of Boston, 1830–1860*. New York, 1971.

Komarovsky, Mirra. *Blue-Collar Marriage*. New York, 1962.

Laing, Ronald David, and Esterton, Aaron. *Sanity, Madness, and the Family: Families of Schizophrenics*. American ed. New York, 1964.

Landes, David S. *The Unbound Prometheus*. Cambridge, 1964.

Larcom, Lucy. *A New England Girlhood, Outlined from Memory*. Boston and New York, 1889.

Lens, Sidney. *Radicalism in America*. New York, 1966.

Letarte, Jacques. *Atlas d'histoire économique et sociale du Quebec, 1851–1901*. Montreal, 1971.

Lewis, George Cornwall. *On Local Disturbances in Ireland*. N.p., 1836.

Lifton, Robert J., ed. *Women in America*. Boston, 1965.

Lipset, Seymour Martin. *Revolution and Counterrevolution: Change and Persistence in Social Structure*. New York, 1968.

————, and Hofstadter, Richard. *Sociology and History: Methods*. New York, 1968.

Lisk, Edward H. *Representative Young Irish-Americans of Troy*. Troy, 1889.

Litwack, Leon. *The American Labor Movement*. Englewood Cliffs, N.J., 1962.

Lockridge, Kenneth A. *A New England Town: The First Hundred Years–Dedham, Massachusetts, 1636–1736*. New York, 1970.

Lynd, Staughton. *Anti-Federalism in Dutchess County, New York: A Study of Democracy and Class Conflict in the Revolutionary Era*. Chicago, 1962.

McGouldrick, Paul F. *New England Textiles in the Nineteenth Century: Profits and Investment*. Cambridge, Mass., 1968.

McGregor, O. R. *Divorce in England: A Centenary Study*. London, 1957.

Manning, James H. *New York State Men*. Albany, 1911.

Masten, Arthur H. *The History of Cohoes, New York, from Its Earliest Settlement to the Present Time*. Albany, 1877.

Mayhew, Henry. *London Labor and the London Poor*. 4 vols. London, 1967 [1861–62].

Meyer, Annie Nathan, ed. *Woman's Work in America*. New York, 1891.

Miller, William, ed. *Men in Business: Essays on the Historical Role of the Entrepreneur*. Cambridge, Mass., 1952.

Montgomery, David. *Beyond Equality: Labor and the Radical Republicans, 1863–1872*. New York, 1967.

Moore, Irving H., ed. *The Great Fire of Troy, New York: May 10, 1862*. Troy, 1862.

More, Louis Bolard. *Wage-Earners' Budgets: A Study of Standards and Costs of Living in New York City*. New York, 1907.

Mount Magdalen School of Industry and Reformatory of the Good Shepherd; Guardian Angel Home and Industrial Home. Troy, 1922.

Neu, Irene D. *Erastus Corning, Merchant and Financier, 1794–1872*. Ithaca, N.Y., 1960.

North, Douglas C. *The Economic Growth of the United States, 1790–1860*. New York, 1966.

O'Broin, Leon. *Fenian Fever, an Anglo-American Dilemma*. London, 1971.

Ouellet, Fernand. *Histoire économique et sociale du Quebec, 1760–1850: structures et conjuncture*. Montreal, 1966.

Ozanne, Robert. *A Century of Labor-Management Relations at McCormick and International Harvester*. Madison, Wis., 1967.

Parker, Amasa Junius, ed. *Landmarks of Albany County, New York*. Syracuse, 1897.

Parsons, Talcott, and Bales, Robert. *The Family: Socialization and Interaction Process*. Glencoe, Ill., 1955.

Pinchbeck, Ivy. *Women Workers and the Industrial Revolution, 1750–1850*. London, 1969 [1930].

Pollard, Sidney. *A History of Labour in Sheffield.* Liverpool, 1959.
Practical Iron Founding. London, 1889.
Proudfit, Margaret Burden. *Henry Burden: His Life.* Troy, 1904.
Rayback, Joseph G. *A History of American Labor.* New York, 1959.
Redfield, Robert. *The Primitive World and Its Transformations.* Ithaca, N.Y., 1953.
Rezneck, Samuel. *Profiles out of the Past of Troy, New York, since 1789.* Troy, 1970.
Rowntree, Benjamin S. *Poverty: A Study of Town Life.* London, 1901.
Rude, George. *The Crowd in History.* New York, 1964.
———. *The Crowd in the French Revolution.* London, 1959.
Saul, S. B. *The Myth of the Great Depression.* London, 1969.
Schumpeter, Joseph A. *Business Cycles: A Theoretical, Historical, and Statistical Analysis of the Capitalist Process.* 2 vols. New York, 1939.
Sennett, Richard. *Families against the City: Middle Class Homes of Industrial Chicago, 1872–1890.* Cambridge, Mass., 1970.
Sennett, Richard. *The Uses of Disorder.* New York, 1970.
———, and Thernstrom, Stephan, eds. *Nineteenth-Century Cities: Essays in the New Urban History.* New Haven, 1969.
Shannon, James P. *Catholic Colonization on the Western Frontier.* New Haven, 1957.
Shannon, William V. *The American Irish.* New York, 1963.
Shlakman, Vera. *Economic History of a Factory Town: A Study of Chicopee, Massachusetts.* Northampton, Mass., 1935.
Shorter, Edward, and Tilly, Charles. *Strikes in France, 1830–1968.* Cambridge, 1974.
Shortt, Adam, and Doughty, Arthur G., eds. *Canada and Its Provinces.* Vols. 15, 16. Toronto, 1914.
Sinclair, Andrew. *The Emancipation of the American Woman.* New York, 1965.
Slater, Philip E. *The Pursuit of Loneliness: American Culture at the Breaking Point.* Boston, 1970.
Smelser, Neil. *Social Change in the Industrial Revolution.* London, 1958.
Smith, Timothy L. *Revivalism and Social Reform in Mid-Nineteenth-Century America.* New York, 1957.
Smuts, Robert W. *Woman and Work in America.* New York, 1959.
Snively, Thaddeus A. *A Half-Century of Parish Life.* Troy, 1881.
Stearns, Peter N. *European Society in Upheaval: Social History since 1740.* 2nd ed., rev. New York, 1975.
———, and Walkowitz, Daniel J., eds. *Workers in the Industrial Revolution.* New Brunswick, N.J., 1974.

Stedman Jones, Gareth. *Outcast London: A Study in the Relationship between Classes in Victorian Society*. Oxford, 1971.

Stevens, Fitz H. *History of Troy's Young Men's Association*. Troy, 1869.

Sylvester, Nathaniel Bartlett. *History of Rensselaer Co., New York*. Philadelphia, 1880.

Sylvis, James. *Life, Speeches, Labors and Essays of William H. Sylvis*. Philadelphia, 1872.

Taft, Philip. *The A. F. of L. in the Time of Gompers*. New York, 1957.

Temin, Peter. *Iron and Steel in Nineteenth Century America: An Economic Inquiry*. Cambridge, Mass., 1964.

Thebaud, Augustus J. *Forty Years in the United States of America (1839–1885)*. New York, 1904.

Thernstrom, Stephan. *The Other Bostonians*. Cambridge, Mass., 1974.

———. *Poverty and Progress: Social Mobility in a Nineteenth Century City*. Cambridge, Mass., 1964.

Thompson, Edward P. *The Making of the English Working Class*. New York, 1963.

Tilly, Charles. *The Vendee*. Cambridge, Mass., 1959.

———; Tilly, Louise; and Tilly, Richard. *The Rebellious Century*. Cambridge, Mass., 1975.

Tocqueville, Alexis de. *Democracy in America*. 2 vols. Trans. Henry Reeve. New York, 1945 [1835].

Trends in the American Economy in the Nineteenth Century: Studies in Income and Wealth. Vol. 24. A Report of the National Bureau of Economic Research, New York. Princeton, 1960.

Turner, Frederick Jackson. *The Significance of the Frontier in American History*. New York, 1963 [1893].

Veblen, Thorstein. *The Theory of the Leisure Class: An Economic Study in the Evolution of Institutions*. New York, 1899.

Wade, Hugh Mason. *The French-Canadian Outlook*. New York, 1946.

———. *The French Canadians, 1760–1945*. Vol. 1, 1760–1911. Rev. ed. Toronto, 1968.

Waite, John G., and Waite, Diana S. *Industrial Archeology in Troy, Waterford, Cohoes, Green Island, and Watervliet*. Troy, 1973.

Waite, Peter B. *Canada, 1874–1896: Arduous Destiny*. Toronto, 1871.

Ware, Caroline F. *The Early New England Cotton Manufacture*. Boston, 1931.

Ware, Norman J. *The Industrial Worker: 1840–1860*. Boston, 1924.

———. *The Labor Movement in the United States, 1860–1895: A Study in Democracy*. New York, 1929.

Warner, Sam Bass. *The Private City: Philadelphia in Three Periods of Its Growth*. Philadelphia, 1968.

————. *Streetcar Suburbs: The Process of Growth in Boston, 1870–1900.* Cambridge, Mass., 1962.

Warner, W. Lloyd, and Low, J. O. *The Social System of the Modern Factory, The Strike: A Social Analysis.* Yankee City Series, vol. 4. New Haven, 1947.

J. M. Warren & Co. *One Hundred Years of Successful Business* (1809–1909). Troy, 1909.

Weise, Arthur James. *The City of Troy and Its Vicinity.* Troy, 1886.

————. *Firemen and Fire Departments of Troy.* Troy, 1876.

————. *History of the City of Troy, from the expulsion of the Mohegan Indians to the present centennial year of the Independence of the United States of America, 1876.* Troy, 1876.

————. *Troy's One Hundred Years, 1789–1889.* Troy, 1891.

Wiebe, Robert H. *The Search for Order, 1877–1920.* New York, 1967.

Williams, Raymond. *Culture and Society, 1780–1950.* New York, 1958.

Wittke, Carl. *The Irish in America.* Baton Rouge, 1956.

————. *We Who Built America: The Saga of the Immigrant.* Rev. ed. Cleveland, 1964.

Woodworth, John. *Reminiscences of Troy, from its settlement in 1790, to 1807, with remarks on its commerce, enterprise, improvements, state of political parties, and sketches of individual characters.* Albany, 1853.

Yellowitz, Irwin. *The Position of the Worker in American Society, 1865–1896.* Englewood Cliffs, N.J., 1969.

Yeo, Eileen, and Thompson, Edward P., eds. *The Unknown Mayhew.* New York, 1972.

Index

McDonnell, Joseph P., 220, 223
Machinists, 37, 111
Machinists and blacksmiths' union, 204
McMulkin, James, 195
Madison, James, 254
Malleable Iron Company, 230, 232–33, 237–43
Maloney, Michael, 41
Mann, Simon F., 87, 94, 172, 243, 244
Manufacturers. *See* Iron founders; Textile industry
Masonic orders, 157–60, 165. *See also* Associations
Mead, George, 235
Meehan, John "Whacker," 213–14
Metal Workers' Association, 230
Methodism. *See* Religion
Middle class: making of an Irish, 109–10, 256, 260; and associational life, 137, 157–60, 164, 165, 172, 173, 234, 235
Mobility: social, 12, 13, 38, 68, 109, 128–29, 253, 254, 255, 256, 259; geographic, 37, 256
Molders, 1, 2, 6, 10, 13, 25, 29, 82, 102, 143, 166, 185, 229–30, 248–52, 254, 257; ethnicity, 31, 32, 37; labor process, 34–35, 154–55; status, 38; ages, 40, 186; property holding among, 41; organize, 86, 90, 91; 1866 lockout, 95–98; standard of living, 106; residential patterns, 111; traditions among, 130–33, 168; wages, 146; as leaders, 170–72; and police, 196, 213, 214; Malleable strike, 237–43. *See also* Iron Molders' International Union; Lockouts; Strikes
Molders' Hall (Troy), 91
Molly Maguires, 168, 169, 207, 209
Morrissey, James, 169
Mullaney, Kate, 174
Mule Spinners' Association, 222
Murphy, Edward, Jr. (mayor of Troy), 25, 160, 164, 184, 195, 201, 232–35, 255, 256
Murphy, Francis, 1, 126
Murray, Joseph, 213

National Amalgamated Association of Iron, Steel and Tin Workers, 126, 230
National Forge, 198, 201, 202. *See also* Puddlers
National Guard, 213, 215
Nationalism, 13

National Labor Union, 174
National Labor Union Congress, 1
National Stove Manufacturers' and Iron Founders' Association, 95, 208
Nativism, 34, 67, 118, 125
New York Central Railroad, 26
New York City Central Labor Union, 225, 226
New York City coopers' union, 162
New York Herald, 188
New York Weekly Tribune, 83
Norton, Thomas, 172, 201

Occupational mobility. *See* Mobility
Ogden Mills, 56, 83, 84, 189
Owen, Silas, 120, 122, 191

Panic of 1857. *See* Depressions
Parnell, Charles Stewart, 163
Paternalism, 57, 58, 70, 105, 107, 111, 150, 151–52, 161, 185–88, 192, 222–23, 227
Paterson, N.J., 117, 220, 223, 250
Pattern fitters, 132
Pattern makers, 31, 33, 37, 96, 111
Pattern Makers' Union, 232
Peekskill, N.Y., 1
Pennsylvania, 20
Philadelphia, 203; iron molders, 86
Philips and Clarks' Foundry, 26
Pinkertons, 238
Pittsburgh: 1875 strike, 204
Police: ex-molders as, 37, 40, 184; ethnicity, 38; iron masters try to use, 185, 192–93, 199; and Troy working class, 194–97; and "reign of terror," 203–5, 210–15; and 1881 Police Bill, 233–37. *See also* Courts; Local politics
Polish Jews, 117
Poor relief: and churches, 123
Potter, Darius, 40
Poughkeepsie and Eastern Railroad, 26
Presbyterians. *See* Religion
Professionals, 28
Progress and Poverty, 163
Protestants. *See* Religion
Protestant work ethnic, 193
Providence Steam Mills, 56
Puddlers, 29, 86, 143, 249–59; ethnicity, 31, 33, 37, 166; labor process, 34, 154–55; early resistance, 87, 88, 91; standard of living, 106, 149, 185; residential patterns,